Microsoft® Windows® 7

ILLUSTRATED

Introductory

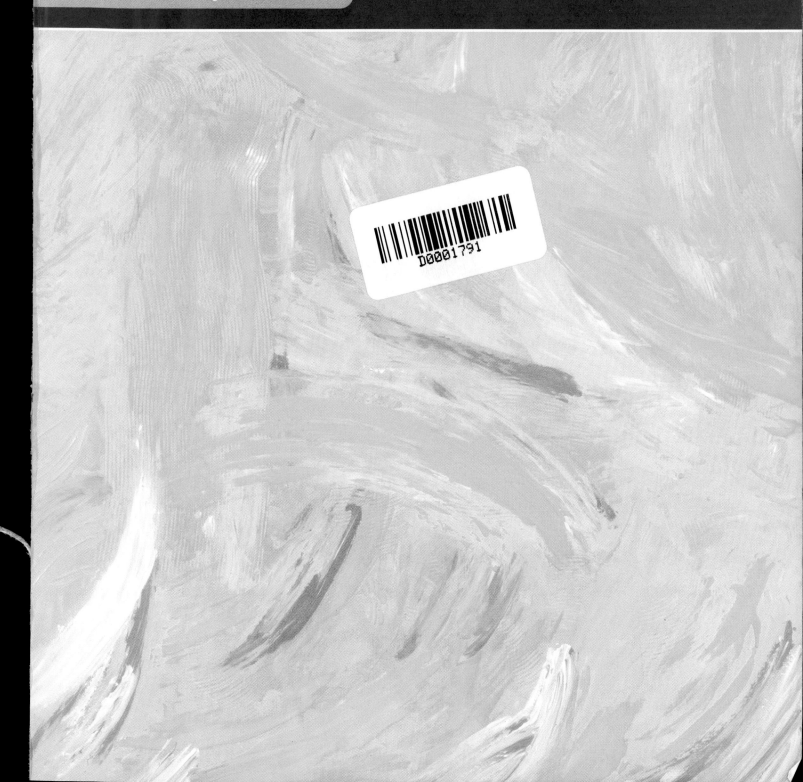

Microsoft® Windows® 7

ILLUSTRATED

Introductory

Steve Johnson

COURSE TECHNOLOGY
CENGAGE Learning·

Australia • Brazil • Japan • Korea • Mexico • Singapore • Spain • United Kingdom • United States

COURSE TECHNOLOGY
CENGAGE Learning

Microsoft® Windows® 7—Illustrated Introductory
Steve Johnson

Executive Editor: Marjorie Hunt

Associate Acquisitions Editor: Brandi Shailer

Senior Product Manager: Christina Kling Garrett

Associate Product Manager: Michelle Camisa

Editorial Assistant: Kim Klasner

Director of Marketing: Cheryl Costantini

Senior Marketing Manager: Ryan DeGrote

Marketing Coordinator: Kristen Panciocco

Developmental Editor: Janice Jutras

Content Project Manager: Matt Hutchinson

Copy Editor: Karen Annett

Proofreader: Harry Johnson

Indexer: Rich Carlson

QA Manuscript Reviewers: John Frietas,
Serge Palladino, Jeff Schwartz, Danielle Shaw

Cover Designer: Derek Bedrosian

Cover Artist: Mark Hunt

Composition: Pre-Press PMG

For product information and technology assistance, contact us at
Cengage Learning Customer & Sales Support, 1-800-354-9706

For permission to use material from this text or product, submit all requests online at **www.cengage.com/permissions**
Further permissions questions can be emailed to
permissionrequest@cengage.com

ISBN-0-538-74905-9

ISBN-978-0-538-74905-3

Course Technology
20 Channel Center Street
Boston, MA 02210
USA

Cengage Learning is a leading provider of customized learning solutions with office locations around the globe, including Singapore, the United Kingdom, Australia, Mexico, Brazil, and Japan. Locate your local office at:

international.cengage.com/region

Cengage Learning products are represented in Canada by Nelson Education, Ltd.

To learn more about Course Technology, visit **www.cengage.com/coursetechnology**

To learn more about Cengage Learning, visit **www.cengage.com**

Purchase any of our products at your local college store or at our preferred online store **www.ichapters.com**

Trademarks:
Some of the product names and company names used in this book have been used for identification purposes only and may be trademarks or registered trademarks of their respective manufacturers and sellers.

Microsoft and the Windows logo are either registered trademarks or trademarks of Microsoft Corporation in the United States and/or other countries. Cengage Learning, Course Technology is an independent entity from Microsoft Corporation, and not affiliated with Microsoft in any manner.

Printed in the United States of America
3 4 5 6 15 14 13 12 11 10

Brief Contents

Contents

Windows 7

630-955-1200

Preface

Welcome to *Microsoft Windows 7—Illustrated Introductory*. If this is your first experience with the Illustrated series, you'll see that this book has a unique design: each skill is presented on two facing pages, with steps on the left and screens on the right. The layout makes it easy to learn a skill without having to read a lot of text and flip pages to see an illustration.

This book is an ideal learning tool for a wide range of learners—the "rookies" will find the clean design easy to follow and focused with only essential information presented, and the "hotshots" will appreciate being able to move quickly through the lessons to find the information they need without reading a lot of text. The design also makes this a great reference after the course is over! See the illustration on the right to learn more about the pedagogical and design elements of a typical lesson.

What's New in this Edition

Microsoft has made many changes and enhancements to Microsoft Windows 7 to make it the best ever. Here are some highlights of what's new:

- **Libraries**—Libraries are special folders that catalog files and folders in a central location, regardless of where you actually store them on your hard drive.

- **Action Center**—The Action Center allows you to set the system and security alerts you want to see, and hide the ones you don't. If you're attention is needed, the Action Center displays an icon in the notification area on the taskbar to make you aware of potential security risks, such as a new virus, out of date antivirus software, or if an important security option is turned off or other security related issues from Microsoft.

- **Internet Explorer 8**—Internet Explorer 8 displays the information you want in your browser with features such as Accelerators and Web Slices. The redesigned

---

Each two-page spread focuses on a single skill.

Introduction briefly explains why the lesson skill is important.

A case scenario motivates the the steps and puts learning in context.

UNIT A
Windows 7

Shutting Down the Computer

When you finish working on your computer, you need to make sure to turn off, or **shut down**, your computer properly. This involves several steps: saving and closing all open files, closing all open windows, exiting all running programs, shutting down Windows itself, and, finally, turning off the computer. Shutting down your computer makes sure Windows and all its related programs are properly closed; this avoids potential problems starting and working with Windows in the future. If you turn off the computer by pushing the power switch while Windows or other programs are running, you could lose important data. If a program is still open when you instruct Windows to shut down, you will be prompted to save the file and close the program before the shut-down process continues. You shut down your computer now.

STEPS

1. If any windows or programs are open on your screen, click the Close button in the upper-right corner of each window

QUICK TIP
To prevent other users from using your computer, you can press [L] to lock the computer and return to the Welcome screen. To unlock, move the mouse and log on at the Welcome screen.

2. Click the Start button on the taskbar, then point to the arrow next to the Power button

A submenu appears, displaying several options for turning off your computer, as shown in Figure A-15. See Table A-4 for a description of each option. The Power button (set by default to Shut down) provides easy access to your preferred shutdown option. Depending on your Windows settings, your shutdown options might be different.

QUICK TIP
If you have a mobile PC, set Power Options in the Control Panel to turn off your computer or put it to sleep by closing the lid.

3. If you are working in a lab, click the Windows desktop to cancel the task; if you are working on your own machine or if your instructor tells you to shut down Windows, click the Shut down button or menu option to exit Windows and shut down your computer

4. If you see the message "It's now safe to turn off your computer," turn off your computer and monitor

Some computers power off automatically, so you might not see this message.

TABLE A-4: Shut down options

option	function	when to use it
Switch user	Maintains your session and changes users	When you want to continue working with Windows, yet allow another user to access another Windows session
Log off	Saves and leaves your session to disk and changes users	When you want to stop working with Windows, yet allow another user to access another Windows session
Lock	Maintains your session, while restricting access to Windows	When you want to stop working with Windows and you want to keep others from using Windows
Restart	Restarts the computer and reloads Windows	When you want to restart the computer and begin working with Windows again (when your programs might have frozen or stopped working)
Sleep	Maintains your session, keeping the computer running on low power	When you want to stop working with Windows for a few moments and conserve power (ideal for a laptop or portable computer); available when a power scheme is selected in Power Options (in the Control Panel)
Hibernate	Saves your session to disk so that you can safely turn off power; restores your session the next time you start Windows	When you want to stop working with Windows for a while and start working again later; available when the Power Options setting (in the Control Panel) is turned on
Shut down	Prepares the computer to be turned off	When you finish working with Windows and you want to shut off your computer

Tips and troubleshooting advice, right where you need it—next to the step itself.

Tables provide helpful summaries of key terms, buttons, or keyboard shortcuts.

Large screen shots keep students on track as they complete steps

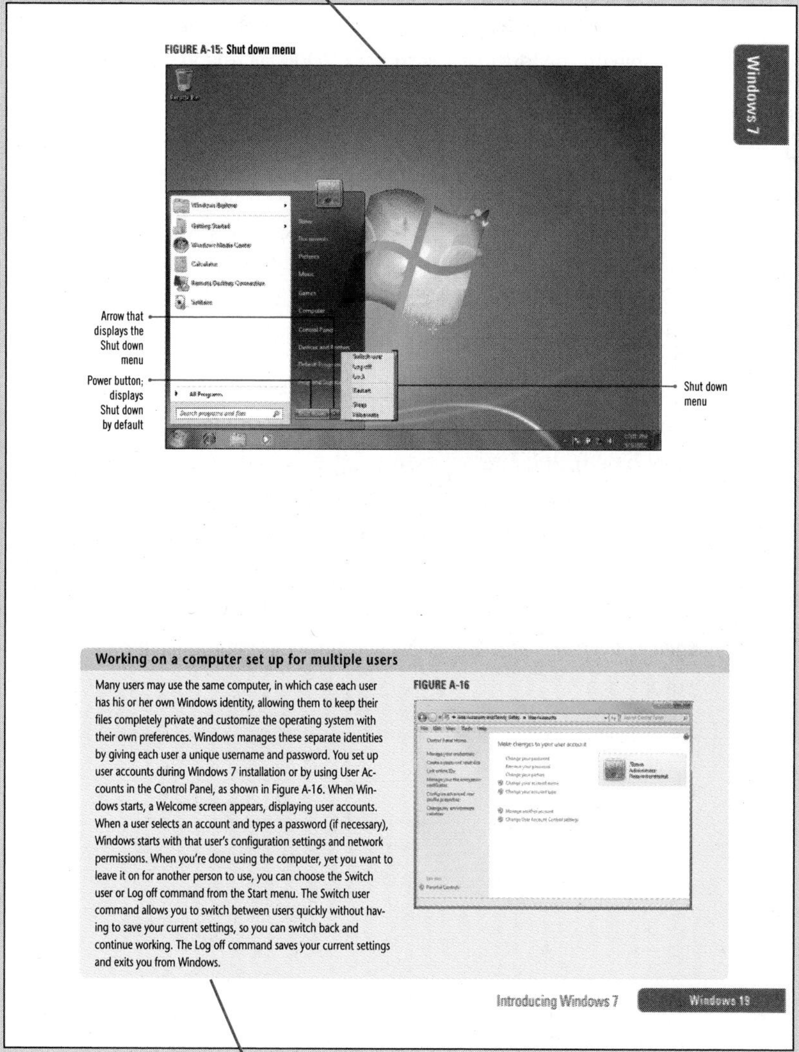

FIGURE A-15: Shut down menu

Arrow that displays the Shut down menu

Power button; displays Shut down by default

Shut down menu

Working on a computer set up for multiple users

Many users may use the same computer, in which case each user has his or her own Windows identity, allowing them to keep their files completely private and customize the operating system with their own preferences. Windows manages these separate identities by giving each user a unique username and password. You set up user accounts during Windows 7 installation or by using User Accounts in the Control Panel, as shown in Figure A-16. When Windows starts, a Welcome screen appears, displaying user accounts. When a user selects an account and types a password (if necessary), Windows starts with that user's configuration settings and network permissions. When you're done using the computer, yet you want to leave it on for another person to use, you can choose the Switch user or Log off command from the Start menu. The Switch user command allows you to switch between users quickly without having to save your current settings, so you can switch back and continue working. The Log off command saves your current settings and exits you from Windows.

FIGURE A-16

Introducing Windows 7   Windows 19

Clues to Use boxes provide useful information related to the lesson skill.

Address bar with domain highlighting and compatibility view, and tabbed browsing with new tab options make it easier to display and work with Web pages. With InPrivate browsing and filtering, you can browse the Web without keeping track of your whereabouts and protect yourself from Web sites gathering information about you.

• **Windows Live Essentials**—Windows Live Essentials is a collection of programs available from Microsoft online that allows you to communicate on the Web and work with and share media. The Windows Live programs include Messenger, Mail, Photo Gallery, Toolbar, Writer, Family Safety, Movie Maker, and Microsoft Silverlight. Many of these programs came installed along with Windows Vista, however in Windows 7, you need to download and install them.

Assignments

The lessons use Quest Specialty Travel, a fictional adventure travel company, as the case study. The assignments on the yellow pages at the end of each unit increase in difficulty. Data files and case studies provide a variety of interesting and relevant business applications. Assignments include:

• **Concepts Review** consist of multiple choice, matching, and screen identification questions.

• **Skills Review** provide additional hands-on, step-by-step reinforcement.

• **Real Life Independent Challenges** are practical exercises in which student perform activities to help them with their every day lives.

• **Advanced Challenge Exercises** set within **Independent Challenges** provide optional steps for more advanced students.

• **Visual Workshops** are practical, self-graded capstone projects that require independent problem solving.

Instructor Resources

The Instructor Resources CD is Course Technology's way of putting the resources and information needed to teach and learn effectively into your hands. With an integrated array of teaching and learning tools that offer you and your students a broad range of technology-based instructional options, we believe this CD represents the highest quality and most cutting edge resources available to instructors today. Many of these resources are available at www.cengage.com/coursetechnology. The resources available with this book are:

- **Instructor's Manual**—Available as an electronic file, the Instructor's Manual includes detailed lecture topics with teaching tips for each unit.

- **Sample Syllabus**—Prepare and customize your course easily using this sample course outline.

- **PowerPoint Presentations**—Each unit has a corresponding PowerPoint presentation that you can use in lecture, distribute to your students, or customize to suit your course.

- **Figure Files**—The figures in the text are provided on the Instructor Resources CD to help you illustrate key topics or concepts. You can create traditional overhead transparencies by printing the figure files. Or you can create electronic slide shows by using the figures in a presentation program such as PowerPoint.

- **Solutions to Exercises**—Solutions to Exercises contains every file students are asked to create or modify in the lessons and end-of-unit material. Also provided in this section, there is a document outlining the solutions for the end-of-unit Concepts Review, Skills Review, and Independent Challenges. An Annotated Solution File and Grading Rubric accompany each file and can be used together for quick and easy grading.

- **Data Files for Students**—To complete most of the units in this book, your students will need Data Files. You can post the Data Files on a file server for students to copy. The Data Files are available on the Instructor Resources CD-ROM, the Review Pack, and can also be downloaded from www.cengage.com/coursetechnology. In this edition, we have included a lesson on downloading the Data Files for this book, see the inside back cover of this text.

Instruct students to use the Data Files List included on the Review Pack and the Instructor Resources CD. This list gives instructions on copying and organizing files.

- **ExamView**—ExamView is a powerful testing software package that allows you to create and administer printed, computer (LAN-based), and Internet exams. ExamView includes hundreds of questions that correspond to the topics covered in this text, enabling students to generate detailed study guides that include page references for further review. The computer-based and Internet testing components allow students to take exams at their computers, and also saves you time by grading each exam automatically.

COURSECASTS   **Learning on the Go. Always Available...Always Relevant.**

Our fast-paced world is driven by technology. You know because you are an active participant—always on the go, always keeping up with technological trends, and always learning new ways to embrace technology to power your life. Let CourseCasts, hosted by Ken Baldauf of Florida State University, be your guide into weekly updates in this ever-changing space. These timely, relevant podcasts are produced weekly and are available for download at http://coursecasts.course.com or directly from iTunes (search by CourseCasts). CourseCasts are a perfect solution to getting students (and even instructors) to learn on the go!

Acknowledgements

Author Acknowledgements

Steve Johnson The task of creating any book requires the talents of many hard-working people pulling together to meet impossible deadlines and untold stresses. I would like to thank the entire team responsible for making this book possible. I would like to especially thank Janice Jutras for making this book easier to read, understand, and follow. I would also like to thank the manuscript reviewers, John Freitas and Jeff Schwartz, for their helpful feedback during the writing process, and the project manager, Christina Kling-Garrett, for keeping this project on track.

And, most importantly, I would like to thank my wife Holly, and three children, JP, Brett, and Hannah, for their support and encouragement during the project.

Read This Before You Begin

Frequently Asked Questions

What are Data Files?

A Data File is a WordPad, Paint, Windows Media Player, or another type of file that you use to complete the steps in the units and exercises to create the final materials that you submit to your instructor. Each unit opener page lists the Data Files that you need for that unit.

Where are the Data Files?

Your instructor will provide the Data Files to you or direct you to a location on a network drive from which you can download them. Alternatively, you can follow the instructions on the next page to download the Data Files from this book's Web page.

What software was used to write and test this book?

This book was written and tested using a typical installation of Microsoft Windows 7 Ultimate Edition, with Aero turned on using the standard Windows 7 Aero theme. The browser used for any steps that require a browser is Windows Internet Explorer 8.

What software do I need to complete the steps and exercises in this book?

The exercises in this book assume that your computer is using a typical installation of Microsoft Windows 7 Home Premium Edition or higher, with Aero turned on using the standard Windows 7 Aero theme. The browser used for this book assumes that your computer is using Windows Internet Explorer 8, which comes installed with a typical Microsoft Windows 7 installation. The e-mail program used for this book requires the download and installation of Windows Live Mail from the Windows Live Essentials Web site; the program doesn't come installed with a typical Microsoft Windows 7 installation.

Do I need to be connected to the Internet to complete the steps and exercises in this book?

Some of the exercises in this book assume that your computer is connected to the Internet. If you are not connected to the Internet, see your instructor for information on how to complete the exercises.

Downloading Data Files

In order to complete many of the lesson steps and exercises in this book, you are asked to open and save Data Files. A **Data File** is a partially completed file that you use as a starting point to complete the steps in the units and exercises. The benefit of using a Data File is that it saves you the time and effort needed to create a file; you can simply open a Data File, save it with a new name (so the original file remains intact), then make changes to it to complete lesson steps or an exercise. Your instructor will provide the Data Files to you or direct you to a location on a network drive from which you can download them. Alternatively, you can follow the instructions in this lesson to download the Data Files from this book's Web page.

1. Start Internet Explorer, type www.cengage.com/coursetechnology/ in the address bar, then press [Enter]

2. Click in the Enter ISBN Search text box, type 9780538749053, then click Search

3. When the page opens for this textbook, click the About this Product link for the Student, point to Student Downloads to expand the menu, and then click the Data Files for Students link

4. If the File Download – Security Warning dialog box opens, click Save. (If no dialog box appears, skip this step and go to Step 6)

5. If the Save As dialog box opens, click the Save in list arrow at the top of the dialog box, select a folder on your USB drive or hard disk to download the file to, then click Save

6. Close Internet Explorer and then open Computer on the Start menu or Windows Explorer on the taskbar and display the contents of the drive and folder to which you downloaded the file

7. Double-click the file 749053.exe in the drive or folder, then, if the Open File – Security Warning dialog box opens, click Run

8. In the WinZip Self-Extractor window, navigate to the drive and folder where you want to unzip the files to, then click Unzip

9. When the WinZip Self-Extractor displays a dialog box listing the number of files that have unzipped successfully, click OK, click Close in the WinZip Self-Extractor dialog box, then close Windows Explorer

   You are now ready to open the required files.

Introducing Windows 7

figure
en miniature

Microsoft Windows 7 is an **operating system**, a computer program that controls the operation of your computer and the programs you run on it. **Programs**, also known as **applications**, help you accomplish specific tasks, such as sending and receiving electronic mail and managing files on your computer. When you work with Windows 7, you will notice **icons** and **thumbnails**, which are small pictures on your screen intended to be meaningful symbols of the items they represent. You will also notice **windows** (thus the name of the operating system), which are rectangular frames on your screen that can contain icons, the contents of a file, or other usable data. A **file** is a collection of information that has a unique name, distinguishing it from other files. This use of icons, thumbnails, and windows is called a **graphical user interface** (**GUI**, pronounced "gooey"), meaning that you interact ("interface") with the computer through the use of graphics. Windows 7 provides two distinct GUI experiences: a "basic" experience for entry-level systems and a more visually dynamic experience called **Windows Aero** for high-level systems. Windows Aero provides expanded visual effects, such as glasslike interface elements that you can see through, subtle window animations, window colors, and live thumbnails that you can display on the taskbar. In this unit, you will be introduced to basic Windows skills.

OBJECTIVES
Start Windows and view the desktop
Use pointing devices
Use the Start button
Use the taskbar
Work with windows
Use menus, toolbars, and panes
Use dialog boxes
Use Windows Help and Support
Shut down the computer

Starting Windows and Viewing the Desktop

When you first start Windows 7, you see the Welcome screen, a way to identify yourself on the computer, or log on. After you log on, you see the Windows desktop, as shown in Figure A-1. The **desktop** is the graphical background on screen that represents a desk. It contains windows, icons, files, and programs, which you can use to access, store, organize, modify, and share information. The horizontal bar at the bottom of your screen is called the **taskbar**; it allows you to start programs and switch among currently running programs. At the left end of the taskbar is the **Start button**, which you use to start programs, find and open files, access Windows Help and Support, and much more. Next to the Start button are taskbar-pinned programs, which you use to quickly start your Internet browser, Windows Explorer, and Windows Media Player. At the right end of the taskbar is the **notification area** (also known as the **system tray**), which displays the program-related icons, time and date, and the **Show the desktop button** (the blank button next to the time and date). If you upgraded your computer to Windows 7 from a previous version of Windows, your desktop might contain additional desktop icons, toolbars, and other elements, such as miniprograms called gadgets. **Gadgets** provide easy access to frequently used tools and information, such as news headlines. Windows 7 automatically starts when you turn on your computer. If your computer is not on, you turn it on now.

STEPS

1. **Turn on your computer and wait for Windows to start**

   Windows automatically starts and displays a security prompt, the Welcome screen, or the desktop. The security prompt provides an additional step to prevent unauthorized users from accessing your computer. If the security feature is turned on, Windows 7 asks you to press several keys at the same time to continue. If the security prompt appears, continue to Step 2; if the Welcome screen appears, skip to Step 3; and if the desktop appears, skip to Step 4.

2. **If prompted on the screen, press and hold [Ctrl] and [Alt] with one hand, then press [Del] with the other to display the Welcome screen**

   At the Welcome screen, you select your username and enter a password to identify yourself on the computer. If you share the computer with other users, you see multiple usernames on the Welcome screen.

   > **TROUBLE**
   > If you are new to using the mouse, read through the next topic, "Using Pointing Devices."

3. **In the Welcome screen, click your username, if necessary, type your password, then press [Enter]**

   A password prevents other users from accessing your computer files without proper authorization. Windows passwords are **case sensitive**, which means that Windows makes a distinction between upper- and lowercase letters and nonalphabetic characters (numbers and symbols). Only bullets appear as you type the password. This helps to prevent other people from learning your password. Once the password is accepted, the Windows desktop appears on your screen, as shown in Figure A-1.

4. **If a message pops up in the notification area, as shown in Figure A-1, click the Close button x in the upper-right corner of the pop-up to dismiss it**

   A **pop-up notification** is an informational message that appears when you need it. For example, when Windows 7 detects the need for updates on your computer, a pop-up notification appears, letting you know. If you don't dismiss a notification, it will fade away on its own. When you start Windows 7 for the first time, the Getting Started window appears, displaying icons for easy access to common options, such as Go online to find out what's new in Windows 7, Personalize Windows, and Transfer files and settings from another computer, to help you get started using Windows 7.

   > **QUICK TIP**
   > To open the Getting Started window later, click the Start button, point to All Programs, click Accessories, then click Getting Started.

5. **If the Getting Started window appears, click the Close button in the upper-right corner of the Getting Started window**

   The Getting Started window closes.

FIGURE A-1: Windows 7 desktop

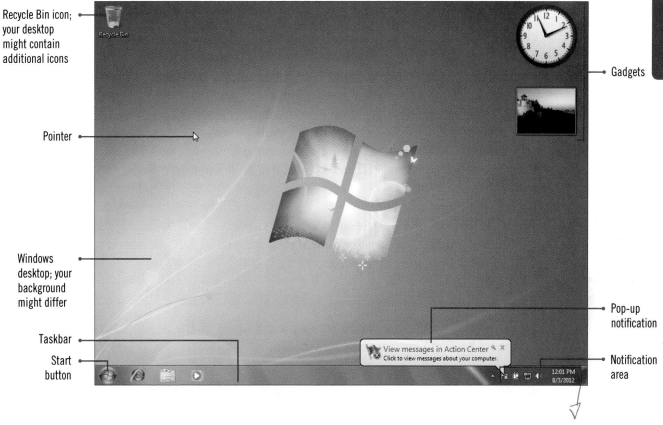

Recycle Bin icon; your desktop might contain additional icons

Gadgets

Pointer

Windows desktop; your background might differ

Pop-up notification

Taskbar

Start button

Notification area

View messages in Action Center
Click to view messages about your computer.

12:01 PM
8/3/2012

desktop Buttom

Using and changing a password

You can set up your computer to require users to log on with a user-name and password to use it. You specify a username and password when you install Windows 7, or an instructor or technical support person (the person in charge of computers at your school or busi-ness) assigns you a username and password on a computer owned by the school or business. If you own your own computer and you want to change your password, or if you don't have one and want to set one up, click the Start button, then click Control Panel. This opens the Control Panel window. Click User Accounts and Family Safety, then click Change your Windows password. The window changes to display the heading "Make changes to your user ac-count." Click Change your password or Create a password for your account, then follow the instructions provided. If you have forgotten your password, you can click Reset password on the Welcome screen to start the Forgotten Password Wizard. The Forgotten Password Wizard takes you step-by-step through a series of instructional win-dows to help you recover user account information (username and password) and personalized computer settings. To use the Forgotten Reset Wizard, you need to insert a password reset disk into a disk drive or USB drive. To create a password reset disk, return to the Make changes to your user account window in the Control Panel, then click Create a password reset disk in the left pane in the win-dow. Follow the instructions provided. Never write down your pass-word on paper or let someone look over your shoulder as you log on to the computer. Always be sure to log off or shut down when you walk away from your computer.

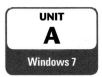

Using Pointing Devices

A **pointing device** is hardware connected to or built into the computer you use to position the **pointer**, the small symbol on the screen that indicates the pointer's position. The most common pointing devices are a **mouse**, as shown in Figure A-2, for desktop computers and a **touch pad** for laptop or notebook computers. When you move the mouse across a flat surface (such as a desk or a mouse pad), or place your finger on the touch pad and drag across it, the pointer on the screen moves in the same direction. The shape of the pointer changes to indicate different activities. Table A-1 shows some common pointer shapes. Once you move the pointer to a desired position on the screen, you use the buttons on the mouse or touch pad to "tell" your computer what you want it to do. If your mouse has a scroll wheel between the two buttons, you can roll the wheel backward (toward you) or forward (away from you) to scroll through windows. Other available pointing devices include trackballs, which function similarly to the mouse, and stylus pens, which work with a tablet pad to move the pointer and enter handwritten information. You want to use the mouse to become familiar with these navigational skills. The steps in this lesson refer to a mouse; if you have another pointing device, use it instead.

STEPS

1. **Place your hand on the mouse, locate the pointer ⟍ on the desktop, then move the mouse back and forth across your desktop**

   As you move the mouse, the mouse pointer moves correspondingly.

TROUBLE

If the pointer changed to a pointing finger when you pointed to the Recycle Bin and a window opened when you clicked it, your system is set up in Web style. See the Clues to Use box in this lesson for more information.

2. **Move the mouse to position the pointer over any icon in the notification area**

   Positioning the mouse pointer over an icon or over any specific item on the screen is called **pointing**. When you point to an item, Windows often displays a **ScreenTip**, identifying the item or displaying status information, as shown in Figure A-3.

3. **Locate the Recycle Bin on the desktop (the default position for this icon is in the upper-left corner of the screen), position the pointer over it, then press and release the left mouse button**

   The act of pressing a mouse button once and releasing it is called **clicking**. The icon is now highlighted, or shaded differently from the other icons. The act of clicking an item, such as an icon, indicates that you have selected it. To perform an operation on an icon, such as moving it, you must first select it.

TROUBLE

If the icon jumps back to the left edge of the screen, Auto arrange icons is turned on. Position the pointer anywhere on the desktop, press the right mouse button, point to View on the menu that appears, then click Auto arrange icons to deselect it.

4. **Point to the Recycle Bin, press and hold down the left mouse button, move the pointer to the center of the desktop, then release the mouse button**

   The icon moves with the mouse pointer. This is called **dragging**, which you use to move Windows elements. If the icon jumps a little when you release the mouse, the desktop is set to align icons automatically with an invisible grid.

5. **Point to the Recycle Bin, then press and release the right mouse button**

   Clicking the right mouse button is known as right-clicking. **Right-clicking** an item displays a shortcut menu, shown in Figure A-4. Shortcut menus display the commands most commonly used for the item you clicked. When a step tells you to "click," it means to click the left mouse button. If you are supposed to click the right mouse button, the step will instruct you to "right-click."

6. **Click anywhere outside the menu to close the shortcut menu without choosing a command**

7. **Drag the Recycle Bin back to its original position on the desktop**

QUICK TIP

You can also press [Esc] to close a shortcut menu without executing a command.

8. **Point to the Recycle Bin, then click the left mouse button twice quickly**

   The Recycle Bin window opens. It might be empty or it might contain file icons that you or someone else wants to delete. (You'll learn more about the Recycle Bin in Unit C.) Clicking the mouse button twice in a row is known as **double-clicking**, and it allows you to open a window, program, or file that an icon represents.

9. **Click the Close button ▣ in the upper-right corner of the window to close it**

FIGURE A-2: Typical mouse

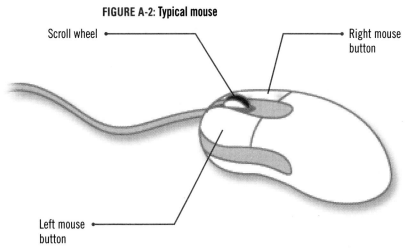

Scroll wheel

Right mouse button

Left mouse button

FIGURE A-3: ScreenTip in notification area

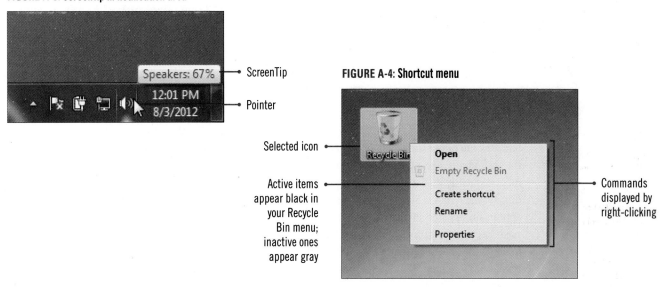

ScreenTip

Pointer

FIGURE A-4: Shortcut menu

Selected icon

Active items appear black in your Recycle Bin menu; inactive ones appear gray

Commands displayed by right-clicking

TABLE A-1: Common mouse pointer shapes

shape	used to
⇱	Select items, choose commands, start programs, and work with programs
I	Position the mouse pointer for editing or inserting text; called the insertion point or cursor
○	Indicate Windows is busy processing a command
⤢ ⤡ ↔ ↕	Position the mouse pointer on the edge of a window to change its size
⟂	Position the mouse pointer to select and open Web-based content

Using the mouse with the Web style

In the default setup for Windows, you click an item to select it, and you double-click an item to open it. However, as you probably are aware, when you use Web sites on the Internet, you don't need to double-click items to open them; you point to them, the pointer changes to ⟂, and you click once. You can choose whether you want to extend the way you click while using the Internet to the rest of the work you do on your computer so that you single-click icons to open items. This is known as Internet or **Web style;**

double-clicking to open icons is known as **Classic style.** To change from one style to the other, click the Start button on the taskbar, click Control Panel, click Appearance and Personalization, click Specify single- or double-click to open, click the Single-click to open an item (point to select), or Double-click to open an item (single-click to select) option button, then click OK. Windows 7 is set by default to double-click to open items, and the steps in this book assume you are using this setting.

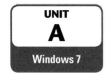

Using the Start Button

The key to getting started with the Windows desktop is learning how to use the **Start button** ⊕ on the taskbar. Clicking the Start button on the taskbar displays the **Start menu**, a list of commands that allows you to start a program, open a document, change a Windows setting, find a file, or display support information. Table A-2 describes the available commands on the Start menu that are installed with Windows 7. As you install more programs on your computer, finding them on the Start menu can sometimes be difficult. Windows 7 allows you to search the Start menu to find installed programs and other Windows items, such as Control Panel programs, documents, music, Web sites you have visited, contacts, e-mail messages, and appointments. To search the Start menu, click in the **Search box** on the Start menu, and then start typing the search text you want. As you type, the Start menu filters out items to show you possible results, with priority given to the programs you use frequently. As you become more familiar with Windows, you might want to customize the Start menu to include additional items that you use most often. ▄▄▄▄ You want to view the Start menu, perform a Start menu search, and open the **Control Panel**, a window containing various programs that allow you to specify how your computer looks and performs.

STEPS

QUICK TIP

To add or remove a program from the pinned items list, right-click the program on the Start menu, then click Pin to Start Menu or Unpin from Start Menu. To remove a program from the Start menu, right-click the program on the Start menu, then click Remove from this list.

1. **Click the** Start button ⊕ **on the taskbar**

   The Start menu opens, as shown in Figure A-5. The left column of the Start menu is separated into two lists: pinned items above the separator line and most frequently used items below. The **pinned** items remain on the Start menu, like a piece of paper held by a push pin on a bulletin board, until you remove them. The most frequently used items change as you use programs: Windows keeps track of the programs you use and displays them on the Start menu for easy access. When a program or Windows item, such as Getting Started, appears on the Start menu with an arrow, the submenu displays a list of recently opened files for the program known as a **jump list** for easy access. The top of the right column in the Start menu indicates the name of the person currently logged on to the computer. Below the username are commands that provide easy access to folders, Windows settings, Help information, and search functionality.

2. **Point to** All Programs

   The All Programs submenu opens on top of the left column on the Start menu. An arrow next to a menu item indicates a **cascading menu** or **submenu**, which is a list of commands for that menu item. Pointing at these menu items displays another list from which you can choose additional commands. The All Programs submenu provides you access to common programs and accessories that come installed with Windows 7.

3. **Click** Back **in the left column on the Start menu**

   The All Programs submenu closes and the original left column of the Start menu reappears. If you find it difficult to locate a program or Windows item, you can use the Search box on the Start menu to help you find it.

4. **Click in the** Search box **at the bottom of the left column on the Start menu, then type** control

   As you type, the Start menu filters out items to show you possible results, with priority given to the programs you use frequently. The search results continue to narrow as you type your topic. If you don't find what you are looking for during a search, you can click "See more results" on the Start menu to display Windows 7 search results or expand the search to other areas, or click the Close button in the Search box to cancel the search.

QUICK TIP

To pin an item on the Start menu, click the item on the Start menu, then drag it to a new location at the top. A black horizontal bar indicates the new location.

5. **In the Search box, click the** Close button ⊠

   The Start menu reappears.

6. **In the right column, click** Control Panel

   The Control Panel window opens, containing categories and icons for various programs that allow you to specify how your computer looks and performs.

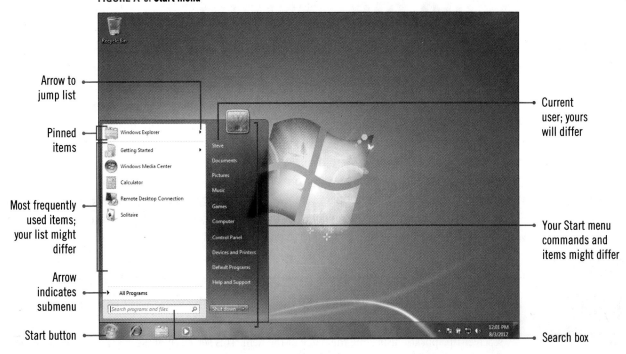

FIGURE A-5: Start menu

Arrow to jump list

Pinned items

Most frequently used items; your list might differ

Arrow indicates submenu

Start button

Current user; yours will differ

Your Start menu commands and items might differ

Search box

TABLE A-2: Start menu commands

command	description
Specific Program	Opens a specific program or submenu; displays pinned and frequently used items on the Start menu
All Programs	Opens a list of all the programs installed on your computer
Search box	Searches the Start menu for installed programs and other Windows items
Username	Opens the personal folder for the current user, where you store personal folders, such as Contacts, Desktop, Downloads, and Favorites
Documents	Opens the Documents folder, where you store and manage files
Pictures	Opens the Pictures folder, where you store and manage photos, images, and graphic files
Music	Opens the Music folder, where you store and manage sound and audio files
Games	Opens the Games folder, where you start and play games, such as Hearts and Minesweeper
Computer	Opens the Computer window, where you access information about disk drives and other hardware devices
Control Panel	Provides options to customize the appearance and functionality of the computer
Devices and Printers	Opens the Devices and Printers window, where you can display and manage currently installed devices, such as monitors, printers, and faxes, and add new devices
Default Programs	Opens the Default Programs window, where you set default programs and computer defaults and associate a file type with a program
Help and Support	Displays Windows Help topics, tutorials, troubleshooting, support options, and tools
Power button (Shut down)	Exits Windows and turns off the computer
Arrow next to Power button	Provides commands to switch users, log off from the computer, lock the computer, restart the computer, or set the computer in sleep or hibernate mode

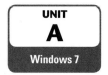

Using the Taskbar

The taskbar is the horizontal bar at the bottom of the desktop. The taskbar includes the Start button on the left end, program buttons and open window buttons in the middle, and the notification area on the right end. The taskbar allows you to start programs and switch among currently running programs and open windows. When you start a program or open a window, a corresponding button appears on the taskbar. If the taskbar becomes too crowded with buttons for open windows, then buttons associated with the same program automatically group together into a single button to conserve space. When you rest the pointer over a taskbar button, Windows Aero displays a live thumbnail, showing the content of that window. Windows Aero provides two other ways to manage windows: Windows Flip 3D and Windows Flip. Windows Flip 3D creates a view of open windows in a three-dimensional stack on your desktop. Windows Flip allows you to flip through open windows (by using [Alt][Tab]), providing a live thumbnail of each window. ▚▚▚ You want to use the taskbar to open and switch between windows.

STEPS

QUICK TIP

To pin a program to the taskbar, right-click a program icon, then click Pin this program to taskbar or Pin to Taskbar. To unpin a program from the taskbar, right-click a program icon on the taskbar, then click Unpin this program from taskbar.

1. **With the Control Panel window still open, point to the** Windows Explorer button ▣ **on the taskbar**

   A ScreenTip appears, displaying the name of the item. This ScreenTip indicates the item is not opened or started. Similar to the Start menu, the taskbar allows you to pin items (to the right of the Start button) to it for easy access. The pinned items remain on the taskbar until you remove them. By default, the pinned items on the taskbar include Internet Explorer, Windows Explorer, and Windows Media Player; your items might differ.

2. **Click the** Windows Explorer button **on the taskbar**

   The Windows Explorer window opens in front of the Control Panel window. The Windows Explorer window allows you to navigate to different locations on your computer and manage files. The Windows Explorer window is now **active**, which means that any actions you perform take place in this window. The taskbar button for the active window (in this case, the Windows Explorer button) is also highlighted.

3. **Point to the** Control Panel button **on the taskbar**

   For Windows Aero, a live thumbnail appears, displaying a miniature version of the Control Panel window, as shown in Figure A-6. When you point to the thumbnail, a Close button appears in the thumbnail and the window temporarily appears on the screen.

4. **Click the** Control Panel button **on the taskbar**

   The Control Panel window moves in front of the Windows Explorer window. The Control Panel window is now active.

5. **Press and hold** ▦ **with one hand, then press [Tab], but do not release** ▦

   Windows Flip 3D displays the windows in a stacked format. The window that is currently active—the Control Panel—appears in the front of the stack.

6. **Still holding down** ▦, **press [Tab] again**

   The Windows Explorer window appears in the front of the stack, as shown in Figure A-7, while the Control Panel window moves to the back.

7. **Release** ▦

   The Windows Explorer window is now active.

QUICK TIP

When you select the Desktop icon in the Windows Flip pop-up window, all open windows are minimized.

8. **Press and hold [Alt] with one hand, then press [Tab], but do not release [Alt]**

   Windows Flip displays a pop-up window with button icons for the open windows, including the desktop.

9. **Release both keys simultaneously**

   The Control Panel window is now active. As you continue to press [Tab], Windows Flip cycles through the icons. In Windows Aero, the selected window appears with the other windows transparent. To display the window represented by the currently selected thumbnail, release both keys. The Control Panel window is now active.

FIGURE A-6: Live thumbnail

Active window

Live thumbnail

Taskbar buttons

FIGURE A-7: Windows Flip 3D

Stacked window display

Working with the taskbar

Similar to the Start menu, the taskbar allows you to pin programs or files to it for easy one-click access. After you pin a program to the taskbar or open a program, you can right-click the taskbar button to display a jump list of recently opened files for the program. The taskbar also provides you with several options for arranging open windows. If you want to show all open windows stacked side by side or overlapped (known as cascading), you can right-click the taskbar, then click the option you want. If you prefer using a mouse, you can drag a window to the side of the screen (where the mouse touches the edge) to resize it for side-by-side comparison. The taskbar is locked by default, so it cannot be accidentally resized or moved. You can unlock the taskbar to resize and move it. To unlock the taskbar, right-click a blank area on the taskbar, then click Lock the taskbar on the shortcut menu to deselect the option. You can move the taskbar by dragging it to any edge (right, left, top, or bottom) of the desktop. You can also change the size of the taskbar in the same way you resize a window by dragging its edge. In addition to buttons, you can also show or hide toolbars on the taskbar. Right-click a blank area of the taskbar, point to Toolbars, then select a toolbar. To create a new toolbar with items from a folder, right-click a blank area of the taskbar, point to Toolbars, click New toolbar, select the folder you want to use, then click Select Folder.

Working with Windows

One of the powerful things about the Windows operating system is that you can open and work with more than one window or program at once. That means, however, that the desktop can get cluttered with many open windows for the various programs. You can identify a window by its name on the title bar at the top of a program window or in the **Address bar** of a Windows Explorer window, which you also use to navigate to different locations on your computer. To organize your desktop, you must sometimes change the size of a window or move it to a different location. Each window, no matter what it contains, is surrounded by a border that you can drag to resize or move the window. Each window also has three buttons in the upper-right corner that allow you to control the size of the window or to close it. In addition to using the resizing buttons in a window, you can also drag a window to the top or side of the screen to resize it. When you have one or more windows open and you want to display the desktop, you can click the Show desktop button (the blank button) located at the right end of the taskbar to minimize all open windows or point to the Show desktop button in Windows Aero to make all open windows transparent to quickly see your desktop. You want to try moving and resizing windows.

STEPS

QUICK TIP

Right-click the Show desktop button, and then click Peek at desktop to turn off peeking.

1. **Point to the Show desktop button ▌in the lower-right corner of the taskbar to show window transparency, click the Show desktop button to show the desktop, then click the Show desktop button again to display the Windows Explorer and Control Panel windows**
   The Show desktop button gives you two ways to view your desktop. Point to the button to temporarily peek at your desktop with transparent windows (in Aero), or click the button to minimize all open windows.

2. **Click anywhere in the Windows Explorer window on the desktop**
   The Windows Explorer window moves in front of the Control Panel window to become active.

QUICK TIP

You can also click a taskbar button for an active window to minimize the window.

3. **Click the Minimize button 🗕 in the upper-right corner of the Windows Explorer window**
   The window no longer appears on the desktop, but you can still see a button named Windows Explorer on the taskbar. When you **minimize** a window, you do not close it but merely reduce it to a button on the taskbar so that you can work more easily in other windows.

4. **Point to the bar at the top of the Control Panel window, click and hold the left mouse button, then drag the window to center it on the desktop**
   The window is relocated. This action is similar to dragging an icon to a new location.

5. **Position the pointer on the lower-right corner of the Control Panel window until it changes to ⬉, then drag the corner up and to the left about two inches**
   The window is now resized smaller. If you resized it small enough, scroll bars—bars with small arrows at either end and a rectangle in the middle—appear on the right and bottom edges of the window, as shown in Figure A-8. You can resize windows by dragging any corner or border.

QUICK TIP

Double-click the bar at the top of a window to switch between maximizing and restoring the size of a window.

6. **Click the Maximize button 🗖 in the upper-right corner of the Control Panel window or drag the bar at the top of the window to the top of your screen and release the mouse**
   When you **maximize** a window, it fills the entire screen. When a window is maximized, the Maximize button is replaced by the Restore Down button.

7. **Click the Restore Down button 🗗 in the upper-right corner of the Control Panel window**
   The **Restore Down button** returns a window to its previous size. The Restore Down button appears only when a window is maximized. When you finish using a window, you can close it with the Close button.

8. **Resize the Control Panel window large enough that the scroll bar doesn't show**

QUICK TIP

You can also right-click a taskbar button, then click Close window to close an open window.

9. **Click the Close button ✖ in the upper-right corner of the Control Panel window, then click the Windows Explorer button on the taskbar**
   The Control Panel window closes, and the Windows Explorer window returns to its original size.

FIGURE A-8: Window controls in the Control Panel

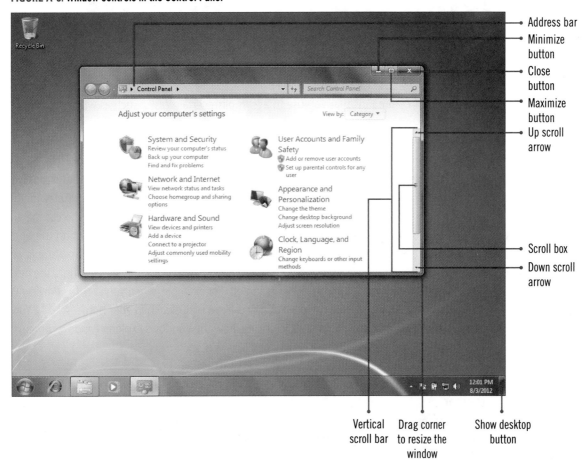

Address bar
Minimize button
Close button
Maximize button
Up scroll arrow
Scroll box
Down scroll arrow

Vertical scroll bar
Drag corner to resize the window
Show desktop button

Using scroll bars

When you cannot see all of the items available in a window, scroll bars appear on the right and bottom edges of the window. **Scroll bars** allow you to display the additional contents of the window. The vertical scroll bar moves your view up and down through a window; the horizontal scroll bar moves your view from left to right. There are several ways you can use the scroll bars. When you need to scroll only a short distance, you can use the scroll arrows. When you need to scroll more quickly, you can click in the scroll bar on either side of the **scroll box** to move the view up or down one window's height or left or right one window's width. Dragging the scroll box moves you even more quickly to a new part of the window. The scroll box, the box in the middle of the scroll bars, indicates your relative position within the window. The size of the scroll box indicates the amount of information available to scroll. A small scroll box indicates a lot of information, whereas a large scroll box indicates a small amount. If you have a mouse with a scroll wheel between the left and right buttons, you can roll the wheel button to scroll up and down quickly, or click the wheel button and move the mouse in any direction. When no scroll bars appear in a window, it means that all the information fits completely in the window.

Using Menus, Toolbars, and Panes

A **menu** is a list of commands that you use to accomplish certain tasks, such as when you used the Start menu to open a window or program. A **command** is a directive that provides access to a program's features. Each Windows program has its own set of menus, which are usually located on a menu bar. The menu bar organizes commands into menus, or groups of related operations, such as File or Help. To access the commands in a menu, you click the name of the menu. You can also carry out some of the most frequently used commands by clicking a button on a toolbar. A **toolbar** contains buttons that display menus, select options, or perform commands. For example, the Organize button displays a menu, whereas the Views button displays a list of options. Note that some buttons have arrows next to them; clicking the button itself causes a default action, whereas clicking the arrow next to the button opens a menu. For example, when you click the Views button arrow, a list of options appears, and when you click the Views button, the next view in the list displays. Other buttons toggle options on and off. For example, when you click the Preview Pane button on the toolbar, it shows or hides the pane; it works like a light switch in your home. ▰▰▰▰ You want to use menus, toolbar buttons, and commands to change how the Windows Explorer window contents appear.

STEPS

1. **With the Windows Explorer window open, point to the** Organize button `Organize ▾` **on the toolbar**

    When you position the pointer over a button, a description of the action associated with the button appears as a ScreenTip. You can use the ScreenTip feature to explore buttons on a toolbar.

> **QUICK TIP**
>
> If a command on a menu includes a keyboard reference, known as a keyboard shortcut, you can quickly perform the action by pressing and holding the first key, and then pressing the second key.

2. **Click the** Organize button **on the toolbar**

    A menu of commands appears. Just like on the Start menu, when an arrow appears on the right side of a menu command, pointing to that command opens a submenu.

3. **Point to** Layout

    The Layout submenu appears, displaying commands, as shown in Figure A-9. A **pane** is a frame within a window where you can quickly access commands or display information. The Layout submenu allows you to show or hide the menu bar and window panes. On a menu, a check mark identifies a currently selected feature, meaning that the feature is **enabled**, or turned on. To **disable**, or turn off the feature, you click the command again to remove the check mark. Menu bar is currently disabled. The icons next to the panel commands on the Layout submenu indicate the same thing.

> **TROUBLE**
>
> If you don't see the menu bar, the menu bar was already enabled. Repeat Steps 2 through 4.

4. **Click** Menu bar **on the submenu**

    A new menu bar appears at the top of the window.

5. **Click** View **on the menu bar**

    The View menu appears, displaying the View commands. In the View menu, the bullet indicates the current view—the way the files are displayed in the window. A bullet next to a command indicates that the option is enabled. To disable a command with a bullet mark next to it, however, you must select another command (within the menu section, separated by gray lines) in its place.

> **TROUBLE**
>
> If the status bar is not visible on your screen, the status bar was already enabled. Click View on the menu bar, then click Status bar again to enable it.

6. **Click** Status bar **to enable it, then click** View **on the menu bar again**

    The status bar appears at the bottom of the Windows Explorer window, and Status bar on the View menu now has a check mark next to it. A description of the View menu appears in the status bar. See Figure A-10.

7. **Click** Status bar

    The status bar is turned off.

8. **Click the** Organize button **on the toolbar, point to** Layout, **then click** Menu bar

    The menu bar is removed from the window.

9. **Click the** Close button `✕` **in the upper-right corner of the Windows Explorer window**

    The Windows Explorer window closes.

FIGURE A-9: Organize button in the Libraries window

Toolbar

Arrow
indicates
submenu

Commands
on menu

Details
pane

Preview
Pane button

Views
button

Disabled
option

Submenu

Enabled
option

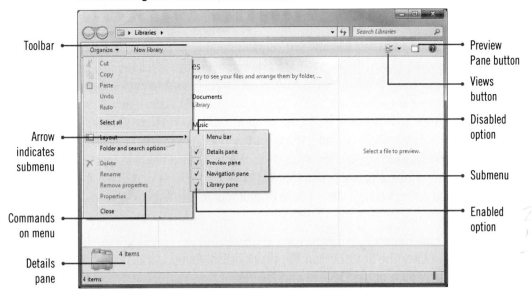

FIGURE A-10: View menu open with the status bar visible

Menu bar

Check mark

Bullet

Navigation pane

Description of menu
in status bar

Commands on your
screen might differ

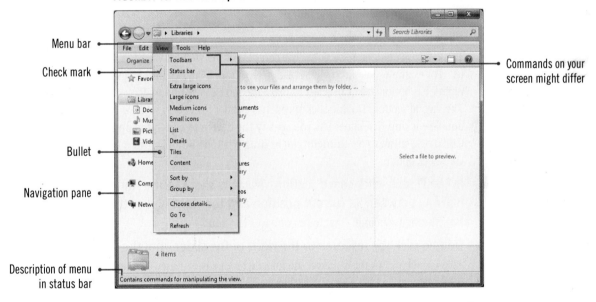

Setting Accessibility for special needs

If you have difficulty using a mouse or typing, have slightly impaired vision, or are deaf or hard of hearing, you can adjust the appearance and behavior of Windows 7 to make your computer easier for you to use. The Accessibility Wizard takes you step-by-step through a series of instructional windows to help you configure Windows for your vision, hearing, and mobility needs. The Accessibility Wizard also enables you to save your settings in a file that you can use on another computer. To open the Accessibility Wizard, click the Start button on the taskbar, click Control Panel, click Ease of Access, then click Ease of Access Center. A window opens with verbal instructions for using the Ease of Access

Center and commands to adjust the way your keyboard, display, and mouse function to suit various vision and motor abilities. Some of the accessibility tools available include Sticky Keys, which enables simultaneous keystrokes while pressing one key at a time; Filter Keys, which adjusts the response of your keyboard; Toggle Keys, which emits sounds when you press certain locking keys; Sound Sentry, which provides visual warnings for system sounds; Narrator, which instructs programs to provide captions; High Contrast, which improves screen contrast; and Mouse Keys, which enables the keyboard to perform mouse functions.

Using Dialog Boxes

A **dialog box** is a window that contains options for completing a task. A dialog box opens when you choose a button on a toolbar or menu command that is followed by an ellipsis (. . .). The **ellipsis** on a menu command indicates that you must supply more information before the program can carry out the command you selected. Dialog boxes open in other situations as well, such as when you open a program in the Control Panel. You can also access a dialog box from the notification area on the taskbar. When you click an icon in the notification area, such as the date and time, a menu appears with links or commands to open a dialog box or Control Panel window. In a dialog box, you specify the options you want using a variety of elements. See Figure A-11 and Table A-3 for some of the typical elements of a dialog box. 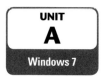 You practice using a dialog box to control your mouse settings.

STEPS

TROUBLE
If your dialog box differs from Figure A-12, read through Steps 2–4 and do not perform any actions, then continue with Step 5.

1. **Click the Start button** ⊕, **click Control Panel, click Hardware and Sound, then click Mouse under Devices and Printers**

   The Mouse Properties dialog box opens, as shown in Figure A-12. The options in this dialog box allow you to control the configuration of the mouse buttons, select the types of pointers that appear, choose the speed of the mouse movement on the screen, and specify what type of mouse you are using. **Tabs** at the top of the dialog box separate these options into related categories. The tabs in the dialog box vary depending on the mouse installed on the computer.

2. **Click the Buttons tab, if necessary**

   This tab has two or more sections. The contents of the sections vary depending on the type of computer you use. For example, a desktop might be different from a laptop. In this case, the first section, Button configuration, has options you can select to make the mouse easier to use for a right-handed or left-handed person. The second section, Double-click speed, has a slider for you to set how fast the mouse pointer responds to double-clicking. The slider lets you specify the degree to which the option is in effect. The third section, ClickLock, allows you to highlight or drag without holding the mouse button when you select the ClickLock option.

3. **In the Double-click speed section, drag the slider to the right to position it about halfway between its current position and the right end of the slider bar**

   Now the mouse pointer is set to respond to a fast double-click.

TROUBLE
If nothing happens when you double-click the test area, try double-clicking faster, with less time between each click.

4. **Double-click the test area to the right of the slider until the graphical icon moves**

   As you double-click the test area, the folder icon opens or closes. The test area allows you to try out the adjusted settings.

5. **Click the other tabs in the Mouse Properties dialog box, and examine the available options in each category**

   The two most common command buttons are OK and Cancel. Clicking OK accepts your changes and closes the dialog box; clicking Cancel leaves the original settings intact and closes the dialog box. Many dialog boxes, including this one, contain a third command button—Apply. Clicking Apply executes the options you selected but keeps the dialog box open so that you can select additional options.

6. **Click Cancel to leave the original settings intact and close the dialog box**

7. **Click the Close button** ⊠ **in the upper-right corner of the Control Panel window to close the window**

FIGURE A-11: Dialog box elements

Check box

Option button

Text box

Up and down arrows

Command buttons

FIGURE A-12: Mouse Properties dialog box

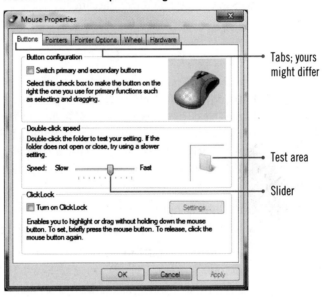

Tabs; yours might differ

Test area

Slider

TABLE A-3: Typical items in a dialog box

item	description
Check box	A square box that turns an option on when the box is checked and off when the box is blank
Command button	A rectangular button with the name of the command on it; it carries out a command in a dialog box
List box	A box containing a list of items; to choose an item, click the list arrow, then click the desired item
Option button	A small circle that selects a single dialog box option (you cannot check more than one option button in a group)
Up and down arrows	A box with two arrows and a text box you can scroll through to choose from numerical increments or type a number
Slider	A shape that you drag to set the degree to which an option is in effect
Tab	A place where related options are organized; similar to tabs on file folders
Text box	A box in which you type text

Using Windows Help and Support

When you have a question about how to do something in Windows 7, you can usually find the answer with a few clicks of your mouse. Microsoft **Help and Support** is a complete resource of information, training, and support to help you learn and use Windows 7. Help and Support is like a book stored on your computer with additional links to the Internet, complete with a search feature, and a table of contents to make finding information easier. If you have an Internet connection, you can get online help from a support professional at Microsoft or from other users on the Windows newsgroup (an electronic forum where people share information), or invite a friend with Windows to chat with you, view your screen, and work on your computer to provide remote support. You want to use Help and Support to learn more about Windows 7.

STEPS

TROUBLE
If your dialog box differs from Figure A-13, click the lower-right button, then click Get online Help.

QUICK TIP
To get help on a specific program, you can click Help on the program's menu bar or click the Help button on the toolbar.

QUICK TIP
To print a Help topic, click the Print button on the toolbar at the top of the Windows Help and Support window.

QUICK TIP
To receive help in a dialog box or window, click the Help button in the upper-right corner of the dialog box or window. The Help and Support window opens, displaying Help information related to the options in that dialog box.

1. **Click the Start button on the taskbar, then click Help and Support**
   The Windows Help and Support window opens with a list of Help and Support categories, as shown in Figure A-13. Help windows always appear on top of the currently active window, so you can see Help topics while you work. You can find answers from the main categories (How to get started with your computer, Learn about Windows Basics, or Browse Help topics), or go online to the Microsoft Web site to get more information, downloads, and ideas. If you need additional help, you can display more support options to ask others online for help.

2. **Click in the Search box, type help, then press [Enter]**
   A list of the best results possible displays. See Figure A-14. To display more results, scroll to the bottom of the window, and then click the more results link. When you point to a Help category or a search result, the pointer changes to , and the Help text becomes underlined to indicate that more information is available by clicking. A single-click opens the Help category or topic. This is similar to the way selecting a hyperlink on the Internet works.

3. **In the results list, click Getting help**
   The Help topic appears in the window. Read the information on getting help.

4. **Click the Help and Support home button on the toolbar at the top of the Windows Help and Support window**
   The main Help and Support window appears again. Now you will display a search pane with more topics.

5. **Click Browse Help topics to open the list of main Help topics, click Getting started, then click Shutting down**
   Help topics in the Shutting down category appear. The list of contents organizes the online Help topics and allows you to browse your way around the Help topics you want to view.

6. **Click Turning off your computer properly**
   The Help topic appears in the window. You can move back and forth between Help topics you have already visited by clicking the Back button and the Forward button on the toolbar.

7. **Click the Back button on the Help and Support toolbar to return to the previous Help screen**
   Help topics in the Shutting down category appear.

8. **Click the All Help link below the Help and Support toolbar to return to the main Help topic list**

9. **Click the Close button in the upper-right corner of the Help and Support window**
   The Help and Support window closes.

FIGURE A-13: Windows Help and Support

Back and
Forward buttons

Help toolbar

Search box

Help
categories

Online
information

Click to set
Help settings

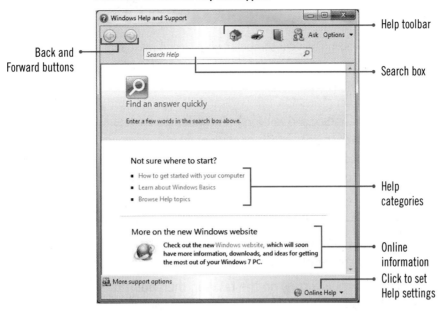

FIGURE A-14: Help topic

Search text

Help topic
search results;
your results
may vary

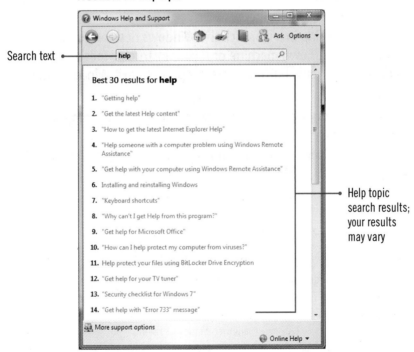

Getting help online

If you need additional help and have an Internet connection, you can use Windows Help and Support to get online help from a support professional at Microsoft or from other users in Windows communities, or you can invite a friend to chat with you, view your screen, and work on your computer to provide remote support. To get help from a friend or offer help to a friend, you use Windows Remote Assistance, which connects two computers over the Internet so that one person can help troubleshoot or fix problems on the other person's computer. While the computers are connected, the person providing assistance can view the other person's screen or take control of the computer to perform a fix. To do this, in Windows Help and Support, click the Ask button on the toolbar at the top of the Windows Help and Support window, click Windows Remote Assistance under Ask a person for help, and follow the step-by-step instructions provided.

Shutting Down the Computer

When you finish working on your computer, you need to make sure to turn off, or **shut down**, your computer properly. This involves several steps: saving and closing all open files, closing all open windows, exiting all running programs, shutting down Windows itself, and, finally, turning off the computer. Shutting down your computer makes sure Windows and all its related programs are properly closed; this avoids potential problems starting and working with Windows in the future. If you turn off the computer by pushing the power switch while Windows or other programs are running, you could lose important data. If a program is still open when you instruct Windows to shut down, you will be prompted to save the file and close the program before the shut-down process continues. ▰▰▰▰▰ You shut down your computer now.

STEPS

1. **If any windows or programs are open on your screen, click the Close button [x] in the upper-right corner of each window**

QUICK TIP

To prevent other users from using your computer, you can press [⊞] [L] to lock the computer and return to the Welcome screen. To unlock, move the mouse and log on at the Welcome screen.

2. **Click the Start button 🕐 on the taskbar, then point to the arrow ▷ next to the Power button**

   A submenu appears, displaying several options for turning off your computer, as shown in Figure A-15. See Table A-4 for a description of each option. The Power button (set by default to Shut down) provides easy access to your preferred shutdown option. Depending on your Windows settings, your shutdown options might be different.

3. **If you are working in a lab, click the Windows desktop to cancel the task; if you are working on your own machine or if your instructor tells you to shut down Windows, click the Shut down button or menu option to exit Windows and shut down your computer**

QUICK TIP

If you have a mobile PC, set Power Options in the Control Panel to turn off your computer or put it to sleep by closing the lid.

4. **If you see the message "It's now safe to turn off your computer," turn off your computer and monitor**

   Some computers power off automatically, so you might not see this message.

TABLE A-4: Shut down options

option	function	when to use it
Switch user	Maintains your session and changes users	When you want to continue working with Windows, yet allow another user to access another Windows session
Log off	Saves and leaves your session to disk and changes users	When you want to stop working with Windows, yet allow another user to access another Windows session
Lock	Maintains your session, while restricting access to Windows	When you want to stop working with Windows and you want to keep others from using Windows
Restart	Restarts the computer and reloads Windows	When you want to restart the computer and begin working with Windows again (when your programs might have frozen or stopped working)
Sleep	Maintains your session, keeping the computer running on low power	When you want to stop working with Windows for a few moments and conserve power (ideal for a laptop or portable computer); available when a power scheme is selected in Power Options (in the Control Panel)
Hibernate	Saves your session to disk so that you can safely turn off power; restores your session the next time you start Windows	When you want to stop working with Windows for a while and start working again later; available when the Power Options setting (in the Control Panel) is turned on
Shut down	Prepares the computer to be turned off	When you finish working with Windows and you want to shut off your computer

FIGURE A-15: Shut down menu

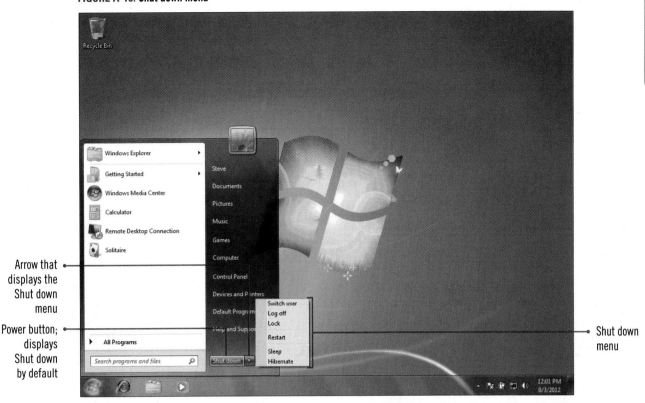

Arrow that displays the Shut down menu

Power button; displays Shut down by default

Shut down menu

Working on a computer set up for multiple users

Many users may use the same computer, in which case each user has his or her own Windows identity, allowing them to keep their files completely private and customize the operating system with their own preferences. Windows manages these separate identities by giving each user a unique username and password. You set up user accounts during Windows 7 installation or by using User Accounts in the Control Panel, as shown in Figure A-16. When Windows starts, a Welcome screen appears, displaying user accounts. When a user selects an account and types a password (if necessary), Windows starts with that user's configuration settings and network permissions. When you're done using the computer, yet you want to leave it on for another person to use, you can choose the Switch user or Log off command from the Start menu. The Switch user command allows you to switch between users quickly without having to save your current settings, so you can switch back and continue working. The Log off command saves your current settings and exits you from Windows.

FIGURE A-16

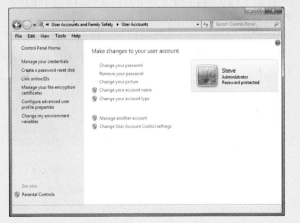

Practice

Concepts Review

For current SAM information including versions and content details, visit SAM Central (http://samcentral.course.com). If you have a SAM user profile, you may have access to hands-on instruction, practice, and assessment of the skills covered in this unit. Since we support various versions of SAM throughout the life of this text, you will want to check with your instructor for instructions and the correct URL/Web site to access those assignments.

Match the statements below with the elements labeled in the screen shown in Figure A-17.

FIGURE A-17

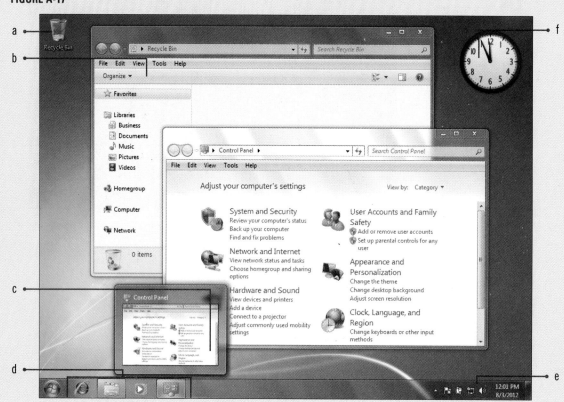

1. Which element points to an icon on the desktop? *a*
2. Which element points to a toolbar? *b*
3. Which element points to the notification area? *e*
4. Which element points to a gadget on the desktop? *f*
5. Which element points to a live thumbnail? *c*
6. Which element points to taskbar buttons? *d*

Match each term with the statement that describes its function.

f 7. **Start button**

e 8. **Recycle Bin**

d 9. **Mouse**

c 10. **Address bar**

a 11. **Sizing buttons**

b 12. **Taskbar**

a. Allows you to minimize, maximize, and restore windows

b. Holds the Start button and buttons for currently open programs and windows

c. Where the name of a Windows Explorer window appears

d. Used to point at screen elements and make selections

e. Where deleted files are placed

f. The item you click first to start a program

Concepts Review (Continued)

Select the best answers from the following lists of choices.

13. Moving an item to a new location on the desktop is called:
    a. Dragging.
    b. Restoring.
    c. Pointing.
    d. Clicking.

14. Which screen element allows you to perform a search?
    a. Desktop
    b. Start menu
    c. Taskbar
    d. Notification area

15. The Maximize button is used to:
    a. Scroll slowly through a window.
    b. Reduce a window to a button on the taskbar.
    c. Return a window to its original size.
    d. Expand a window to fill the entire screen.

16. The Minimize button is used to:
    a. Scroll slowly through a window.
    b. Reduce a window to a button on the taskbar.
    c. Return a window to its original size.
    d. Expand a window to fill the entire screen.

17. The menu provides access to a program's functions through:
    a. Commands.
    b. Dialog box elements.
    c. Toolbar buttons.
    d. Scroll buttons.

18. An ellipsis after a menu command indicates:
    a. Another menu will display.
    b. A keyboard shortcut to that command.
    c. The menu command is not currently available.
    d. A dialog box will open.

19. Which shutdown option turns off your computer and reloads Windows?
    a. Shut down
    b. Restart
    c. Hibernate
    d. Sleep

Skills Review

1. **Start Windows and view the desktop.**
   a. Start Windows and log on, if necessary.
   b. Identify and write down as many desktop items as you can, without referring to the lesson.
   c. Compare your results with Figure A-1.

2. **Use pointing devices.**
   a. Move the mouse on your desk, and watch how the mouse pointer moves across the screen.
   b. Point at an icon on the desktop.
   c. Click the icon once. Notice the icon's highlighted title.
   d. Press and hold down the mouse button, then drag the icon to the opposite side of the desktop. (*Hint*: release the mouse button when you finish dragging.)
   e. Drag the icon back to its original location.
   f. Double-click the Recycle Bin icon.
   g. Close the Recycle Bin.

3. **Use the Start button.**
   a. Open the Start menu.
   b. Open the All Programs submenu.
   c. Display the list of programs in the Accessories folder.
   d. Return to the Start menu.
   e. In the Search box, type **access** to find Ease of Access Center.
   f. Close the search.
   g. Open the Control Panel window.

4. **Use the taskbar.**
   a. Open the Recycle Bin window.
   b. Make the Control Panel window active.

Skills Review (Continued)

    c. Display live thumbnails on the taskbar.

    d. Use Windows Flip 3D to display the Recycle Bin window.

    e. Use Windows Flip to display the Control Panel window.

5. Work with windows.

    a. Show the desktop, then display the Recycle Bin and Control Panel windows.

    b. Make the Recycle Bin window active.

    c. Minimize the Recycle Bin window.

    d. Resize the Control Panel window to make it smaller.

    e. Drag the Control Panel window to the center of the desktop.

    f. Maximize the Control Panel window.

    g. Restore the Control Panel to its original size.

    h. Close the Control Panel window.

    i. Restore and close the Recycle Bin window.

6. Use menus, toolbars, and panes.

    a. Open the Games window using the command in the right column on the Start menu.

    b. Display the menu bar.

    c. Click View on the menu bar, then click Content.

    d. Click View on the menu bar, then click Tiles.

    e. Hide the menu bar.

    f. Click the Views button arrow on the toolbar to display a list of all the views.

    g. Click Large Icons on the Views button menu.

    h. Close the Games window.

7. Use dialog boxes.

    a. In the Control Panel window, click Change desktop background (under Appearance and Personalization).

    b. Click a background.

    c. Change the Picture position to Center.

    d. Minimize the window and view the changes to the desktop.

    e. Maximize the Control Panel window, then click Cancel.

    f. Close the Control Panel window.

8. Use Windows Help and Support.

    a. Click the Start button on the taskbar, then click Help and Support.

    b. In the Search text box, type **computer**, then press [Enter].

    c. In the list of search results, click a Help topic, then read the Help topic in the window.

    d. Click the Print button, select a printer, then click Print.

    e. Click the Help and Support home button.

    f. Click the Help and Support window Close button.

9. Shut down the computer.

    a. Click the Start button on the taskbar, then point to the arrow next to the Power button.

    b. If you are not working in a lab or if your lab manager approves of shutting down the computer, click Shut down. Otherwise, click a blank area of the desktop.

Independent Challenge 1

You are a student in a Windows 7 course and want to find out what's new in Windows 7. Use the Getting Started window to access the latest online information about Windows 7 and manage the open windows.

    a. Open the Start menu, type **Getting Started** in the Search box, then click Getting Started in the search results on the Start menu. You can also click the Start button, point to All Programs, click Accessories, then click Getting Started.

Independent Challenge 1 (Continued)

b. Make sure you are connected to the Internet, click the Go online to find out what's new in Windows 7 icon, then click Go online to learn more in the upper-right area of the window.

c. Drag the title bar to the top of the screen or use the Maximize button to maximize your browser window.

d. Read the Windows 7 Web page to learn more about Windows 7.

e. Drag your browser window to either side of the screen to resize it for comparison or use the Restore Down button.

f. Activate the Getting Started window.

g. Right-click a blank area of the taskbar, then use commands to show windows side by side, show windows stacked, and cascade windows.

h. Use Windows Flip and Windows Flip 3D to display the different open windows.

i. Show the desktop to minimize all open windows, then show all the open windows.

j. Close your Web browser and the Getting Started window.

Independent Challenge 2

Windows 7 provides extensive online help and support. At any time, you can select Help and Support from the Start menu and get the assistance you need. Explore more of the topics available in Help and Support.

a. Start Help and Support.

b. Click a link in the main Help and Support window to Learn about Windows Basics.

c. Use the Search text box to search for information about Windows keyboard shortcuts and customer support. Print the information about keyboard shortcuts.

d. Click a link in the main Help and Support window to Browse Help topics, then find information about accessibility features. Use the list of categories in Help Contents. Click Customizing your computer, then click Ease of Access (Accessibility). Click and read the information on two or more topics.

Advanced Challenge Exercise

- In the main Help and Support window, click the More support options button (at the bottom of the window) or Ask button on the toolbar.
- Make sure you are connected to the Internet, click the Microsoft Customer Support link (under Ask a person for help) to open your browser and access Microsoft Help and Support with more technical help and support information.
- Type **Windows 7 help** in the Search box, then click Search Site to display links to Windows 7–related help and support topics.
- View the topics, then click a link to a topic.
- When you're done, click the Close button to exit your browser, then close all tabs.

e. Close the Help and Support window.

Independent Challenge 3

You can customize many Windows features to suit your needs and preferences. One way you do this is to change the items that appear in the notification area on the desktop. Another way is to change the desktop background.

a. Open the Control Panel window, click Appearance and Personalization, click Customize icons on the taskbar (under the Taskbar and Start Menu heading), then click Turn system icons on or off.

b. Click the Behaviors list arrow for Clock, Volume, Network, and Power (if possible), then set them to Off. What happens in the notification area?

c. Click the Behaviors list arrow for the same options, set them back to On, then click OK twice.

d. Go Back to the main Control Panel window.

e. In the Control Panel window, click Change desktop background (under Appearance and Personalization). In the Choose your desktop background screen, click various backgrounds to change the display behind the Control Panel window.

f. Click Cancel.

Independent Challenge 3 (Continued)

Advanced Challenge Exercise

- In the Control Panel window, click Change the theme (under Appearance and Personalization).
- In the themes list, click Windows Classic (under Basic and High Contrast Themes) to apply it.
- Click Desktop Background, select a different color to see it applied, then click Cancel.
- In the themes list, click Windows 7 (under Aero Themes) to apply it.

g. Close the Control Panel window.

Real Life Independent Challenge

Many people move through different time zones as they travel, either on vacation or business. It is usually a good idea to set up your computer to reflect local time. You can do this in the Control Panel window.

a. Open the Control Panel window, click Clock, Language, and Region, then click Change the time zone.

b. On the Date and Time tab in the Date and Time dialog box, click Change time zone.

c. In the Time Zone Settings dialog box, click the Time zone list arrow.

d. Note the current time zone on your computer, and then scroll through the list of time zones.

e. Select a time zone for a location you have visited (or would like to visit) for vacation or business from the list (scroll if necessary). Note that a line is added below the Current date and time in the dialog box telling you what the date and time will be after you apply the new time zone setting.

f. Click OK. Note the changed time in the notification area.

g. Restore the original time zone setting, then close the Date and Time dialog box.

h. Close the Control Panel window.

Visual Workshop

Re-create the screen shown in Figure A-18, which shows the Windows desktop with the Libraries and the Control Panel open.

FIGURE A-18

Working with Windows Programs

Now that you know how to work with common Windows graphical elements, you're ready to work with programs. A **program** is software you use to accomplish specific tasks, such as word processing and managing files on your computer. Windows comes with several **accessories**—built-in programs that, although not as feature-rich as many programs sold separately, are extremely useful for completing basic tasks. In this unit, you work with some of these accessories. You're a tour developer for Quest Specialty Travel, a growing company that uses Windows 7 on its computers. You want to prepare a document outlining ideas for travel packages, so you plan to use two Windows accessories, WordPad and Paint, to create it. You also want to use two other multimedia accessories, Windows Media Player and Windows Media Center, to play travel videos and sound clips and to create a travel movie.

OBJECTIVES

Start a program
Open and save a WordPad document
Modify text in WordPad
Work with a graphic in Paint
Copy data between programs
Embed or link an object
Print a document
Play a video or audio clip
Work with Windows media

Starting a Program

A **Windows program** is software designed to run on computers using the Windows operating system. The most common way to start a Windows program is to use the Start menu, which provides easy access to programs installed on your computer. Clicking the Start button 🌐 on the taskbar displays the Start menu, which lists common and recently used programs, and the All Programs submenu, which you can click to list all the programs installed on your computer. In this lesson, you start a Windows accessory called **WordPad**, a word-processing program that comes with Windows. A **word processor** is a program that you use to enter, edit, and format text and graphics. As you look for WordPad on the All Programs sub-menu under Accessories, you might notice an accessory called **Notepad**. The accessory names are similar, and both programs work with text. Notepad is a **text editor**, in which you can enter and edit text only with basic document formatting. With both programs, you can open only one document per open pro-gram window at a time. ▰▰▰ Before you can use WordPad to prepare a text document of tour package ideas, you need to start the program.

STEPS

1. **Click the Start button 🌐 on the taskbar**

   The Start menu opens. If you frequently use a program, it appears on the left column of the Start menu for easy access. When a program, such as WordPad, appears on the Start menu with an arrow, the submenu displays a list of recently opened files for the program known as a **jump list** for easy access. If the program you want to start doesn't appear in the frequently used list, you can use the Search box at the bottom of the Start menu, or you can use the All Programs submenu to locate and start it.

2. **Point to All Programs on the Start menu**

   The All Programs submenu opens, listing the programs and subfolders for programs installed on your com-puter. WordPad is in the folder called Accessories.

3. **Click Accessories on the All Programs submenu**

   The Accessories folder list opens, as shown in Figure B-1. The Accessories folder contains several programs to help you complete common tasks. The All Programs submenu remains open and displays the Back com-mand at the bottom.

4. **Point to Back on the All Programs submenu**

   The Start menu reappears, displaying the recently used programs in Windows 7.

5. **Click All Programs on the Start menu, then click WordPad on the All Programs submenu under Accessories**

   Your mouse pointer changes momentarily to ⟳, indicating that Windows is starting the WordPad pro-gram. The WordPad window then opens on your screen.

6. **Click the Maximize button 🔲 in the upper-right corner of the WordPad window, if necessary**

   The WordPad window expands to fill the screen, as shown in Figure B-2. The WordPad window includes a title bar at the top with the filename (currently untitled with the name "Document") and program name, a customizable toolbar, called the **Quick Access toolbar**, the **WordPad button** to select file-related commands, a **Ribbon** with two tabs—Home and View—to quickly select document-related commands, as well as the ruler, the work area, and the status bar. A blinking line, known as the **insertion point**, appears in the work area of the WordPad window, indicating where new text will appear. A button, called a taskbar button, appears on the taskbar. **Taskbar buttons** represent open windows on the desktop. In the next lesson, you open and save a document in WordPad.

FIGURE B-1: Starting WordPad using the Start menu

WordPad on the Start menu

Accessories folder list; yours might differ

FIGURE B-2: Windows desktop with the WordPad window open

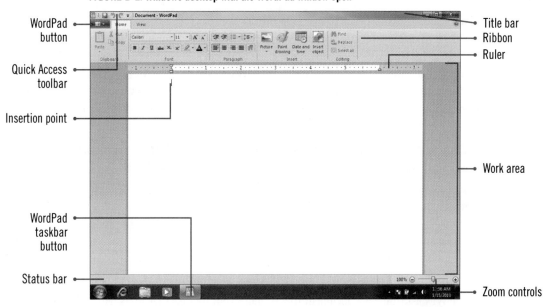

WordPad button

Quick Access toolbar

Insertion point

WordPad taskbar button

Status bar

Title bar

Ribbon

Ruler

Work area

Zoom controls

Creating documents in other languages

You can install multiple languages on your computer, such as Hebrew, Arabic, Japanese, French, Spanish, German, and many others. You can choose which language you want to use when you create a document, then Windows makes the characters for that language available. To install additional languages, click the Start button, click Control Panel, then click Change keyboards or other input methods (under Clock, Language, and Region) to open the Region and Language dialog box. Click Change keyboards to open the Text Services and Input Languages dialog box with the General tab on top, then click Add to open the Add Input Language dialog box. The languages you can add appear in a list. Scroll down the list, click the plus sign next to the language you want to add, click the plus sign next to Keyboard or Speech, then click the check box next to the language element you want to add. If you have more than one language installed, the Language bar allows you to select the language you want to use. To set Language bar settings, click the Language Bar tab in the Text Services and Input Languages dialog box, and then click the option to display the Language bar, either Docked in the taskbar or Floating On Desktop. The Language bar will not appear unless you have more than one language installed. To compose a document that uses more than one language, click the Input language button on the Language bar, click the language you want to use in the list that opens, then type your message. The language setting remains in place until you change it or shut down your computer. Any recipient of multilanguage documents must also have the same languages installed on their computer to read and edit the documents.

Opening and Saving a WordPad Document

A **document** is a file you create using a word-processing program, such as a letter, memo, or resume. When you start WordPad, a blank document opens which is known as the **document window**. You can enter information to create a new document and save the result in a file, or you can open an existing file and save the document with changes. Until you save a document, it is stored in the computer's **random access memory (RAM)**, temporary storage whose contents are erased when you turn off the computer. To store a document permanently, you save it as a file. The first time you save a file, you need to specify a filename and folder in the Save As dialog box. The next time you save, the program saves the file with the same name in the same folder. If you want to change a file's name or location, you can use the Save As dialog box again to create a copy of the original file. You have been brainstorming some new tour ideas. Rather than typing the information from scratch, you open an existing document. You want to preserve the original tour ideas so you save it with a new name before making changes to it.

STEPS

QUICK TIP
To quickly open a recently used file, point to the WordPad button, then click a file in the right column of the menu.

1. **Click the WordPad button ▮▼, then click Open**
    The Open dialog box opens. You use the Open dialog box to locate and choose the file you want to open. The **Navigation pane**, located on the left side of the dialog box, is used to navigate to common locations and recently used files and folders. The **Address bar** at the top of the dialog box indicates the current folder location. The folder location, which appears as a series of links separated by arrows, creates a **path** from the drive to the folder. You select a location by clicking a drive or folder location name in the Address bar, or by clicking a link arrow to the right of the location to select a subfolder location.

TROUBLE
In this book, files are displayed with file extensions. Your display might differ.

2. **Click Computer in the Navigation pane, or click the leftmost link arrow in the Address bar and click Computer, then, in the window, double-click the drive and folder where you store your Data Files**
    A list of files and folders appears in the file list, as shown in Figure B-3. The files shown are determined by the option chosen in the Files type list. The Files type list box indicates that the documents shown in this list are in the All Wordpad Documents (.rtf), the default format for WordPad files. **Rich Text Format (RTF)** is a file format that includes formatting for text files and can be opened and read by many other programs.

TROUBLE
If there aren't any filenames in the file list, click the Files of type list arrow, then click Rich Text Format (*.rtf).

3. **In the list of files, click WIN B-1.rtf, then click Open**
    The WIN B-1.rtf file is a document that contains your tour package ideas. The only way to prevent accidental changes from occurring to an original document is to save it in another file with a new name.

4. **Click the WordPad button ▮▼, point to Save as, click Rich Text document, then click Browse Folders, if necessary, to expand the dialog box**
    The Save As dialog box opens, as shown in Figure B-4. You use the Save As dialog box to save an existing document with a new name and in a different folder or drive. The Save as submenu allows you to select a file format for the new document. In addition to RTF, you can also save documents in **Office Open XML Document (DOCX)**, which is for Microsoft Word 2007, **OpenDocument Text (ODT)**, which is for exchanging Office documents, and **Text Document (TXT)**, which is for plain text.

5. **Type Tour Ideas in the File name text box**
    As soon as you start typing, the text you type replaces the selected text in the File name text box. When you type a name in the File name text box, **AutoComplete** suggests possible matches with previous filename entries. You can continue to type or click the File name list arrow, then click the correct filename from the list.

6. **Click Save**
    The file is saved as Tour Ideas.rtf in the same folder and drive as the WIN B-1.rtf file.

FIGURE B-3: Open dialog box

Link arrows •

Click to access • your Data Files

Navigation pane •

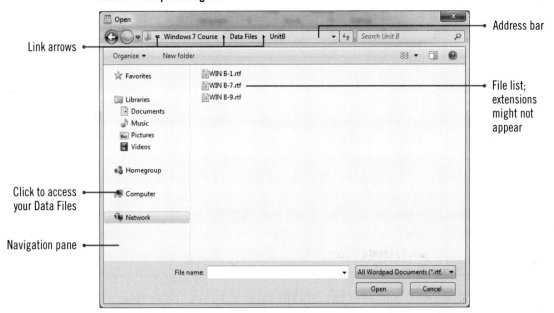

Address bar

File list; extensions might not appear

FIGURE B-4: Save As dialog box

File name text box •

Toggles between • Browse Folders and Hide Folders

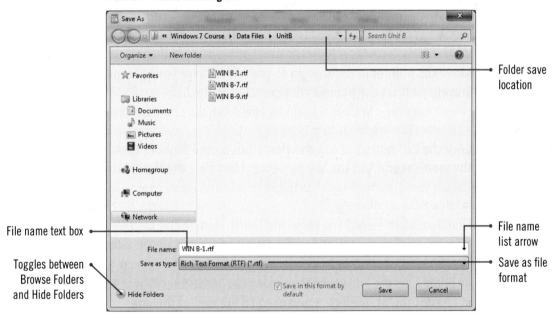

Folder save location

File name list arrow

Save as file format

Working with filename extensions

The program Windows uses to open a document depends on a three- or four-letter extension to the document's filename, called a **filename extension**. You might have never seen a document's filename extension because your system might be set up to hide it. The filename extension for simple text files is ".txt" (pronounced "dot t-x-t"), and many graphic filenames have the extension ".bmp." This means that the full name for a text file named Memo is Memo.txt. If you double-click a document whose filename ends with the three-letter extension ".txt," Windows automatically opens the document with Notepad, a text-only editor. If you want to display or change filename extension settings, open the Control Panel,

click Appearance and Personalization, then click Folder Options. If you want to display filename extensions in dialog boxes and windows, click the View tab in the Folder Options dialog box, then click the Hide extensions for known file types check box to deselect it in the Advanced settings list box. If you want to change the program Windows automatically starts with a given filename extension, right-click the file that you want to change, point to Open with, click Choose default program, then click the program you want to use to open this file. If you want all files of that type to open with the same program, select the Always use the selected program to open this kind of file check box, then click OK.

Modifying Text in WordPad

When you use a word-processing program, you can **edit**, or change, the contents of the document without re-creating it. You can move text from one place to another using the Cut and Paste commands or the **drag-and-drop** method, which allows you simply to drag text from one location to another. When selected text is cut from a document, Windows removes it from the document and places it on the **Clipboard**, a temporary storage place where it remains available to be pasted elsewhere. You can also change the **format**, or the appearance, of the text and graphics in a document so that the document is easier to read or more attractive. For special emphasis, you can combine formats, such as bold and italic. In addition, you can change the font style and size. A **font** is a set of characters with the same typeface or design, such as Arial or Times New Roman, that you can increase or decrease in size. Font size is measured in points; one **point** is 1/72 of an inch high. ▓▓▓▓ You want to add an introduction and modify and move text in the Tour Ideas document, then make the document more attractive.

STEPS

1. **Press [↓] three times to place the insertion point in the fourth line, type** Quest Specialty Travel (QST) takes the toil out of travel and puts the thrill back in! Each tour includes adventure, culture, and education (ACE)., **then press** [Enter]

   WordPad keeps the text on multiple lines together in the same paragraph, using a process called **word wrap**. The text wraps to the edge of the window or to the right margin of the ruler depending on your word-wrap settings. When you press [Enter], you create a new paragraph. To correct a mistake or to change text, press [Backspace] to delete the character to the left of the insertion point until you delete the text, then retype the text.

2. **Move the pointer in the margin to the left of "Live your dreams with Quest Specialty Travel!," so that the pointer changes to ↗, then click**

   When the pointer is in the left margin, clicking selects the entire line. Table B-1 describes several methods for selecting text in a document.

QUICK TIP

When the pointer is positioned in the WordPad work area, it changes to ⌶, which you can click to reposition the insertion point.

3. **Click the Cut button ✂ on the Home tab on the Ribbon, click ⌶ after the space after the word "world." in the last sentence, then click the Paste button 📋 on the Home tab**

   The text you selected in Step 2 is cut from the document, placed on the Clipboard, and is now pasted at the location of the insertion point.

4. **Double-click the word French in the fourth item in the bulleted list to select the entire word, then click the selection and drag it to the left of the word "farm"**

   As you drag the pointer, a vertical line next to the pointer indicates where the selection will be placed.

QUICK TIP

To change text color, select the text, click the Text color button **A** ▾ on the Home tab, then select a color.

5. **Position ⌶ to the left of the first character in the line "Quest Specialty Travel" at the top of the document, then click and drag to the end of the line**

   The text you dragged over is selected.

6. **Click the Center button ☰, the Bold button B, and the Italic button ⁄ on the Home tab**

   The title is now centered and in bold and italic. Note that the Center button is selected ("turned on"), and the Align Left button is deselected ("turned off"). Related buttons on a toolbar, such as Align text left, Center, and Align text right, act like options in a dialog box—click one to turn it on, and the other related ones turn off. Some buttons, such as Bold, Italic, Underline, and Start a list, act as **toggle** switches—click once to turn the format feature on, click again to turn it off.

QUICK TIP

To add buttons to the Quick Access toolbar, click the Customize Quick Access Toolbar button ▾ on the Quick Access toolbar, then click a button to select it.

7. **Click the Undo button ↶ on the Quick Access toolbar**

   Italics are removed from the selected text. The **Undo** command reverses the last change made.

8. **Click the Font list arrow** Arial ▾ **on the Home tab, scroll down the font list, click Times New Roman, click the Font Size list arrow** 10 ▾ **on the Home tab, click 18, then click the Save button 💾 on the Quick Access toolbar**

   The size of the selected text changes to 18-point Times New Roman, as shown in Figure B-5.

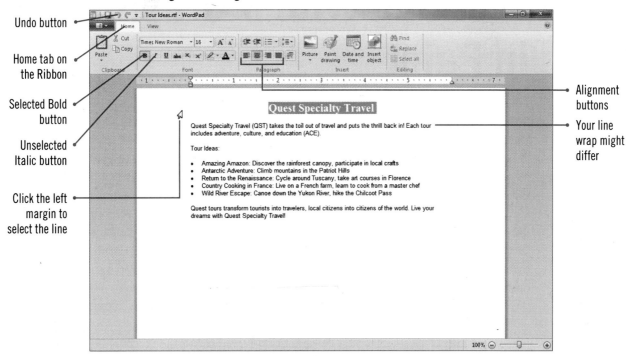

FIGURE B-5: Editing and formatting a WordPad document

Undo button

Home tab on the Ribbon

Selected Bold button

Unselected Italic button

Click the left margin to select the line

Alignment buttons

Your line wrap might differ

TABLE B-1: Methods for selecting text

to select	do this
A single word	Double-click the word
A single line	Click the left margin to the left of the first character in the line
A single paragraph	Triple-click a word within the paragraph or double-click in the margin to the left of the paragraph
Any part of a document	Drag the pointer over the text you want to select
A large selection	Click at the beginning of the text you want to select, press and hold [Shift], then click at the end of the text you want to select
The entire document	Triple-click in the left margin, press [Ctrl][A], or click the Select all button on the Home tab

Setting paragraph tabs and indents

Tabs set how text or numerical data aligns in a document. A **tab stop** is a predefined stopping point along the document's typing line. Default tab stops are set every half-inch on the ruler, but you can set multiple tabs per paragraph at any location. Each paragraph contains its own set of tab stops. The default tab stops appear as small hash marks below the ruler, and the manual tab stops appear as dark marks on the ruler itself. To display the tab stops for a paragraph on the ruler, click any word in the paragraph. To set a tab stop, click the ruler where you want to set it. Once you place a tab stop, you can drag the tab stop to position it where you want. To delete a tab stop, drag it off the ruler. If you want to add or adjust tab stops in multiple paragraphs, simply select the paragraphs first. When you indent a paragraph, you move its edge in from the left or right margin. You can indent the entire left or right edge of a paragraph or just the first line. The markers on the ruler control the indentation of the current paragraph. The left side of the ruler has three markers. The top triangle, called the **first-line indent marker**, controls where the first line of the paragraph begins. The bottom triangle, called the **hanging indent marker**, controls where the remaining lines of the paragraph begin. The small square under the bottom triangle, called **the left indent marker**, allows you to move the first-line indent marker and the left indent marker simultaneously. When you move the left indent marker, the distance between the hanging indent and the first-line indent remains the same. The triangle on the right side of the ruler, called the **right indent marker**, controls where the right edge of the paragraph ends. You can also click the Paragraph button on the Home tab to open the Paragraph dialog box and manually set paragraph indents.

Working with a Graphic in Paint

Paint is a Windows accessory you can use to create and work with graphics or pictures. You can open and save pictures created in, or for, other graphics programs and the Internet using several common file formats, such as .bmp, .tiff, .png, .gif, or .jpeg. A **bitmap** file is a map of a picture created from small dots, or pixels. The value of each dot is stored in one or more bits. One bit is used to represent a dot in black and white, or monochrome graphics, whereas multiple bits are used to represent a dot in graphics with color or shades of gray. With a 4-bit graphic, you can use 16 unique colors, an 8-bit graphic 256 colors, and a 24-bit graphic 16 million colors. To draw or modify graphics in Paint, you use buttons, including those in the Tools and Shapes groups, on the Home tab on the Ribbon, and described in Table B-2. The Colors group on the Home tab allows you to select the colors you want to use in Paint. You can open more than one Windows program at a time, called **multitasking**, so while WordPad is still running, you can open Paint and work on drawings and pictures. ▓▓▒▓ You decide you want to include the Quest logo in the Tour Ideas document you created. However, you need to modify it before you can insert the logo.

STEPS

1. **Click the Start button 🌐 on the taskbar, point to All Programs, click Accessories, click Paint, then click the Maximize button 🔲 in the Paint window, if necessary**

   The Paint window opens and is maximized in front of the WordPad window. The Paint window includes a title bar at the top with the filename (currently "Untitled") and program name, a customizable toolbar called the **Quick Access toolbar**, the **Paint button** used to select file-related commands, and a Ribbon with two tabs—Home and View—to quickly select document-related commands. In addition, the Paint window contains the status bar and the canvas area. The **canvas area**, or **work area**, is the white drawing area within the Paint window that doesn't include the gray area.

2. **Click the Paint button ◼▾, then click Open**

   The Open dialog box opens with all the picture files in the selected folder listed.

3. **Navigate to the drive and folder where you store your Data Files, click WIN B-2.bmp in the file list, then click Open**

   The file named WIN B-2.bmp, which is a logo, opens in the Paint window, as shown in Figure B-6.

QUICK TIP

To change the file format, click the Save as type list arrow, select the format you want, then click Save.

4. **Click the Paint button ◼▾, click Save as, then save the file as QST Logo.bmp to the drive and folder where you store your Data Files**

   As you type the new name of the file, Windows automatically determines the file type and changes the format in the Save as type list. In this case, the format changes to 24-bit Bitmap.

QUICK TIP

To resize the canvas, drag the white resize handle in the lower-right corner of the canvas.

5. **Click the Magnifier tool 🔍 on the Home tab, then click the canvas area**

   Notice that the pointer changed to 🔍 when you positioned it over the canvas area. The image magnifies to display the logo larger. A tool remains turned on until another tool is selected.

6. **Click the Fill with color tool 🖌 on the Home tab, click Color 1 on the Home tab if necessary, click the fourth small square from the left in the first row of the Color Box, then move the pointer into the canvas area**

   The pointer changes to 🖌. Color 1 indicates the foreground color and Color 2 indicates the background color. If you want to change the background color, click Color 2 instead of Color 1 before you select a color.

QUICK TIP

To set a picture as your desktop background, click the Paint button, point to Set as desktop background, then click an option.

7. **Position 🖌 so that the pour tip of the icon is in the right unfilled section of the top part of the compass, then click**

   The closed area you clicked filled with red, the current foreground color. See Figure B-7.

8. **Click the Save button 💾 on the Quick Access toolbar**

   Now you can use the recolored logo in other documents.

FIGURE B-6: Company logo in Paint

Home tab
on the Paint
Ribbon

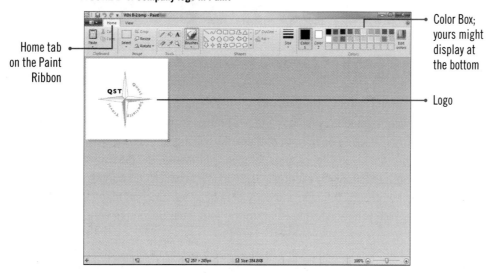

Color Box;
yours might
display at
the bottom

Logo

FIGURE B-7: Company logo with a new color fill

Fill with
color button

Fill bucket
pointer

Click in here to
fill with color

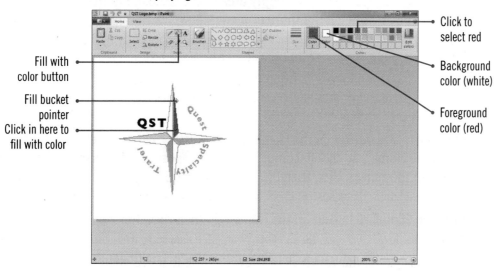

Click to
select red

Background
color (white)

Foreground
color (red)

TABLE B-2: Tools on the Home tab

tool	used to	tool	used to
Paste	Paste Clipboard or file to the canvas	Eraser/Color Eraser	Erase or color part of a drawing
Cut	Remove selection to the Clipboard	Color picker	Pick up a color from the picture for drawing
Copy	Copy selection to the Clipboard	Magnifier	Magnify part of an image
Crop	Remove contents outside selection	Brush	Draw a brush stroke using a brush with the selected size and shape
Resize	Resize or skew selection	Shapes	Draw a shape
Rotate	Rotate or flip selection	Shape outline	Draw a shape with an outline color or brush
Rectangular selection	Select a square or rectangular shape	Shape fill	Draw a shape with a fill color or brush
Free-form selection	Select a free-form or irregular shape	Size	Draw a shape with a line thickness
Pencil	Draw a freehand line	Color 1	Select a foreground color
Fill with color	Fill a closed shape with the current color or texture	Color 2	Select a background color
Text	Enter text in drawings	Edit colors	Change the selected color

Copying Data Between Programs

One of the most useful features Windows offers is the ability to use data created in one file in another file, even if the files were created in different Windows programs. To work with more than one program or file at a time, you simply need to open both of them. To switch from one open window to another, click the correct taskbar button. If you **tile**, or arrange open windows on the desktop so that they are visible, you can switch among them simply by clicking in the window in which you want to work. You can use the Cut, Copy, and Paste commands to move and copy data between different files. ▓▓▓▓▓ You want to add the company logo, which you modified in Paint, to the Tour Ideas document containing your ideas for travel packages.

STEPS

TROUBLE
If your windows aren't tiled, click the taskbar buttons and ensure that both windows are maximized, then repeat Step 1.

1. **Place the mouse pointer on an empty area of the taskbar, right-click, then click** Show windows side by side **on the shortcut menu**
   The windows (Paint and WordPad) are tiled next to one another vertically, so you can maneuver quickly between them while working. Neither window is active at the moment.

2. **Click the** QST Logo.bmp – Paint taskbar button **on the taskbar**
   Clicking a taskbar button makes the window associated with that button the **active window**, so the Paint program window becomes the active window.

TROUBLE
If you have trouble selecting the logo, click the Zoom in button on the status bar to display 100%, then repeat Step 3.

3. **Click the** Image button **on the Home tab if necessary, click the** Select tool button arrow **on the Home tab, click** Rectangular selection, **position the cursor in the upper-left corner of the canvas, click, then drag around the QST logo to select it**
   Dragging with the Select tool selects an object in Paint for cutting, copying, or performing other modifications.

4. **Click the** Clipboard button **on the Home tab, then click the** Copy button
   A copy of the logo is placed on the Clipboard, but it also remains in its original place in the file.

5. **Click anywhere in the WordPad window to make it active, then click at the top of the WordPad document, above the first line of text**
   Clicking in an inactive window is another way to make that window active. The WordPad program becomes active, and the insertion point is blinking near the left margin in the first line on the Tour Ideas document page, where you want the logo to appear.

6. **Click the** Clipboard button **on the Home tab, if necessary, click the** Paste button **in the WordPad window, then click the logo to select it**
   The logo is pasted into the document. A selection rectangle with resize handles, as shown in Figure B-8.

7. **Click the** Maximize button **in the WordPad window, click the** Center button **on the Home tab, then click a blank area of the document window, if necessary**
   The logo is deselected, and is now centered horizontally on the page.

8. **Click the** Save button **on the Quick Access toolbar in the WordPad window**
   You're finished working with Paint. To close a program and any of its currently open files, click Exit on the Paint menu or click the Close button in the upper-right corner of the program window.

9. **Click the** QST Logo.bmp – Paint taskbar button **on the taskbar, click the** Save button , **then click the** Close button **in the Paint window**

FIGURE B-8: Logo copied from one program to another

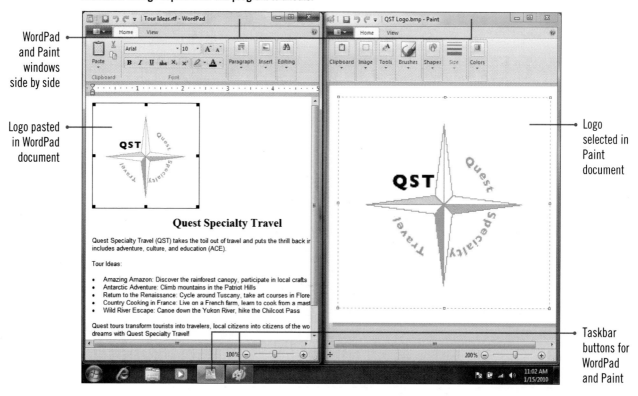

WordPad and Paint windows side by side

Logo pasted in WordPad document

Logo selected in Paint document

Taskbar buttons for WordPad and Paint

Switching between files

When you open many file and program windows, the taskbar groups windows from the same program together in one taskbar button to reduce the clutter on the taskbar and save space. For example, if you have five windows open, and two of them are WordPad files, the two WordPad files are grouped together on the taskbar within the one button named *WordPad*. When you click the *WordPad* button on the taskbar, a thumbnail appears for each open WordPad file, from which you can choose the file you want to view, as shown in Figure B-9. You can point to the thumbnail to temporarily view it or click the thumbnail to switch to it. (To open more than one WordPad window, you need to start two versions of the program using the Start menu.)

FIGURE B-9: WordPad taskbar buttons grouped on taskbar

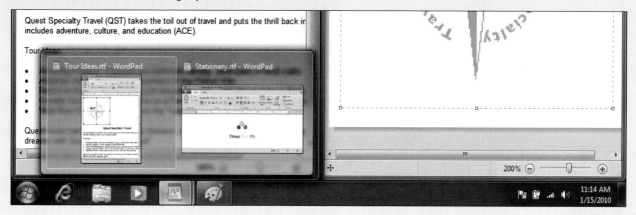

Embedding or Linking an Object

Object Linking and Embedding (OLE) is a way to share information—an object—between two programs. An **object** can be a picture from a graphics program, a chart from a spreadsheet program, a video clip, text, or almost anything else you can create on a computer. The program that creates the object is the **source program**; the program that creates the file into which you want to insert the object is the **destination program**. Likewise, the file that originally contained the object is called the **source file**, and the file where you want to insert the object is called the **destination file**. With **embedding**, a copy of the object becomes part of the destination file, which also increases the size of the file. If you want to edit the object, you make changes in the destination file using the source program, and the original file remains intact. With **linking**, a representation of the object appears in the destination file, but the object is actually stored in the source file. Because a linked object is not stored in the destination file, the object doesn't increase the size of the destination file. If you want to edit the linked object, you make changes in the source file, and the changes will be reflected in the other file the next time you open or update it. The company logo is not final yet, so you want to link the source file to the document. Then, you can quickly update the document once the logo is finalized.

STEPS

QUICK TIP

To create a new object from Paint, click the Paint drawing button on the Home tab, draw the image you want, click the Paint button , then click Exit and return to document. Double-click the object to edit it.

1. **In the WordPad document, click the QST logo image to select it, then press [Delete]**
   The nonlinked logo is now deleted from the Tour Ideas document.

2. **Click the Insert object button on the Home tab to open the Insert Object dialog box, then click the Create from File option button**

3. **Click Browse to open the Browse dialog box, navigate to the drive and folder where you store your Data Files, click QST Logo.bmp, then click Open**
   The file you selected is listed in the Insert Object File text box. So far, you have completed the same steps to insert a new version of the logo as a linked file that you would have done if you planned to embed the object.

4. **Click the Link check box to select it, as shown in Figure B-10, then click OK**
   The two files are now linked. The linked object—the QST logo—remains outlined on the WordPad page.

QUICK TIP

When you open a destination file with a linked object, the destination program checks the source file location to reestablish the link. If it doesn't find the file, it displays an alert, asking you to locate it and reestablish the link.

5. **Right-click the QST logo image, then click Links**
   The Links dialog box opens, as shown in Figure B-11. The box lists the linked objects in the document; in this case, it contains just one—the logo.

6. **Click the Manual option button, then click Close**
   The Links dialog box closes. Now the linked logo will be updated only when you choose to do so.

7. **Double-click the QST logo image in WordPad**
   The QST Logo.bmp file is opened in Paint, and the Paint window becomes the active window.

TROUBLE

If your circle doesn't match Figure B-12, use the Undo button on the Quick Access toolbar, then repeat Step 8.

8. **Maximize the Paint window, click the Oval tool in the Shapes Box, select the second color in the second row in the Colors Box, drag to draw a circle around the logo, then save the image and close Paint**

9. **Right-click the QST logo image, then click Links, click Update Now, click Close, then save your changes and deselect the logo**
   WordPad updates the QST logo from the Paint file. See Figure B-12.

FIGURE B-10: Insert Object dialog box

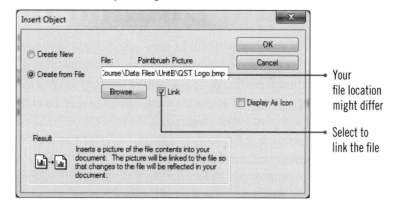

Your file location might differ

Select to link the file

FIGURE B-11: Links dialog box

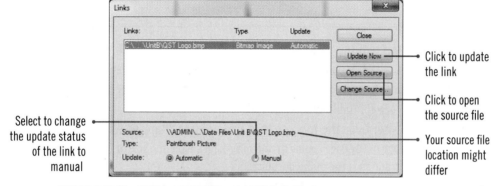

Click to update the link

Click to open the source file

Select to change the update status of the link to manual

Your source file location might differ

FIGURE B-12: WordPad document with updated linked object

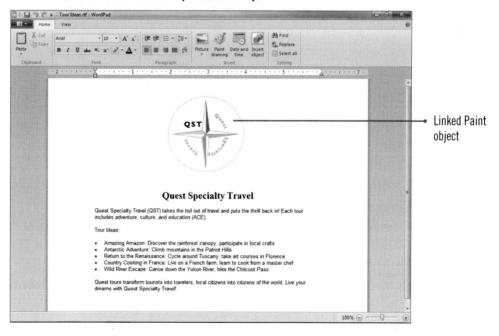

Linked Paint object

Finding, changing, and breaking a linked object

Instead of opening the source file to make changes to a linked object, you can open a linked object from within the destination file using the Open Source button in the Links dialog box. The Open Source button finds the source file containing the linked object and opens that file. The Links dialog box keeps track of the source file location. You can change the source file to a different file or location by using the Change Source button. If you want to disregard a link and change it to an embedded object, right-click the linked object in the destination file, click Object properties to open the Linked Bitmap Image Properties dialog box, click the Link tab, click Break Link, click Yes in the message box, then click OK. On the Link tab in the Linked Bitmap Image Properties dialog box, you can also open or change the source file, change update options, and update the source for the selected object.

Printing a Document

Printing a document creates a **printout** or **hard copy**, a paper document that you can share with others or review as a work in progress. Most Windows programs have print options that you can set using a Print dialog box. Although printing options vary from program to program, the process works similarly in most of them. Typically, you can access the Print dialog box using a Print command on a menu. If you want to use the current print options and bypass the Print dialog box, you can use the Quick Print command on the Print submenu. It is a good idea to use the **Print Preview** feature to look at the layout and formatting of a document before you print it. You might catch a mistake, find that the document fits on more pages than you wanted, or notice formatting that you want to do differently. Making changes before you print saves paper. ▰▰▰▰ You decide to preview the Tour Ideas document to ensure you are satisfied with how it looks before printing it. When satisfied with the result, you print the Tour Ideas document.

STEPS

1. **In the WordPad window, add your name to the bottom of the document, click the WordPad button ▰▰▾▰, point to Print, then click Print preview**

   The Print preview window opens and a reduced but proportionate image of the page appears in the Print preview window, as shown in Figure B-13.

2. **Move the pointer over the logo so that the pointer changes to 🔍, then click the screen**

   The preview image of the page zooms in to appear larger. Note the size of the **margin**, which is the space between the text and the edge of the document.

3. **Click the Page setup button 🖳 on the Print preview tab**

   The Page Setup dialog box opens. In this dialog box, you can change the margin setting to decrease or increase the area outside the dotted rectangle. You can also change other printing options, including the paper size and page orientation. Page **orientation** describes the direction text is printed on the page. When the page is taller than it is wide, its orientation is **portrait**; when the page is wider than it is tall, its orientation is **landscape**.

4. **If necessary, drag to select the number in the Left text box, type 1, select the number in the Right text box, type 1, then click OK**

   The document appears in the Print preview window with the smaller page margins.

5. **Click the Print button 🖨 on the Print preview tab**

   The Print dialog box opens, as shown in Figure B-14, showing various options available for printing.

6. **Select the printer you want to use if necessary, then click Print**

   The Tour Ideas document prints. While a document prints, a printer icon appears in the notification area of the taskbar that you can point to in order to get status information. The Print preview window closes, and you return to the Tour Ideas document.

7. **Click the Save button 🖫, then click the Close button ▰✕▰ in the WordPad window**

   WordPad saves your changes in the documents and the program closes.

FIGURE B-13: WordPad document in Print Preview

Click to open Page setup dialog box

Click to open Print dialog box

Click to magnify the view

Click to close Print Preview

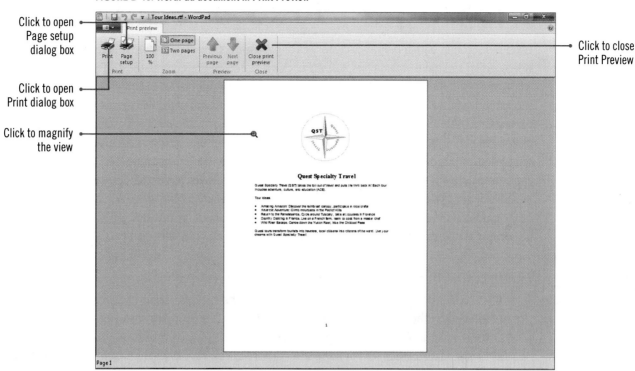

FIGURE B-14: Print dialog box

Double-click icon to add a printer

Selected printer; your name and view might differ

Printer Information

In a multiple page document, set which pages to print

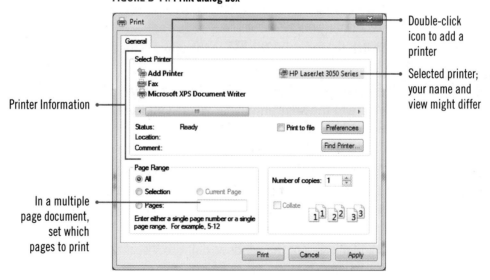

Creating an XPS document

XML Paper Specification (XPS) is a secure fixed-layout format—similar to an Adobe PDF file—developed by Microsoft that retains the format you intended on a monitor or printer. An XPS document is useful when you want to create a document primarily intended to be read and printed, not modified. Windows 7 allows you to save a document as an XPS file, which you can send to others for review in an e-mail. To create an XPS file, select the Microsoft XPS Document Writer in the Print dialog box instead of a printer, click Print, specify a filename and location, then click Save. To view an XPS file, you need to have a viewer—free downloadable software from Microsoft Office Online—installed on your computer.

Playing a Video or Audio Clip

Windows 7 comes with a built-in accessory called **Windows Media Player**, which you can use to play video, audio, and mixed-media files, known as **clips**, stored on your computer, a CD, a DVD, a local network, or the Internet. You can also copy, or **rip**, individual music tracks or entire CDs to your computer and create your own jukebox or playlist of media. In addition, you can create, or **burn**, your own audio CDs or data DVDs, and copy music and videos to portable digital audio players and PCs, such as an MP3 player, cell phone, or mobile device. You can also access online stores to purchase music and other media. With Windows Media Player, you can modify the media, control the settings, and change the player's appearance, or **skin**. Windows 7 comes with Windows Media Player version 12; however, new versions are periodically released. To check online for the most recent version of Windows Media Player, right-click the taskbar in Windows Media Player, point to Help, then click Check for updates. ░▒▓ You want to learn how to use Windows Media Player to play travel video and audio clips for customers.

STEPS

> **TROUBLE**
> If a dialog box opens asking you to choose Recommended settings or Custom settings, click the option you prefer, then click Finish. If you are working in a lab, ask your instructor or technical support person for help.

1. **Click the** Windows Media Player button ▶ **on the taskbar, then click the** Maximize button ▭ **in the Windows Media Player window, if necessary**

   The Windows Media Player window opens. A taskbar with tabs is at the top of the window and player controls that look and function similarly to those on a CD or DVD player are along the bottom. The Library window opens by default, as shown in Figure B-15, displaying the media you currently have stored on your computer.

2. **Right-click a blank area of the Windows Media taskbar, point to** File **on the menu, click** Open, **navigate to the drive and folder where you store your Data Files, click** WIN B-3.wmv, **then click** Open

   A video clip of wildflowers appears in the Now Playing window, a smaller more compact window, as shown in Figure B-16. The video clip plays once.

3. **Click the** Switch to Library button ⊞ **in the upper-right corner of the Now Playing window**

   The Library window opens in Windows Media Player.

> **QUICK TIP**
> To play an audio track from the Library, double-click the track you want to play.

4. **Right-click a blank area of the Windows Media taskbar, point to** File **on the menu, click** Open, **navigate to the drive and folder where you store your Data Files, if necessary, click** WIN B-4.wma, **then click** Open

   The video clip is closed and the audio clip plays once. You can play the media clip continuously, or **loop**.

> **QUICK TIP**
> To play a music CD, insert the CD in the disc drive and wait for Windows Media Player to start playing the CD.

5. **Click the** Turn repeat on button ↻ **at the bottom of the Media Player to turn on the option, then click the** Switch to Now Playing button ⇄ **at the bottom of the Media Player window**

   The Now Playing window opens. When you play audio in the Now Playing window, you can display a **visualization** (a visual effect), which displays color and shapes that change with the beat of the sound.

6. **Right-click a blank area of the window, point to** Visualizations, **point to** Battery, **then click** eletriarnation

   The visual effect continuously displays while the audio plays. The Play tab from the Library window can be accessed from the Now Playing window as well.

7. **Right-click a blank area of the window, then click** Show list

   The Play tab from the Library window opens in the Now Playing window.

8. **After the audio repeats several times, click the** Stop button ▪ **at the bottom of the Windows Media Player window**

   You can control the playback of media in the Now Playing window.

9. **Right-click a blank area of the window, then click** Hide list, **click the** Switch to Library button ⊞, **click the** Turn repeat off button ↻ **to turn off the option, then click the** Close button ✕ **in the Windows Media Player window**

FIGURE B-15: Library window in Windows Media Player

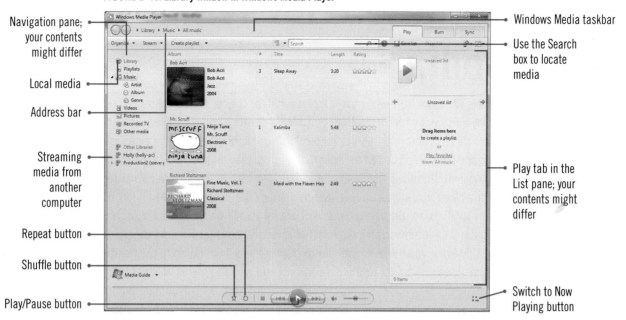

Navigation pane; your contents might differ

Local media

Address bar

Streaming media from another computer

Repeat button

Shuffle button

Play/Pause button

Windows Media taskbar

Use the Search box to locate media

Play tab in the List pane; your contents might differ

Switch to Now Playing button

FIGURE B-16: Playing a video clip in the Now Playing window

Media information

Video clip

Press and hold to rewind

Stop button

Drag to review or forward media

Switch to Library button

Resize window to view more playback controls

Press and hold to fast-forward

Mute button

Volume button

Play/Pause button

Playing media from other computers or the Internet

You can use Windows Media Player to play media available on the Internet or from other networked computers, such as videos, live broadcasts, and music tracks. You can stream the media directly from another computer on your network or over the Internet or from a Web site, or you can download the media file to your computer. Delivering high-quality, continuous video, live broadcasts, sound, and music playback is known as **streaming media**. When you stream the media, the video or music starts playing while the file is transmitted to you from another networked computer or over the Internet. The streaming media is not stored on your computer. If you have media on another computer over a network, HomeGroup (a home-sharing network), or the Internet, you can use commands on the Stream menu to allow access and control of the media on your computer. You can access the streaming media from

the Navigation pane just your like local media. You can also use the Media Guide button in the Windows Media Player to help you find media—music, movies, and radio—on the Internet. To stream media from the Internet, locate the Web site that contains the media you want to play, click the link to the media, then wait for Windows Media Player to start (if necessary) and the first data bits to be transmitted to a temporary memory storage area called a **buffer** and for the media to start playing automatically. The buffer continues to download the media until it's done as Windows Media Player plays the media in the buffer. When you download a media file, you wait for the entire file to be transferred to your computer. To download a file, use a Web browser to locate the media you want to download from the Internet, then click the download link to download and save it locally.

Working with Windows Media

If you have Windows Home Premium, Professional, or Ultimate edition you can use Windows Media Center to play and work with media. Windows Media Center is an entertainment system integrated into your computer that lets you watch live or recorded TV or Netflix movies, play video and look at pictures, listen to music and radio using an FM tuner or the Internet, play and burn CDs and DVDs, browse online media, and play games. Windows Media Center is designed with a display and navigation unlike other Windows programs. When you start Windows Media Center, the program window fills the entire screen and no menus or toolbars are displayed. You navigate by scrolling through a list of main categories, and then scrolling through commands for the selected category. Play, Record, and other VCR/DVD type commands are available when you move the pointer to display them. In addition to the pointer, you can use a remote control or a touch screen to navigate the system and play the media you want. To play FM radio or watch TV, you need to have an FM tuner and a TV tuner card installed on your computer. 🎬 After creating a DVD for the latest marketing promotion, you want to use Windows Media Center to play it.

STEPS

TROUBLE
If you're asked to set up Windows Media Center, click Continue, choose Express Setup, and follow the on-screen instructions.

1. **Click the Start button 🟠 on the taskbar, point to All Programs, then click Windows Media Center**

   The Windows Media Center window opens with its categories listed. When you move your mouse, the Home button moves to the upper-left corner along with the Back button. The Home button brings you back to the main menu screen. The lower-right corner displays VCR and TV tuner controls.

QUICK TIP
If you prefer a desktop view, you can use Windows Media Center as a desktop gadget.

2. **Click the Maximize button 🔲 if necessary, point to the list in the middle of the start screen, then move the pointer to the top or bottom edge of the screen above or below the list to display an arrow and scroll the list**

   You can click the up or down arrow to scroll categories one at a time.

3. **Click the up or down arrow to scroll to the Tasks category, as shown in Figure B-17, click the settings command, then click the Media Libraries command**

   The settings command allows you to customize Windows Media Center and add media libraries.

QUICK TIP
To play music, click Home button, click the Music category, click music library, scroll left or right, select an album, select a track, then click play song.

4. **Click the Videos option, click Next, click the Add folders to the library option, click Next, click the destination option where you store your Data Files, click Next, navigate to the drive and folder where you store your Data Files, select the UnitB check box, click Next, click the Yes, use these locations option, click Finish, then click the Back button ⬅**

   The media files in the UnitB folder are added to their respective libraries, available for use. The Windows Media Center Home screen window opens.

5. **Press [Up Arrow] or [Down Arrow] to scroll to the Pictures + Videos category**

   The category is selected with the picture library, play favorites, and video library commands displayed.

TROUBLE
If you're asked to add more videos to Media Libraries, click Cancel.

6. **Click the video library command**

   The video library category is now active. The Data Files from UnitB are cataloged in the video library.

7. **Click <folders> at the top of the video library category screen, if necessary, click UnitB, point to WIN B-5, then click the thumbnail**

   After a moment, the video plays, as shown in Figure B-18. If the playback and navigation controls autohide, move the mouse to display them again.

8. **Move the pointer to display the controls, then click the Home button 🟠**

   The Windows Media Center Home screen window reopens. If the video has not completed playing, the Home screen controls display with the video playing in the background.

9. **Click the Close button ❎ in the Windows Media Center window**

FIGURE B-17: Navigating in Windows Media Center

Back button

Home button

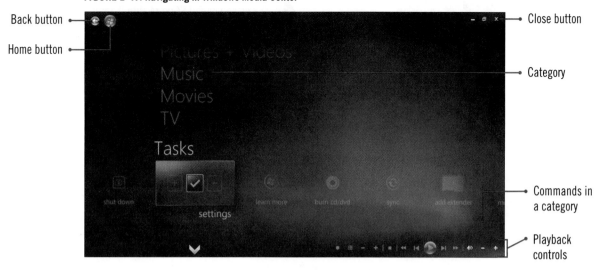

Close button

Category

Commands in a category

Playback controls

FIGURE B-18: Playing a video in Windows Media Center

Playback controls

Changing Windows Media Center settings

You can set up and customize Windows Media Center by selecting the Tasks category on the Home screen, and then selecting the settings command. You can set general options for Windows Media Center and specific options for each of the media types, including TV, Pictures, Music, and DVD. You can also set options for extenders and libraries. A Windows Media Center Extender is a device you connect to your computer, such as a TV, DVD player, digital camera, or Xbox 360.

When you connect an extender, you can control the device from Windows Media Center within a networked environment. Before you get started with Windows Media Center, it's a good idea to set general options, which include startup and window behavior, visual and sound effects, program library options, Windows Media Center setup, parental controls, automatic download options, optimization, and privacy.

Practice

For current SAM information including versions and content details, visit SAM Central (http://samcentral.course.com). If you have a SAM user profile, you may have access to hands-on instruction, practice, and assessment of the skills covered in this unit. Since we support various versions of SAM throughout the life of this text, you will want to check with your instructor for instructions and the correct URL/Web site to access those assignments.

Concepts Review

Match the statements below with the elements labeled in the screen shown in Figure B-19.

FIGURE B-19

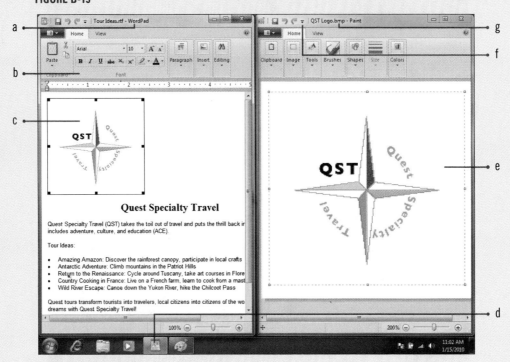

1. Which element points to the Ribbon? *b*
2. Which element points to the Quick Access toolbar? *f*
3. Which element points to the active window? *A*
4. Which element points to the nonactive window? *g*
5. Which element points to the copied logo? *e*
6. Which element points to the original logo? *e*
7. Which element points to a taskbar button? *d*

Match each term with the statement that describes its function.

8. Copy *b*	**a.** Removes selected text or an image from its current location and places it on the Clipboard
9. Cut *a*	**b.** Copies selected text or an image from its current location and places it on the Clipboard
10. Embed *c*	**c.** Copies a representation of an image from its current location into a file
11. Link *e*	**d.** Copies an image from its current location into a file
12. OLE *d*	**e.** A way to share information between programs

Select the best answers from the following lists of choices.

13. RAM stands for:

   a. Random access memory.
   b. Random available memory.

   c. Regular access memory.
   d. Regular available memory.

Concepts Review (Continued)

14. What program can save a file in the Rich Text Format (.rtf) file format?

a. Notepad

b. WordPad

c. Paint

d. Windows Media Player

15. What program can save a file in the bitmap (.bmp) file format?

a. Notepad

b. WordPad

c. Paint

d. Windows Media Player

16. When WordPad automatically moves words to the next line, it is called:

a. Word wrap.

b. Format insert.

c. Margin.

d. Tab.

17. What program command makes a copy of a file?

a. Duplicate

b. Save

c. Copy

d. Save As

18. What is the name of the Windows location that stores cut or copied information?

a. Hard drive

b. Clipboard

c. Start menu

d. Paint

19. Which of the following is not a way to select text?

a. Click the left margin in a line of text.

b. Double-click a word.

c. Drag over the text.

d. Click File on the menu bar, then click Select.

20. What type of object is stored in its destination file?

a. A linked object

b. An embedded object

c. A text placeholder

d. None of the above

21. Which type of object is stored only in its source file?

a. A linked object

b. An embedded object

c. A text placeholder

d. None of the above

22. Which of the following is true about linked objects?

a. To edit a linked object, you must open its source file.

b. A linked object is an independent object embedded directly into a document.

c. You can access a linked object even when the source file is not available.

d. A linked object substantially increases your destination file size.

23. Which of the following controls the size of the empty border around a document?

a. Print Preview

b. Margins

c. Paper Size

d. Orientation

Skills Review

1. Open and save a WordPad document.

a. Start WordPad.

b. Open the WordPad file named WIN B-7.rtf from the drive and folder where you store your Data Files.

c. Save the file as **QST Company Info.rtf** to the drive and folder where you store your Data Files.

2. Modify text in a WordPad document.

a. Insert the name **Derek Opazo** after the text "Tour Developer, the Americas:"

b. Change the CEO name "Holly Todd" to **Jessica Long**.

c. Move the paragraph "VP, Finance: ..." below the paragraph "CEO: ...".

d. Select all the title text "Company Information Sheet".

e. Center the text, change the text font to Georgia (or another available font), and change its size to 16 points.

f. Use the Underline button on the Home tab to underline the text "Corporate Office Location," "Internet," and "Executive Staff"; use the Text color button list arrow on the Home tab to change the color of the three headings to Professional red; then change the font to Georgia, the point size to 12, and the style to bold.

g. Click anywhere in the WordPad window outside of the selected text, then save the document.

Skills Review (Continued)

3. Work with a graphic in Paint.

   a. Start Paint, then open the file WIN B-8.bmp from the drive and folder where you store your Data Files.

   b. Save this file as **QST Logo 2.bmp** to the drive and folder where you store your Data Files.

   c. Draw a green circle around the logo.

   d. Fill the top unfilled section of the left point with the light blue color (third small square from the right in the second row of the Colors Box).

   e. Save the file.

4. Copy data between programs.

   a. Arrange the WordPad and Paint windows side by side. (*Hint*: Maximize both windows first.)

   b. Copy the logo in the Paint window to the Clipboard.

   c. In WordPad, position the insertion point in the blank line at the beginning of the document, then maximize the WordPad window.

   d. Paste the logo in the blank line, then center it.

   e. Save the QST Company Info.rtf file. Close the QST Logo 2.bmp file, then close Paint.

FIGURE B-20

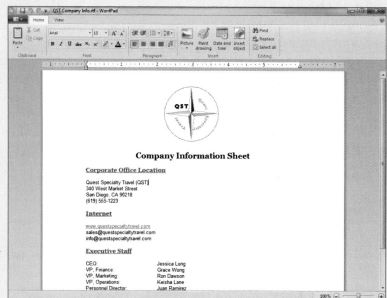

5. Embed or link an object.

   a. Click the QST logo in the WordPad document, then delete it.

   b. Insert the QST logo as a linked object using the file QST Logo 2.bmp.

   c. Change the link update option to manual.

   d. Open the linked file in the source program.

   e. Change the color of the lower-left section in the bottom point in the logo to green.

   f. Save the logo document and close Paint.

   g. Manually update the linked file in WordPad. Compare your final document with Figure B-20.

   h. Save the document.

6. Print a document.

   a. If necessary, change the left and right margins to 1 inch in the QST Company Info.rtf file.

   b. Add your name to the bottom of the document.

   c. Preview and print the document, then save the document.

   d. Close all open documents, then close WordPad.

7. Play a video or audio clip.

   a. Start Windows Media Player.

   b. Open the file named WIN B-4.wma from the drive and folder where you store your Data Files.

   c. Play the audio clip, set the audio to repeat, then switch to Now Playing view.

   d. Change the visualization to Ocean Mist (in the Bars and Waves category).

   e. Stop the playback, then close Windows Media Player.

8. Work with Windows media.

   a. Start Windows Media Center.

   b. Open the video library.

   c. Display the videos for UnitB.

   d. Play the video WIN B-6.wmv.

   e. Close Windows Media Center.

Independent Challenge 1

You own a bookstore that specializes in international books, and you need to create a list of international titles that you want to recommend to customers. Use WordPad to create a document that lists your favorite international books in stock. In the document, include the name of your bookstore and its street address, city, state, zip code, and phone number, and for each book, the author's name (last name first), title, and publication date. You will make up this information.

    a. Start WordPad, then open the file WIN B-9.rtf from the drive and folder where you store your Data Files.

    b. Insert a blank line and then enter the heading (the name of your bookstore, and the address, city, state, zip code, and phone number), pressing [Enter] after the name, address, and zip code.

    c. Center the heading information.

    d. Change the Font for the heading to Verdana. Format the name of the bookstore so it is 14 points and italic.

    e. Insert a blank line, then enter the title **Bestsellers List** below the heading you just entered, center it, then change the font size to 18 point. Insert another blank line between this title and the table.

    f. Italicize the title of each book, then format the last and first names of each author with boldface.

Advanced Challenge Exercise

    ■ Add color to the title (Bestsellers List).

    ■ Underline the entire line containing the column headings, make this text bold, then add a color to this text.

    ■ Change the second column tab stops to 2 inches and the third column tab stops to 4 inches.

    g. If necessary, change the top and bottom margins to 0.75, then add your name to the end of the document.

    h. Save the list as **Bestsellers List.rtf** to the drive and folder where you store your Data Files.

    i. Preview and print the document, then close WordPad.

Independent Challenge 2

As vice president of Things That Fly, a kite and juggling store, you need to design a new type of logo, consisting of three simple circles, each colored differently. You use Paint to design the logo, then you paste the logo into a WordPad document.

    a. Start Paint, then create a small circle, using the [Shift] key and the Ellipse tool.

    b. Select the circle using the Select tool, then copy the circle.

    c. Paste the circle from the Clipboard in the Paint window, then use the mouse to drag the second circle below and a bit to the right of the first.

    d. Paste the circle again, then use the mouse to drag the third circle below and a bit to the left of the first.

    e. For each circle, use the Fill with color tool on the Home tab, select the color in the Colors Box you want the circle to be, then click inside the circle you want to fill with that color.

    f. Using the Select tool, select the completed logo, then copy it.

    g. Save the Paint file as **Stationery Logo.bmp** to the drive and folder where you store your Data Files.

    h. Open WordPad, place the insertion point on the first line, center it, then press [Enter].

    i. Paste the logo in the document, deselect the logo, press [Enter] twice, then type **Things That Fly**.

    j. Change the text to 18-point boldface, then format each word in a different color; make sure the colors you choose coordinate with the logo, then add your name to the end of the document.

    k. Save the WordPad document as **Stationery.rtf** to the drive and folder where you store your Data Files.

    l. Preview the document, make any changes necessary, print the document, then close WordPad and Paint.

Independent Challenge 3

You are the president of Garfield Graffiti Removal, Inc. The company's patented RemoveX system removes paint from all types of surfaces. After removing the paint, GGRI restores surfaces with PreventX, a special clear coating that makes graffiti easier to clean up in the future. Write a letter to persuade your city or town council to award GGRI the contract to remove graffiti from city property. Open and view a short video of the graffiti problem in Windows Media Player that you might send along with the letter.

    a. Start Paint, then create a logo for GGRI.

    b. Save the logo as **GGRI Logo.bmp** (24-bit Bitmap file format) to the drive and folder where you store your Data Files, then close Paint.

Independent Challenge 3 (Continued)

c. Start WordPad, then write a letter to convince the city council to award GGRI the contract, and format the letter as needed, then add your name at the end of the document.

d. Save the document as **Graffiti.rtf** to the drive and folder where you store your Data Files.

e. In your letter, link the file GGRI Logo.bmp from the drive and folder where you store your Data Files.

f. Start Paint and open the GGRI Logo.bmp.

g. Add graffiti to the GGRI Logo.bmp using the Airbrush tool (fourth brush in the first row of the Brushes palette), then close Paint.

h. Update the linked file in your document.

i. Preview and print the document, save the file, then close WordPad.

j. Start Windows Media Player, open the file WIN B-11.wmv from the drive and folder where you store your Data Files to play it, then close Windows Media Player.

Real Life Independent Challenge

You and some of your friends want to have a party. Using WordPad, you want to create an invitation. Using Paint, you then want to paste a map of the party location onto the invitation.

a. Start WordPad, then type the information for the invitation, which includes the invitation title; date, time, and location of the party; directions; your name and phone number; and the date to respond by.

b. Change the title text to a larger size, boldface, center align, then add color.

c. Change the rest of the text to a smaller size and a different font type.

d. Save the WordPad document as **Invitation.rtf** to the drive and folder where you store your Data Files.

e. Start Paint, then open the file WIN B-10.bmp from the drive and folder where you store your Data Files.

f. Copy the map to the Clipboard.

g. Place the insertion point above the instructions in the invitation, then paste the map into the WordPad document.

h. Add your name to the end of the document.

i. Save the document, preview the document, make any necessary changes, then print the document.

j. Close WordPad and Paint.

Advanced Challenge Exercise

- Open Windows Media Center.
- Add a folder with a family video to the media library. (If you don't have one, you can use WIN B-12.wmv in the Unit B folder.)
- Open the video library, then navigate to the family video.
- Play the video in Windows Media Center.
- Close Windows Media Center.

FIGURE B-21

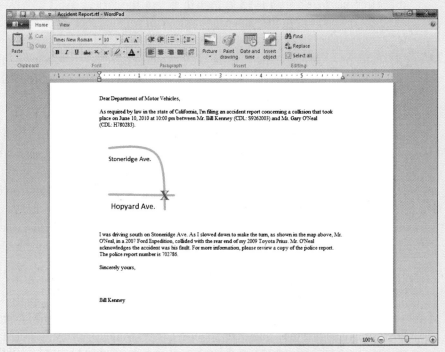

Visual Workshop

Create a document that looks like the example in Figure B-21. Use WordPad as the destination program and Paint as the source program; use linking to save disk space. Add your name to the end of the document. Save the document as **Accident Report.rtf** and the map you create as **Accident Map.bmp** to the drive and folder where you store your Data Files. Print the document.

Managing Files and Folders

File management is organizing and keeping track of files and folders. Working with poorly managed files is like looking for a needle in a haystack—it is frustrating and time consuming to search through irrelevant, misnamed, and out-of-date files to find the one you want. Windows allows you to organize folders and files in a file hierarchy, imitating the way you store paper documents in real folders. Just as a filing cabinet contains several folders, each containing a set of related documents and several dividers grouping related folders together, a **file hierarchy** allows you to place files in folders, then place folders in other folders, so that your files are organized and easier to find. Windows 7 provides you with a main file management window called **Windows Explorer**. Windows Explorer provides access to files, folders, drives, and disks on your local, Homegroup (a shared home network), and network computers. You have just been hired as a marketing specialist. Ron Dawson, the vice president of Marketing, wants you to review the files on your computer and organize them for some upcoming projects.

OBJECTIVES

Open Windows Explorer

View files and folders

Navigate a folders list

Create and rename files and folders

Search for files and folders

Organize files and folders

Copy and move files and folders

Delete and restore files and folders

Work with libraries

Opening Windows Explorer

The keys to organizing files and folders effectively within a file hierarchy are to store related items together and to name folders informatively. Proper hierarchy and relevant names allow you to get a good idea of what's on your system just by looking at the higher levels of your file hierarchy; you don't have to examine every individual file or memorize a coding system. Drives, folders, and files are represented by icons. Table C-1 lists the typical drives on a computer and how you use them. Each drive is assigned a drive letter, denoted with parentheses and a colon to help make it easier to identify. Typically, the hard drive is listed as Local Disk (C:), while the CD or DVD is (D:). If your computer includes additional hard or removable drives, they are assigned letters by your computer in alphabetical order. Windows Explorer provides access to files, folders, drives, and disks on your local, Homegroup (a shared home network), and network computers. The Windows Explorer window contains a toolbar, a Navigation pane, a Details pane, a menu bar (which might not be visible), a status bar (which might not be activated) providing information about the contents of the window, and a list of contents. The Navigation pane displays links to common folder and drive locations, including Favorites, Libraries, Homegroup, Computer, and Network. **Libraries** are special folders that catalog files and folders in a central location, regardless of where you actually store them on your hard drive, to make finding files easier. A library can contain links to files, other folders, and other subfolders anywhere on your computer. The file hierarchy on your disk contains several Quest Specialty Travel folders and files organized by topic. You want to open the Windows Explorer window and review its organization to see if it needs changes.

STEPS

QUICK TIP
To display disks and drives, click the Start button on the taskbar, then click Computer.

1. **Click the Windows Explorer button 📁 on the taskbar**

   The Windows Explorer window opens, displaying the contents of the Libraries folder. Windows 7 comes with four default libraries: Documents, Music, Pictures, and Videos.

2. **Point to Libraries, click the Expand indicator ▷ next to Libraries if necessary to expand the list, then click Documents in the Navigation pane under Libraries**

   The contents of the Documents library folder open in your Windows Explorer window.

TROUBLE
If your Data Files are not stored on a USB drive, locate the drive where you store your Data Files, and substitute that drive for "USB drive" in the steps in this unit.

3. **If you want to save your Data Files to a USB drive, make sure the USB drive where you store your Data Files is plugged into your computer, then click Computer in the Navigation pane**

   The Computer window opens, displaying the contents of your computer, including all disk drives, removable storage devices, and network locations.

4. **Click the drive where you store your Data Files**

   The bottom pane of the Computer window changes to display details about the selected drive, as shown in Figure C-1. This figure shows a USB drive labeled "Removable Disk (G:)," which might be different on your computer. Because computers differ, the contents of your Computer window are also probably different from the figure. If you selected a hard drive, the Details pane displays additional information, including free space and total disk size.

5. **Double-click the drive where you store your Data Files**

   The folders contained on the disk drive open in the Computer window. When you open a disk drive or folder, the Address bar adds the new location to the list. In this example, Removable Disk (G:) is listed in the Address bar after Computer.

TROUBLE
If Microsoft Word or another word-processing program is installed on your computer, your document icons might differ.

6. **Double-click the UnitC folder, then double-click the Quest Travel folder**

   The files and folders in the Quest Travel folder are represented by icons that indicate the application they were created with. For example, the To Do List.rtf file was created in WordPad.

7. **Double-click the Company folder**

   The Company folder opens, displaying four files, which were created in WordPad.

FIGURE C-1: Computer window

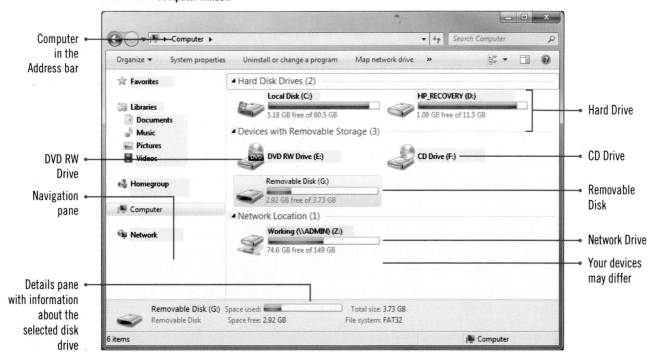

Computer in the Address bar

DVD RW Drive

Navigation pane

Details pane with information about the selected disk drive

Hard Drive

CD Drive

Removable Disk

Network Drive

Your devices may differ

TABLE C-1: Typical disk drives on a computer

icon	type	description
	Local	A hard magnetic disk on which you can store large amounts of data. The disk is typically not removable from the computer.
	Removable	A removable disk on which you can store computer data, such as a Flash memory card or Flash or USB drive.
	Compact Disc-Read-Only Memory (CD-ROM)	An optical disc on which you can stamp, or burn, up to 1 GB (typical size is 650 MB) of data in only one session. The read-only disc cannot be erased or burned again with additional new data.
	Compact Disc-Recordable (CD-R)	A type of read-only CD on which you can burn up to 1 GB of data in multiple sessions. The disc can be burned again with additional new data, but cannot be erased.
	Compact Disc-Rewritable (CD-RW)	A type of CD on which you can read, write, and erase data, just like a removable or hard disk.
	Digital Video Disc (DVD)	A type of read-only optical disc that holds a maximum of 4.7 GB, enough for a full-length movie.
	Digital Video Disc-Recordable (DVD-R)	A type of read-only DVD on which you can burn up to 4.7 GB of data in multiple sessions. The disc can be burned again with new data, but cannot be erased.
	Digital Video Disc-Rewritable (DVD-RW)	A type of DVD on which you can read, write, and erase data, just like a hard disk.
	Network drive	A location on a network drive.

Opening a document with a different program

Most documents on your desktop are associated with a specific program. For example, if you double-click a document whose filename ends with the three-letter extension ".txt," Windows automatically opens the document with Notepad, a text-only editor. There are situations, though, when you need to open a document with a program other than the one Windows chooses, or when you want to choose a different default program. For example, you might want to open a text document in WordPad rather than Notepad so that you can add formatting and graphics. To do this, right-click the document icon you want to open, point to Open with on the shortcut menu, then click the application you want to use to open the document, or click Choose default program to access more program options.

Viewing Files and Folders

Once you have opened more than one folder, the Address bar helps you move quickly between folders in a window. When you open a folder, Windows keeps track of where you have been. To go back or forward to a folder you already viewed, click the Back or Forward button to the left of the Address bar. To go to a folder you viewed two or more locations ago, click the Recent Pages list arrow next to the Forward button to display a menu of places you viewed. The Address bar displays the path you have taken, separated by arrows, to get from a disk drive to your current folder location. To quickly go back to a folder within the path, click the folder name in the Address bar or click an arrow to view the contents of each folder. When you view a folder, you can use the Views button on the toolbar to change the way you view file and folder icons. The available views include Extra Large, Large, Medium, and Small Icons, and List, Details, Tiles, and Content. Icon views display icons in different sizes, sorted alphabetically in horizontal rows, with the name of the file or folder below each icon. When you view files using one of the Icon views, some file types, such as a bitmap, display **Live icons** (or thumbnails), which display the first page of documents, the image of a photo, or the album art for individual songs, making it easier to find exactly what you are looking for. The other views—Details, Tiles, and Content—display additional information, such as file type, date modified, and size, about the file or folder. ▓▓▓ As you continue to browse company files and folders, you want to move between them and, depending upon the information you need, change the way you view your files and folders.

STEPS

1. **Click the Back button ◎ to the left of the Address bar**

   The contents of the Quest Travel folder open in the Quest Travel window in Tiles view, as shown in Figure C-2. Each time you click ◎, you are brought back to the previous folder or drive you viewed.

2. **Click the drive where you store your Data Files in the Address bar**

   In this example, Removable Disk (G:) is listed in the Address bar after Computer. The contents of the drive open in the window, which includes the UnitC folder. Instead of continuously double-clicking between folder icons, the ◎ will return you to the previous folder you viewed.

3. **Click ◎ to the left of the Address bar**

   The Quest Travel folder and its contents open in the Computer window.

4. **Double-click the Advertising folder in the window**

   The contents of the Advertising folder open in the window. Instead of using the Back button, you can use the Recent Pages list arrow to display a list of the drives and folders you recently viewed.

5. **Click the Recent Pages list arrow ⯆ between the Forward button and the Address bar**

   The Recent Pages menu opens, displaying a list of drives and the folders you viewed recently.

6. **Click Quest Travel in the menu**

   The contents of the Quest Travel folder reopens in the window.

7. **Click the Views button arrow ▤ ▾ on the toolbar, then click Details**

   The Quest Travel window changes to Details view, which shows the name, the date that each file or folder was last modified, and the type and size of file, as shown in Figure C-3.

8. **Click the Views button ▤ on the toolbar, then click ▤ again**

   The display changes to Tiles view, which is the next view in the Views menu, then changes to Content view. When you click the Views button, you cycle through the following five views: List, Details, Tiles, Content, and Large Icons. The Tiles and Content views display summary information next to each icon.

9. **Click Computer in the Address bar or click the double arrow «« next to the folder icon in the Address bar and then click Computer**

   The Computer window opens. The «« icon in the Address bar indicates the path is too big to fit in the Address bar, similar to the way the ellipse (. . .) works in a limited space with text.

FIGURE C-2: Viewing files and folders in Tiles view

Back button

Forward button

Recent Pages
list arrow

Views button
arrow

Views button

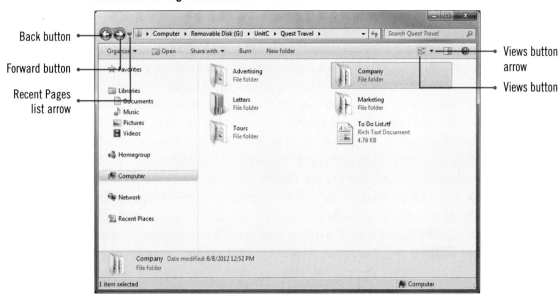

FIGURE C-3: Viewing files and folders in Details view

Views
button
arrow

Files and
folder details;
yours might differ

Details view

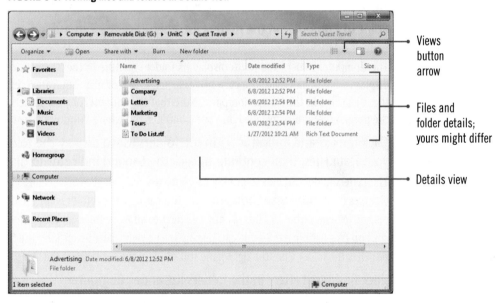

Customizing Details view

When you view files and folders in Details view, a default list of file and folder information appears, which consists of Name, Size, Type, and Date Modified. If the default list of file and folder details doesn't provide you with the information you need, you can add and remove any file and folder information from Details view. If you need to change the way Windows sorts your files and folders, you can use the column indicator buttons in the right pane of Details view. Clicking one of the column indicator buttons, such as Name, Size, Type, or Date Modified, in Details view sorts the files and folders by the type of information listed in the column. To change the details shown, right-click a column heading in Details view, and then click the detail you want to show or hide. To see more details or to change the list order, right-click a column title, then click More. You can also drag a column heading to move it quickly to a new position.

Navigating a Folders List

If you are working in Windows Explorer, you can use the Navigation pane to display and manage files and folders. Windows Explorer splits the window into two panes, or frames, as shown in Figure C-4, which allows you to view information from two different locations. The Navigation pane on the left displays all drives and folders on your computer or network, and the right pane displays the contents of the selected drive or folder. This arrangement enables you to view the file hierarchy of your computer or network and the contents of a folder simultaneously. The Navigation pane is organized into five categories: Favorites, Libraries, Homegroup, Computer, and Network. The Navigation pane displays the file hierarchy of the drives and folders for each category in a **folders list**. Using the Expand indicator ▷ and Collapse indicator ◢ to the left of an icon in the Navigation pane allows you to display different levels of the drives and folders on your computer without opening and displaying the contents of each folder. With its split window, the folders list in the Navigation pane makes it easy to copy, move, delete, and rename files and folders. In an effort to learn how to manage company files effectively, you want to use the folders list in the Navigation pane to quickly move to folders within folders without opening and displaying the contents of each folder in the file hierarchy.

STEPS

QUICK TIP
To change the size of the Navigation pane, place the mouse pointer on the vertical bar separating the two window panes so that it changes to ↔, then drag to change the size of the panes.

1. **Click the Back button ⊙ to the left of the Address bar, then click the Views button ▤▤ on the toolbar until Tiles view appears**

   The Quest Travel folder opens, displaying folders and files in Tiles view.

2. **Point to Computer in the folders list, then click the Expand indicator ▷ that appears next to it, if necessary**

   The Computer folder expands to display its folder structure in the Navigation pane. The Navigation pane displays a file hierarchy of the currently selected folder or disk. You can access all folders and drives from the folders list in the Navigation pane. Note that the contents of your folders list will vary, depending on the programs and files installed on your computer and where Windows is installed.

QUICK TIP
To automatically expand folders in the Navigation pane, right-click a blank area in the Navigation pane, then click Expand to current folder to display a check mark.

3. **Click the Expand indicator ▷ in the folders list to display the folder where you store your Data Files, then continue to click the Expand indicator to display the Letters folder**

   The Letters folder expands to display its folder structure, as shown in Figure C-4. The Expand indicator ▷ changes to the **Collapse indicator ◢**, indicating the subfolders on the drive or in the folder are displayed. When neither ▷ nor ◢ appears next to an icon, the item has no folders in it. However, it might contain files, whose names you can display in the right pane by clicking the folder name. Because you did not click the folder icon, the right pane still displays the contents of the Quest Travel folder as it did before.

4. **Click Business Letters in the folders list under Computer**

   When you click a folder or drive in the folders list, its contents open in the right pane. Figure C-5 shows the contents of the Business Letters folder in the right pane.

5. **Click ◢ next to the Letters folder in the folders list under Computer**

   The folders in the Letters folder collapse and no longer appear in the folders list. Because you did not click the Letters folder icon, the right pane still displays the contents of the Business Letters folder.

QUICK TIP
To show all folders in the Navigation pane, right-click a blank area in the Navigation pane, then click Show all folders to display a check mark.

6. **Click Letters in the folders list under Computer**

   The right pane shows the contents of the Letters folder.

7. **Double-click the Business Letters folder in the right pane**

   The right pane now displays the contents of the Business Letters folder. When you double-click a drive or folder in the right pane, the right pane of the window shows the contents of that item. When you double-click a file, the program associated with the file starts and opens the file in the program window.

Windows ☒ Unit B

FIGURE C-4: Folders on the Removable drive

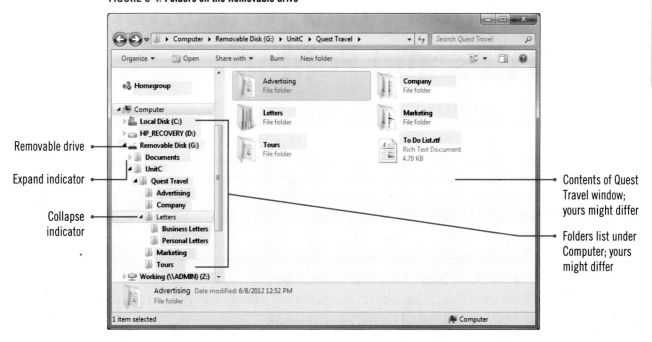

Removable drive

Expand indicator

Collapse indicator

Contents of Quest Travel window; yours might differ

Folders list under Computer; yours might differ

FIGURE C-5: Business Letters folder

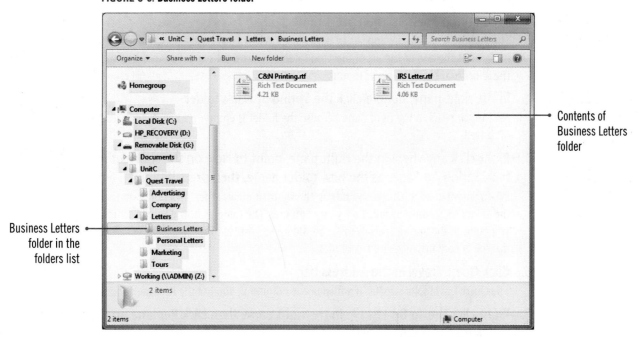

Contents of Business Letters folder

Business Letters folder in the folders list

Customizing the Favorites list

The Favorites list in the Navigation pane provides links to commonly used folders and saved searches to reduce the number of clicks it takes to locate a file or folder. Windows provides a default list of Favorites, including Desktop, Downloads, and Recent Places. You can customize the Favorites list in the Navigation pane to include the folders or saved searches you want for your everyday use. You can move current links, add or rename folders, save searches, or remove an item. To move a link, drag an item in the Navigation pane to a higher or lower position. To add a link to the Favorites list, drag an item from its original location in a folders list or in the Folder window to a position in the Favorites list. You can also rename or remove a link. Right-click the link, then click Rename or Remove on the shortcut menu. If the Navigation pane gets cluttered, you can restore it back to the original default items and start from there. Right-click Favorites in the Navigation pane, then click Restore favorite links on the shortcut menu.

Creating and Renaming Files and Folders

A hierarchy allows you to place files in folders, then place folders in other folders, so that your files are organized and easier to find. To create a hierarchy, you create new folders within disks or folders and you store files within them. To create a folder, you select the location where you want the new folder, create the folder, then name the folder. You should name each folder meaningfully, so that just by reading the folder's name you know its contents. After you name a folder or file, you can rename it at any time. You decide to create a set of new folders to hold the files for the Quest Travel Spring Specials and to rename at least one file with a more appropriate name.

STEPS

1. **Click Quest Travel in the folders list under Computer**

   The Quest Travel folder opens. To create a new folder, you use the New folder button on the toolbar.

TROUBLE

If the folder name is not highlighted, click the folder, then click New folder so that a rectangle surrounds it and the folder name is highlighted.

2. **Click the New folder button on the toolbar**

   A new folder, temporarily named New folder, appears highlighted with a rectangle around the title in the right pane of the window, as shown in Figure C-6. To enter a new folder name, you simply type the new name; the text you type replaces the selected text.

3. **Type Spring Specials, then press [Enter]**

   The Spring Specials folder appears in both panes. When you create a new folder, the icon for the new folder is placed at the end of the list of files and folders in the right pane. You can rearrange, or sort, the icons in the folder to make them easier to find.

QUICK TIP

To create a new file, right-click a blank area in Windows Explorer, point to New, then click the type of file you want.

4. **In the right pane, double-click the Spring Specials folder**

   Nothing appears in the right pane because the folder is empty; no new files or folders have been created or moved.

5. **Right-click anywhere in the right pane, point to New on the shortcut menu, click Folder, type Spring Ad Pages as the new folder name, then press [Enter]**

   When you right-click, the commands on the shortcut menu differ, depending on the item you right-click or the Windows features installed on your computer. The folder is now named Spring Ad Pages. Notice when you point to the Spring Specials folder in the folders list that the Expand indicator appears, indicating that this folder contains other folders or files.

6. **Click Quest Travel in the Address bar**

   The Quest Travel folder opens. If a filename is not useful, you use the Rename command to change it.

QUICK TIP

To quickly change a file or folder name, select the icon, click the name, then type a new name.

7. **Right-click the To Do List file in the right pane, then click Rename on the shortcut menu**

   The filename appears highlighted, while the extension doesn't, as shown in Figure C-7.

8. **Type Important, then press [Enter]**

   The file is renamed Important as a Rich Text Document.

FIGURE C-6: Creating a new folder

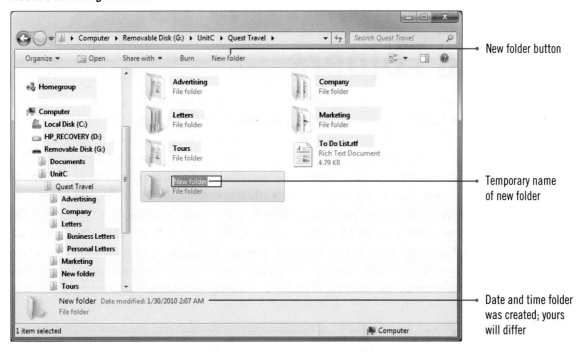

New folder button

Temporary name of new folder

Date and time folder was created; yours will differ

FIGURE C-7: Renaming a file

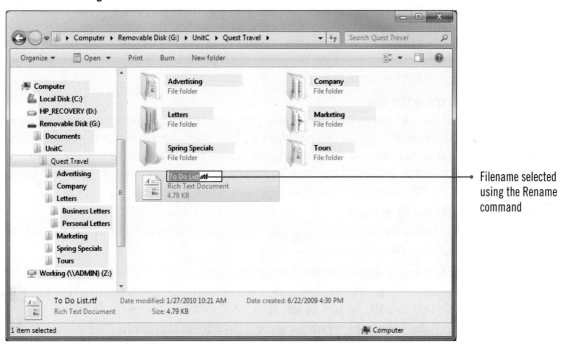

Filename selected using the Rename command

Changing the layout of Explorer windows

Windows gives you the option to customize the layout for each Explorer window depending on the information the window contains. The layout for each Explorer window can include a menu bar, Details pane, Preview pane, and Navigation pane. The Details and Navigation panes appear by default. The Organize menu shows or hides the layout elements. If you prefer working with menus like the previous version of Windows, you can show the menu bar and use traditional menus. To change the Explorer layout, open the folder window you want to change, click the Organize button on the toolbar, point to Layout, then select the layout item you want to show or hide: Menu bar, Details pane, Preview pane, or Navigation pane. Layout options vary depending on the type of Explorer window.

UNIT
C
Windows 7

Searching for Files and Folders

Sometimes remembering precisely where you stored a file can be difficult. Windows provides a Search box and Search Results folder to help you find and view all of the files or folders that meet your search criteria in one place. The Search Results folder provides easy access to all of your files, such as documents, pictures, music, and e-mail, and folders that match search criteria you set in a single view. Items that match the search criteria appear highlighted. If you don't find the files or folders you're looking for, you can perform an advanced search. An advanced search gives you the option to find files or folders by other criteria, such as name, title, author, location, date (taken, modified, or created), size, or **tags**, which are user-defined file properties. The Search Results folder is accessible from any folder window with the Search box to help you locate files and folders on your computer, Homegroups, and Internet. ▰▰▰▰ You want to find a file you created several months ago with preliminary notes for the Spring Specials, so you can move it to the Spring Specials folder. You cannot remember the exact title of the file or where you stored it, so you perform a search.

STEPS

1. **Click in the Search box to the right of the Address bar**

   A Search box menu opens, displaying recently performed searches and advanced search options, known as filters. A **filter** narrows the search to display only items that meet the criteria. After a moment, the menu closes. By default, a search occurs in the folder that is currently open, as well as any subfolders in it, but you can specify any location on your computer to search. Just type the name of the folder or file you want to find or the part you know for certain in the Search box. If you didn't know the name of the file, but did know some text contained in the file, you could enter that text. You want to search in the Quest Travel folder, which is the current folder.

   > **QUICK TIP**
   > Use the * (asterisk) symbol in a filename when you're unsure of the entire name. For example, type "S*rs" to find all files beginning with "S" and ending with "rs," such as Stars and Sports cars.

2. **Type qst in the box**

   As you type, files that contain the text you typed as part of their filename display highlighted in the window, as shown in Figure C-8. You don't have to press [Enter]. If any folders in the Quest Travel folder or its subfolders had names that contained QST, their names would appear as well. Notice that the Address bar displays "Search Results in Quest Travel" to indicate the location of the search. If you don't find the file you want, you can perform an advanced search.

   > **QUICK TIP**
   > To delete an entry on the Search box menu, point to the entry on the menu, then press [Delete].

3. **Click in the Search box**

   A Search box menu opens, displaying recent searches and filter search options at the bottom. The current menu displays Date modified and Size.

4. **Click Size at the bottom of the Search box menu**

   The Search box menu now lists size options, which include Empty (0 KB), Tiny (0–10 KB), Small (10–100 KB), Medium (100 KB–1 MB), Large (1–16 MB), Huge (16–128 MB), and Gigantic (>128 MB).

   > **QUICK TIP**
   > To expand the search to other locations or perform a search, scroll to the bottom, then click a search option, such as Libraries, Homegroup, Computer, Internet, File Contents, and Custom (for location change).

5. **Click Medium (100 KB–1 MB) on the Search box menu for Size**

   You have specified that you only want to find document files that are larger than 100 KB, yet smaller than 1 MB in size. Once you select a search criteria filter, the Search program finds and lists all the corresponding files and folders that meet the criteria. See Figure C-9. Notice that the criteria in the Search box changes to "qst size:medium" to reflect the search options in the Quest Travel folder.

6. **Click the Close button ✖ in the Search box**

   The search criteria are removed from the Search box. Windows Explorer displays all the files and folders in the Quest Travel folder.

Managing Files and Folders

FIGURE C-8: Performing a search

Address bar
changes to indicate
search results

Search criteria

Filter options

Highlighted
search results

Files with "qst" in
their filenames

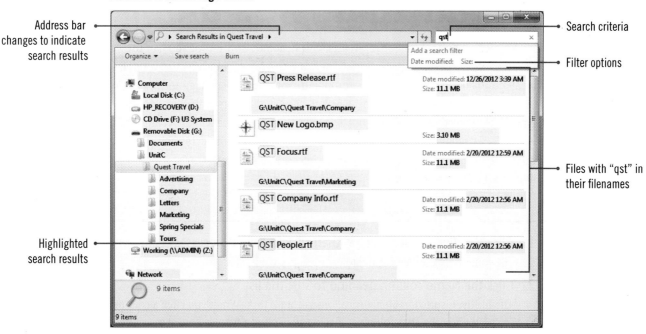

FIGURE C-9: Results from a filtered search

Filtered search
criteria

Close button in
Search box

Filtered search
results

Search location
options

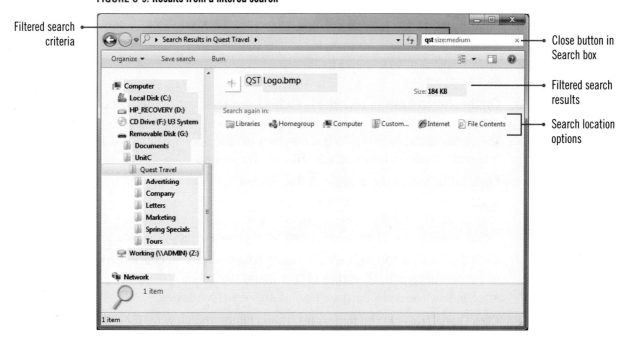

Saving a search

If you frequently perform the same search, you can save your search results like any file and perform or modify the search again later. Once your search is completed, click the Save search button on the toolbar to open the Save As dialog box. The default file type in the Save as type box is Saved Search (*.search-ms). Type a name for the search, then click Save. The search is saved by default in the Searches folder, which you can open by clicking Favorites or Searches in the Navigation pane. To run a saved search, double-click it in the Searches window or click it in the Navigation pane. Like any file or folder icon, you can move a saved search from the Searches folder to the Favorites section in the Navigation pane to make it more accessible. When you no longer need a saved search, you can select it, press [Delete], then click Yes to confirm.

Organizing Files and Folders

In Explorer windows, files appear in lists with headings at the top. You can use the headings to change how files are displayed in the window. There are several ways to organize your files by using file list headings, including sorting, filtering, and grouping. **Sorting** displays files and folders in alphabetical order, either A to Z or Z to A. **Filtering** displays only files and folders with the properties you select by heading type. When you apply a filter to a heading, a check mark appears in the column heading, indicating a filter is enabled. If a filter doesn't display the files you want in the selected folder, you can use the Subfolders option to include them in an expanded search. You want to use sorting and filtering to help you find specific Quest Specialty Travel files.

STEPS

1. **Click the Views button arrow, then click Details, if necessary**

   The contents of the Quest Travel folder open in Details view.

2. **Click the Name column heading to sort the list**

   The file list is sorted in alphabetical order from Z to A. When you click a column heading, the file list is sorted in order by that column. Clicking the column toggles between sorting the list in ascending to descending order and descending to ascending order.

3. **Click the Name column heading again to re-sort the list**

   The file list is sorted in alphabetical order from A to Z. Notice that a list arrow appears at the end of the Name column heading. The list arrow allows you to access additional filtering and grouping commands.

4. **Point to the Name column heading, then click the Name column heading list arrow**

   A shortcut menu opens, as shown in Figure C-10. The menu displays commands to filter files and folders to help you find what you're looking for. If you only want to view files in a certain group, you can select one of the filtering options.

5. **On the shortcut menu, click the I - P check box to select it, then click off the menu to close it**

   The window displays only the files that meet the I - P filter, as shown in Figure C-11. A check mark appears in the column heading to indicate a filter is applied to the view.

6. **Click Subfolders at the bottom of the window**

   A search is applied to the I - P filter to include any files and folders in the Quest Travel subfolders. In this case, the IRS Letter.rtf file appears at the bottom of the list in Contents view. The Address bar displays "Search Results in Quest Travel > I - P" to indicate the results of the search along with the I - P filter.

7. **Click the Back button ⊙, click the Name column heading check mark, click the I - P check box to clear it, then click off the menu to close it**

   All of the search results for the Quest Travel folder open in Details view.

8. **Click Quest Travel in the folders list, then change the view to Tiles, if necessary**

   The file list in the Quest Travel folder is restored back to its original state.

FIGURE C-10: Menu to filter files and folders

Click to sort by heading type

Name column heading list arrow

Menu to filter files and folders

FIGURE C-11: Filtering files and folders

Check mark indicates a filter is applied

Files and folders in the filtered list

Extends the filter to subfolders in the Quest Travel folder

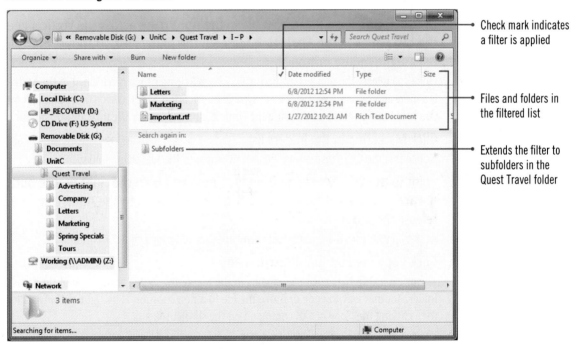

Adding property tags to files

When you create a file, Windows automatically adds **properties** to the files, such as the filename, creation date, modified date, and size. These properties are important to Windows; however, they might not be useful when you are searching for a file. You can create your own custom properties called **tags** to make it faster and easier to locate files in the future. A tag can be anything you choose, such as "QST" or "Important." You can add or modify tag properties for most files.

However, there are some exceptions, such as plain text (.txt) or Rich Text Format (.rtf) files. You can add or modify properties using the Tags box in the Details pane in an Explorer window, the Details tab in the Properties dialog box, or in the Save As dialog box. If you want to remove some or all of the property information in a file, you can quickly remove it using the Properties dialog box. To open the Properties dialog box for a file, right-click the file, then click Properties.

Copying and Moving Files and Folders

Sometimes you will need to move or even copy a file from one folder to another. This can be accomplished using a variety of methods. If the file or folder and the location where you want to move it are visible in a window or on the desktop, you can simply drag the item from one location to the other. Moving a file or folder on the same disk relocates it, whereas dragging it from one disk to another copies it so that it appears in both locations. One way to make sure that you move or copy an item properly is to right-click the file or folder, drag the item to the destination location while still holding down the right mouse button, then choose the appropriate command from the shortcut menu. When the destination folder or drive is not visible, you can use the Cut, Copy, and Paste commands on the Edit menu or the Organize button on the toolbar. As you continue to organize Quest Specialty Travel files, you want to remove some files you no longer need, then make a copy of another file and place it in a folder.

STEPS

QUICK TIP
To select files or folders that are not consecutive, press and hold [Ctrl], then click each item in the right pane.

1. **Click Company in the folders list**

   The contents of the Company folder open in the window. When moving or copying files or folders, make sure the files or folders you want to move or copy appear in the right pane. To move a file, you drag it from the right pane to the destination folder in the folders list.

2. **Drag the QST Press Release.rtf file in the right pane across the vertical line separating the two panes to the Marketing folder in the folders list, as shown in Figure C-12, then release the mouse button**

   Once you release the mouse button, the QST Press Release.rtf file is relocated to the Marketing folder, which is a more appropriate location for this type of information. If you decide that you don't want the file moved, you could move it back easily using the Undo command on the Organize button menu.

3. **Click Marketing in the folders list**

   Notice that the QST Press Release file is now stored in the Marketing folder.

4. **Point to the QST New Logo.bmp file, press and hold the right mouse button, drag the file across the vertical line separating the two panes to the Advertising folder, then release the mouse button**

   As shown in Figure C-13, a shortcut menu appears, offering a choice of options.

QUICK TIP
To copy a file quickly from one folder to another on the same disk, select the file, press and hold [Ctrl], then drag the file to the folder.

5. **Click Copy here on the shortcut menu**

   The original QST New Logo file remains in the Marketing folder, and a copy of the file is in the Advertising folder. Another way to copy or move the file to a new location is by right-clicking a file in the right pane, then clicking the Copy or Cut command on the shortcut menu.

6. **Click Advertising in the folders list**

   A copy of the QST New Logo file is now located in the Advertising folder.

FIGURE C-12: Moving a file from one folder to another

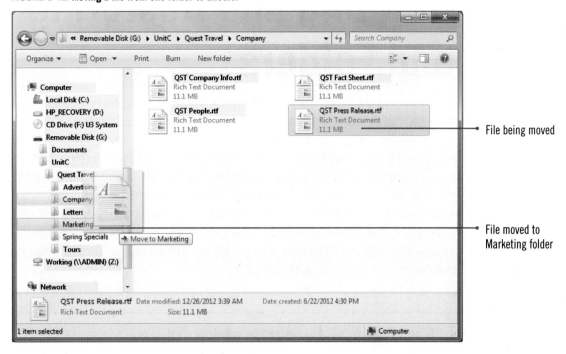

File being moved

File moved to Marketing folder

FIGURE C-13: Copying a file from one location to another

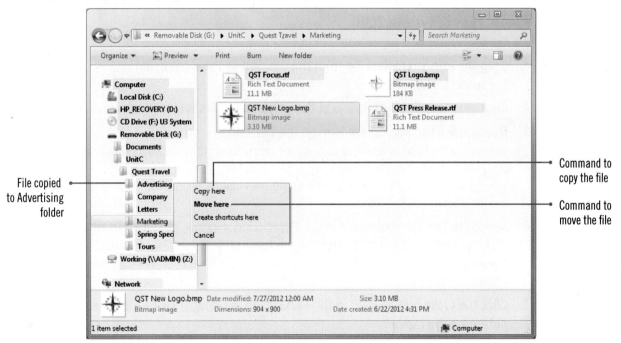

File copied to Advertising folder

Command to copy the file

Command to move the file

Sending files and folders

When you right-click most objects on the desktop or in the Windows Explorer window, the Send to command is one of the choices on the shortcut menu. This command enables you to move a file or folder to a new location on your computer. For example, you can send a file or folder to a USB drive to make a quick backup copy of the file or folder,

to a mail recipient as an electronic message, or to the desktop to create a shortcut. You can also use the Send to command to move a file or folder to the Documents folder. To send a file or folder, right-click the file or folder you want to send, point to Send to on the shortcut menu, then click the destination you want.

Deleting and Restoring Files and Folders

When you organize the contents of a folder, disk, or the desktop, you might find items that you no longer need. You can **delete**, or remove, these items from the disk. If you delete a file or folder from the desktop or from the hard drive, it goes into the Recycle Bin. The **Recycle Bin**, located on your desktop, is a temporary storage area for deleted files. The Recycle Bin stores all the items you delete from your hard disk, so that if you accidentally delete an item, you can remove it from the Recycle Bin to restore it. If the deletion is a recent operation, you can also use the Undo command on the Organize button menu to restore a deleted file or folder. Be aware that if you delete a file from a removable disk, such as a USB drive, it is permanently deleted, not stored in the Recycle Bin. Table C-2 summarizes deleting and restoring options. You decide to delete some files from the Quest Travel folder you no longer need. When you delete a file by mistake, you use the Recycle Bin to restore it.

STEPS

> **TROUBLE**
> If not visible, click the Expand indicator ▷ next to the Letters folder.

1. **If necessary, move and resize the window so that you can see the Recycle Bin icon on the desktop, then click Personal Letters in the folders list**

   Because you cannot restore files deleted from a removable disk, you start by copying a file from the drive where your Data Files are located to the desktop.

2. **Point to the Eric Schubel.rtf file in the right pane, press and hold [Ctrl], drag it to the desktop, then release [Ctrl]**

   The Eric Schubel file is copied to the desktop, as shown in Figure C-14.

> **TROUBLE**
> If a message box appears, click Yes to confirm the deletion.

3. **Drag the Eric Schubel.rtf file from the desktop to the Recycle Bin**

   The Recycle Bin icon looks like it contains paper.

4. **Click the Minimize button ▬ in the Personal Letters folder window**

5. **Double-click the Recycle Bin icon on the desktop**

   The Recycle Bin window opens, containing the Eric Schubel.rtf file and any other deleted files. Like most other windows, the Recycle Bin window has an Address bar, a Search box, a toolbar, and the Details pane. Your deleted files remain in the Recycle Bin until you empty it, permanently removing the contents of the Recycle Bin from your hard drive.

6. **Select the Eric Schubel.rtf file in the Recycle Bin window, as shown in Figure C-15, then click the Restore this item button on the toolbar**

   The file is restored back to its previous location on the desktop. It is intact and identical to the form it was in before you deleted it.

7. **Click the Close button ▣ in the Recycle Bin window, then click the Personal Letters button on the taskbar**

   The Recycle Bin window closes, and the desktop opens with the Eric Schubel.rtf file and the Personal Letters window restored.

8. **Select the Eric Schubel.rtf file on the desktop, press [Delete], then click Yes in the dialog box that opens**

   The Eric Schubel.rtf file is again moved to the Recycle Bin.

9. **Right-click the Recycle Bin, click Empty Recycle Bin, then click Yes in the dialog box that opens**

   The Eric Schubel.rtf file is permanently deleted from the Recycle Bin and your computer.

FIGURE C-14: Selecting a file to drag to the Recycle Bin

Recycle Bin

Selected file copied from the Personal Letters folder to the desktop

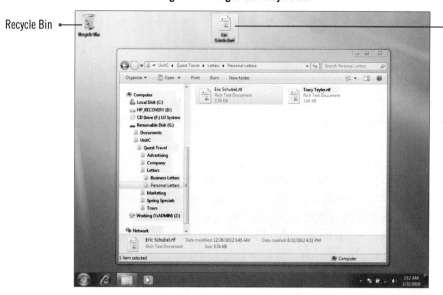

FIGURE C-15: Deleted file from the desktop in the Recycle Bin

Empty the Recycle Bin button

Restore this item button

Contents of the Recycle Bin; yours might differ

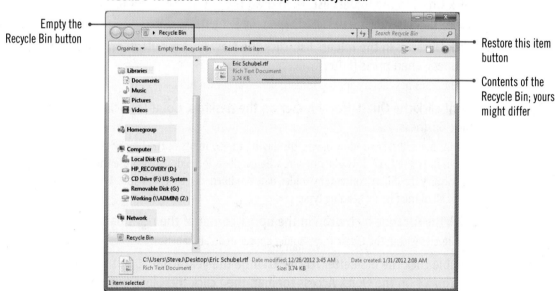

TABLE C-2: Deleting and restoring files

ways to delete a file or folder	ways to restore a file or folder from the Recycle Bin
Select the file or folder, click the Organize button, then click Delete	Select the file or folder, then click a Restore button: Restore this item, Restore the selected items, or Restore all items
Select the file or folder, then press [Delete]	Click the Organize button, then click Undo
Right-click the file or folder, then click Delete	Right-click the file or folder, then click Restore
Drag the file or folder to the Recycle Bin	Drag the file or folder from the Recycle Bin to any location

Recycle Bin properties

You can adjust several Recycle Bin settings by using the Properties option on the Recycle Bin shortcut menu. For example, if you do not want to place files in the Recycle Bin when you delete them, but, rather, want to delete them immediately, right-click the Recycle Bin, click Properties, then click the "Don't move files to the Recycle Bin. Remove files immediately when deleted." option. Also, if you find that the Recycle Bin is full and cannot accept any more files, you can increase the amount of disk space allotted to the Recycle Bin by changing the value in the Maximum size text box.

Working with Libraries

Libraries are special folders that catalog files and folders in a central location, regardless of where you actually store them on your hard drive. A library can contain links to files, other folders, and other subfolders anywhere on your system. You can also share entire libraries as easily as you can share individual directories or files. Windows 7 comes with four libraries already in place: Documents, Music, Pictures, and Videos. You can create additional ones at any time. After you have a library in place, you can use your mouse or the Properties dialog box to include or remove folders and set options to optimize, share, and display the library. After you add one or more folders to a library, Windows 7 tracks your selected folders and updates them automatically in libraries whenever you change their contents. When you open a library, a detailed grouping view of the library indicates the files and subfolders within the monitored folders, letting you easily browse for the file or folder you want to open. ▓▓▓▓ You access the same Quest Specialty Travel company files on a regular basis. Rather than locating the folder using the traditional method, you decide to create a library and place the folder in it for easy access and use.

STEPS

1. **Click UnitC in the folders list, then drag the Quest Travel folder to the desktop**
   A duplicate of the Quest Travel folder appears on the desktop.

QUICK TIP
To restore default libraries, right-click Libraries in the Navigation pane, then click Restore default libraries.

2. **Click Libraries in the folders list, click the New library button on the toolbar, type Business, then press [Enter]**
   The new Business library appears in both panes, as shown in Figure C-16.

3. **Right-click the Quest Travel folder on the desktop, point to Include in library, then click Business**
   The Business library window opens, displaying the contents of the library in a detailed grouping view, as shown in Figure C-17. If you're not sure where a file is located, you can use the Arrange by option to group and display the library contents by folder, date modified, tag, type, or name. **Grouping** displays a sequential list of all of the files by heading type.

4. **Click the Arrange by button in the upper corner of the right pane, then click Name**
   All the files within the Quest Travel folder appear in an alphabetical list.

TROUBLE
Depending on your file association settings, another word-processing program might open instead of WordPad.

5. **Double-click the IRS Letter.rtf file, change the year from 2010 to 2011, click the Save button 🖫 on the Quick Access toolbar, then click the Close button ▄✖▄ in the upper-right corner of the WordPad window**
   The updated file and the WordPad program both close.

6. **Double-click the Quest Travel folder on the desktop, double-click the Letters folder, double-click the Business Letters folder, double-click the IRS Letter.rtf file to see the change, add your name to the bottom of the document, print it, click the Save button, then click the Close button in WordPad and the Business Letters folder windows**
   The file change you made appears when you access the file from the original or library location. The file and the WordPad program close.

7. **Right-click the Quest Travel folder in the Business library in the Navigation pane, click Remove location from library, then click the Close button ▄✖▄ in the Business window**
   The folder location monitored in the Business library is removed from the library.

8. **Click the Business library in the Navigation pane, press [Delete], then click Yes**
   The Business library is permanently deleted from your computer.

9. **Click the Quest Travel folder on the desktop, press [Delete], click Yes to confirm the deletion, then click the Close button in the Libraries window**
   The Quest Travel folder on the desktop is deleted and the Libraries window closes.

FIGURE C-16: Creating a library

Copy of Quest Travel folder on the desktop

New library button

New library

FIGURE C-17: Adding a folder to a library

Library name

Arrange by button

Actual location of the Quest Travel folder

Contents of Business library

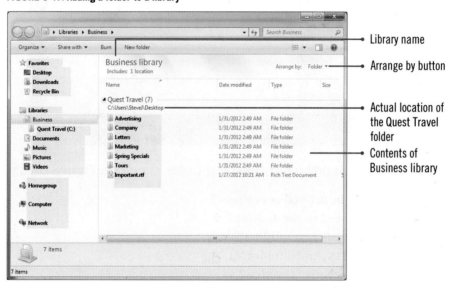

Creating and working with shortcuts

It could take you a while to access a file or folder buried several levels down in a file hierarchy. You can create shortcuts to the items you use frequently. A **shortcut** is a link that you can place in any location to gain instant access to a particular file, folder, or program on your hard disk or on a network just by double-clicking. The actual file, folder, or program remains stored in its original location, and you place an icon representing the shortcut in a convenient location, such as a folder or the desktop. To create a shortcut, right-click an icon, then click Create shortcut. All shortcuts are named the same as the files to which they link, but with the word "Shortcut" at the end of the original name and the file icon includes an arrow. You can also place shortcuts to

frequently used files, folders, and programs on the Start menu or taskbar. To do this on the Start menu, simply drag the shortcut file, folder, or program to the Start button, wait until the Start menu opens, drag the shortcut to a place on the Start menu or to the All Programs submenu, wait until the submenu opens, then drag the shortcut to the appropriate place on the menu. You can drag a shortcut to the taskbar using the same method. When you release the mouse, the item appears on the menu or toolbar. To run a program when Windows starts, right-click the Startup folder on the All Programs submenu, click Open, then drag the shortcut to the program into the Startup folder.

Practice

For current SAM information including versions and content details, visit SAM Central (http://samcentral.course.com). If you have a SAM user profile, you may have access to hands-on instruction, practice, and assessment of the skills covered in this unit. Since we support various versions of SAM throughout the life of this text, you will want to check with your instructor for instructions and the correct URL/Web site to access those assignments.

Concepts Review

FIGURE C-18

Label each component of the desktop personal computer shown in Figure C-18.

1. Which element holds items to be deleted or restored? *A*
2. Which element is copied or moved to the desktop? *b*
3. Which element do you click to collapse a folder? *c*
4. Which element do you click to expand a folder? *e*
5. Which element do you click to change the view? *g*
6. Which element is stored in its original location? *d*
7. Which element is stored in a library? *f*

Match each term with the statement that best describes it.

8. Recycle Bin *c*	**a.** A display of drives and disks
9. Filtering *e*	**b.** A display of files and folders
10. Grouping *d*	**c.** A storage area for deleted files
11. Computer window *a*	**d.** A display of library files
12. Explorer window *b*	**e.** A display of files by properties

Select the best answer from the list of choices.

13. The Windows Explorer window is used to:
   a. Delete files.   **c.** Manage drives and disks.
   b. Add folders.   **d.** All of the above

14. Which of the following is NOT an available view in Windows Explorer?
   a. Content   **c.** Icon
   b. Tiles   **d.** List

Concepts Review (Continued)

15. **Which of the following is NOT a column heading in Details view?**
    - **a.** Content
    - **b.** Size
    - **c.** Type
    - **d.** Date Modified

16. **Which of the following is NOT a layout pane?**
    - **a.** Details
    - **b.** Search
    - **c.** Preview
    - **d.** Navigation

17. **Which of the following displays only files and folders with properties you select by heading type?**
    - **a.** Sort
    - **b.** Group
    - **c.** Filter
    - **d.** Stack

18. **Which of the following is a method for copying a file or folder?**
    - **a.** Press and hold [Ctrl], then drag the folder or file.
    - **b.** Drag the folder or file on the same disk drive.
    - **c.** Double-click the folder or file.
    - **d.** Click the folder or file, then click Copy.

19. **Which of the following locations is NOT a valid place from which to delete a file and send it to the Recycle Bin?**
    - **a.** Removable disk
    - **b.** Explorer window
    - **c.** Hard drive
    - **d.** Computer window

20. **Which of the following is NOT a default library?**
    - **a.** Documents
    - **b.** Music
    - **c.** Movies
    - **d.** Pictures

Skills Review

1. **Open Windows Explorer.**
   a. Open Windows Explorer using the taskbar, then display the Music library.
   b. If you want to save your Data Files to a USB drive, make sure it's plugged in.
   c. Display the Computer window, then navigate to the Quest Travel folder on the drive.
   d. Double-click the Letters folder, then double-click the Personal Letters folder.

2. **View files and folders.**
   a. Change to List view.
   b. Click the Back button to the left of the Address bar, then open the Business Letters folder.
   c. Click the Quest Travel list arrow in the Address bar, then click Tours.
   d. Click the Recent Pages list arrow, then click Quest Travel.
   e. Change to Details view, then change to Content view.
   f. Change to Tiles view without clicking the Views button arrow.

3. **Navigate a folders list.**
   a. Collapse the folders list for the drive under Computer.
   b. Expand the folders list for the drive, then click the drive where you store your Data Files.
   c. Expand the UnitC folder in the folders list, then click the Quest Travel folder in the folders list.
   d. Double-click the Marketing folder in the right pane.

4. **Create and rename files and folders.**
   a. In the Marketing folder, right-click a blank area of the window, point to New, then click Folder.
   b. Name the new folder **Sales & Marketing**.
   c. Rename the Sales & Marketing folder to **Sales**.
   d. Rename the file QST Focus.rtf to **About QST.rtf**.

5. **Search for files and folders.**
   a. Search in the Quest Travel folder for files or folders that are named or contain the word "logo" as part of the filename.
   b. Narrow down the search to only files with a size greater than 1 MB (Large).
   c. Click the Close button in the Search box to clear the search criteria.

Skills Review (Continued)

6. **Organize files and folders.**

   a. Display the Marketing folder in Details view.

   b. Filter the Name column by Q–Z.

   c. Search subfolders review results, then click the Back button.

   d. Sort the contents of the window alphabetically.

   e. Remove the filter Q–Z, then display the Marketing folder.

7. **Copy and move files and folders.**

   a. Select QST New Logo.bmp in the right pane, click the Organize button on the toolbar, then click Copy.

   b. Display the Company folder, click the Organize button on the toolbar, then click Paste.

   c. Move the copy of the QST New Logo file into the Tours folder.

   d. Move the Tours folder into the Marketing folder.

8. **Delete and restore files and folders.**

   a. Open the Quest Travel folder, then resize it, if necessary, to display part of the desktop.

   b. Move the Marketing folder from the drive where you store your Data Files to the desktop.

   c. Drag the Marketing folder from the desktop to the Recycle Bin, then click Yes to confirm the deletion, if necessary.

   d. Double-click the Recycle Bin. Right-click a blank area of the taskbar, then click Show Windows Side by Side.

   e. Click Empty the Recycle Bin on the toolbar in the Recycle Bin window, then click No to cancel the action.

   f. Drag the Marketing folder back to the Quest Travel folder to restore it, then close the Recycle Bin window.

9. **Work with libraries.**

   a. Open the Marketing folder, then drag the Marketing folder to an empty area of the desktop.

   b. Display the Libraries folder, then create a library named Business.

   c. Include the Marketing folder on the desktop in the Business library.

   d. Arrange the library contents by Type.

   e. Remove the Marketing folder from the library, then delete the Business library.

   f. Delete the Marketing folder on the desktop, then close the Windows Explorer window.

Independent Challenge 1

You are vice president of a packaging manufacturing company, Xpress Packaging, and you need to organize your Windows files and folders. In addition to folders for typical business-related functions, such as correspondence, contracts, inventory, and payroll, you have folders related to company functions, such as manufacturing and material suppliers.

   a. Create a new folder named **Xpress Packaging** on the desktop within which the files and folders for this independent challenge will reside.

   b. Open Windows Explorer, display Libraries, then create a library named **Xpress**.

   c. Include the Xpress Packaging folder in the Xpress library.

   d. Create folders in the Xpress Packaging folder named **Manufacturing**, **Material Suppliers**, **East Coast**, and **West Coast**.

   e. Move the East Coast and West Coast folders into the Material Suppliers folder.

   f. Create a blank file using WordPad, add your name, print, and save it as **Suppliers Bid.rtf** in the Manufacturing folder.

   g. Move the Suppliers Bid.rtf file into the Material Suppliers folder.

   h. Copy the Suppliers Bid.rtf file into the Manufacturing folder and rename the copied file **Manufacturing Bids.rtf**, then display the Manufacturing folder.

Advanced Challenge Exercise

   ■ Display the contents of the Xpress Packaging folder in the Explorer window, then drag the Manufacturing folder onto the Favorites list in the Navigation pane.

   ■ Drag the Manufacturing folder link in the Favorites list to a new location in the Favorites list.

   ■ Right-click the Manufacturing folder link in the Favorites list, then click Remove on the shortcut menu.

   i. Copy the Xpress Packaging folder to the drive and folder where you store your Data Files.

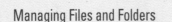

j. Remove the Xpress Packaging folder from the Xpress library, then delete the Xpress library.

k. Delete the Xpress Packaging folder on the desktop, then close the window.

Independent Challenge 2

You are the president of MO PC, a mobile computer accessories company, and you use Windows to organize your business files. You want to create folders to keep your computer organized. As you create files, you save them in the appropriate folders.

a. Create a new folder named **MO PC** on the desktop within which the files and folders for this independent challenge will reside.

b. Open Windows Explorer, display Libraries, then create a library named **Company**.

c. Include the MO PC folder in the Company library.

d. Create folders in the MO PC folder named **Advertising** and **Customers**.

e. Use WordPad to create a letter welcoming new customers. Add your name, print, and save it as **Customer Letter.rtf** in the Customers folder.

f. Use WordPad to create a list of five business management tasks to do. Save it as **Business Plan.rtf** in the MO PC folder.

g. Use Paint to create a simple logo, add your name, print, and save it as **MO Logo.bmp** in the MO PC folder.

h. Move the MO Logo file into the Advertising folder.

i. Create a shortcut to the MO Logo file in the MO PC folder.

j. Delete the Business Plan file, then restore it.

k. Copy the MO PC folder to the drive and folder where you store your Data Files.

l. Remove the MO PC folder from the Company library, then delete the Company library.

m. Delete the MO PC folder on the desktop, then close the window.

Independent Challenge 3

As a human resources manager at Just in Time Books, you need to organize the folders and files on the company's computer for new employees at store locations around the world. Your job is to create and organize company files and folders.

a. Open the Computer window, open the drive and folder where you store your Data Files.

b. Create a new folder named **Just in Time Books** on the desktop within which the rest of the organization of files and folders for this independent challenge will reside.

c. Open Windows Explorer, display Libraries, then create a library named **JITB**.

d. Include the Just in Time Books folder in the JITB library.

e. Create a file using WordPad listing at least six international store locations (city and country). Save it as **New Store Locations.rtf** in the Just in Time Books folder.

f. Create a file using WordPad listing at least four employee names with your name being the last one. Print and save it as **Employee App.rtf** in the Just in Time Books folder.

g. In the Just in Time Books folder, create folders named **Store Locations** and **Employees**.

h. In the Employees folder, create four new folders with employee names, one of which is yourself.

i. Copy the Employee App.rtf file into each of the employee folders, then rename each file as **Employee _Name_.rtf**, replacing "Name" with each employee's name.

j. In the folder named Store Locations, create a new folder named **New Stores**.

k. Move the New Store Locations file to the New Stores folder.

l. Display the contents of the Just in Time Books folder in the Explorer window, then search for "Employee."

m. Create an advanced search using the Date modified option as it relates to when you created the files.

Advanced Challenge Exercise

- Save the search as JITB Employees in the Just in Time Books folder.
- Switch to the Just in Time Books folder, then display the saved search file using the Navigation pane. (Expand the folders list if necessary.)
- Run the saved search.
- Switch to the Just in Time Books folder, then delete the saved search in the folder and Favorites list.

n. Copy the Just in Time Books folder to the drive and folder where you store your Data Files.

o. Remove the Just In Time Books folder from the JITB library, then delete the JITB library.

p. Delete the Just in Time Books folder on the desktop, then close the window.

Real Life Independent Challenge

Many people have collections of something—recipes, books, music, DVDs, and so on. Take something you have collected and organize the different items into categories to help keep files and folders organized in the future.

a. Create a new folder named **My Collection** within which the files and folders for this independent challenge will reside. Replace the word "Collection" in the folder name with the items you collect; for example, if you collect books, name the folder My Books.

b. Open Windows Explorer, display Libraries, then create a library named **Collections**.

c. Include the My Collection folder in the Collections library.

d. Create four files using WordPad, add your name to them, print them, and save them with names relating to your collection in the My Collection folder; for example, a collection of recipes might include files named French Bread.rtf, Torte.rtf, Sweet Bread.rtf, and 7-Layer Chocolate.rtf.

e. In the My Collection folder, create at least two folders related to your collection; for example, if you collect DVDs, you might create folders named Comedies and Thrillers. Move the files into the appropriate folders.

f. Open one of the folders, then create at least two subfolders.

g. Move files into the subfolders if appropriate.

h. Copy the My Collection folder to the drive and folder where you store your Data Files.

i. Remove the My Collection folder from the Collections library, then delete the Collections library.

j. Create a shortcut on the desktop to one of the files in the My Collection folder.

k. Drag the My Collection folder on the desktop to the Recycle Bin.

l. Open the Recycle Bin, then restore the folder.

m. Delete the My Collection folder and the shortcut file, then close the Computer window.

Visual Workshop

Re-create the screen shown in Figure C-19, which displays the Search Results window with files from the drive and folder where you store your Data Files.

FIGURE C-19

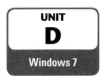

Customizing File and Folder Management

As you work with files and folders, you'll discover that navigating through a long list of folders can be time consuming. To be more efficient, you can customize the way you work with files and folders to save time and effort and to suit your personal needs and preferences. In this unit, you'll learn how to change the layout of Windows Explorer windows, change folder view options to display the file and folder information you need, view the contents of personal folders, create a personal folder and customize the view options, display disk and folder size information, compress files and folders to save disk space, and use a CD or DVD to back up and store files for later use in case of problems. As a new employee of Quest Specialty Travel, you want to customize some file management tasks so you can work more effectively.

OBJECTIVES

Change the layout of Explorer windows

Change folder options

Change file details to list

Change search options

Use personal folders

Customize personal folders

Display disk and folder information

Compress files and folders

Manage files and folders on a CD or DVD

Changing the Layout of Explorer Windows

Windows 7 gives you the option to customize the layout for each Explorer window depending on the information the window contains. The layout for each Explorer window includes a menu bar, Details pane, Preview pane, and Navigation pane, but only the Details and Navigation panes appear by default. If you prefer working with menus like the previous version of Windows, you can show the menu bar and use traditional menus. The Details pane displays information about the selected file, folder, or disk at the bottom of the window, whereas the Preview pane displays the contents of a selected file on the right side of the window. The Navigation pane displays Favorite links and the folders list. For some Explorer windows, such as the personal folder labeled with your user account name, the layout also includes the Search pane, which displays basic and advanced search options to help you find the files you're looking for. If you open the Explorer window in one of the library folders, you can also use the Library pane, which displays the current library name, included folder locations, and an arrange by option. **◢◣◤◥** Instead of opening a file on your computer to determine its contents, you want to display the Preview pane for the Quest Travel folder, so you can quickly determine the contents of a selected file.

STEPS

1. **Click the Start button ⊛ on the taskbar, then click Computer**

   The Computer window opens, displaying the contents of your computer, including all disk drives and common folders.

2. **Navigate to the drive and folder where you store your Data Files, double-click the UnitD folder, then double-click the Quest Travel folder**

   The Quest Travel window opens, displaying the contents of the Quest Travel folder. The folder includes five folders (Advertising, Company, Letters, Marketing, and Tours) and one file (To Do List).

3. **Double-click the Marketing folder, click the Views button arrow ▦▾ on the toolbar, then click Tiles if necessary**

   The Marketing window opens, displaying the contents of the Marketing folder.

4. **Click the Organize button on the toolbar, then point to Layout**

   The Organize menu opens, displaying the Layout submenu, as shown in Figure D-1.

5. **Click Preview pane**

   The Preview pane displays on the right side of the window.

6. **Click the QST New Logo.bmp file**

   A preview of the new Quest Specialty Travel logo opens in the Preview pane, as shown in Figure D-2.

7. **Click the QST Focus.rtf file**

   A preview of the QST Focus.rtf file opens in the Preview pane.

8. **Click the Preview Pane button ▢ on the toolbar**

   The Preview pane is hidden and the Marketing window becomes active.

FIGURE D-1: Explorer window layout options

Layout option in Organize menu

Windows Layout submenu; your list might differ

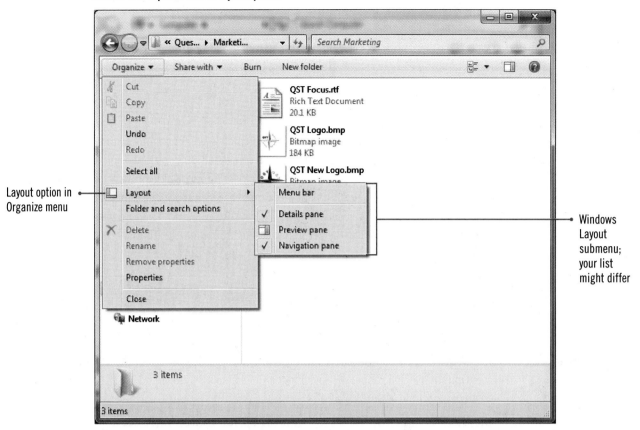

FIGURE D-2: The Preview pane in an Explorer window

Navigation pane

Preview pane displaying the contents of the selected file; your pane size might differ

Details pane

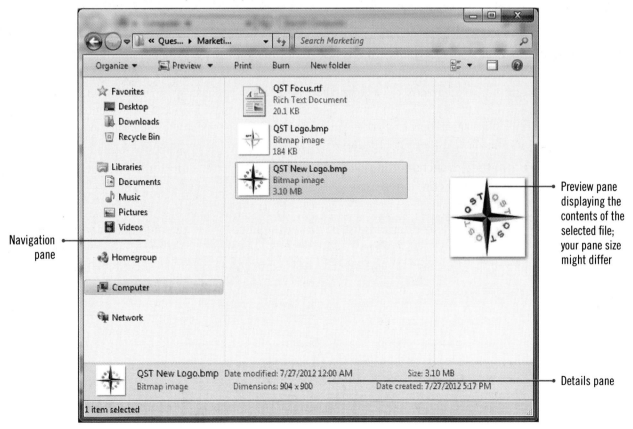

Changing Folder Options

When you work with files and folders, Windows displays folder contents in a standard way, known as the **default**. The default folder view settings (expect for libraries) are as follows: Tiles view displays files and folders as icons; folders show Details and Navigation panes; folders open in the same window; and items open when you double-click them. Depending on previous installations or users, your folder view settings might differ. Instead of changing the folder view to your preferred view—one of the icon or list views, or Details view—each time you open a folder, you can change the view permanently to the one you prefer. In addition to the defaults, you can change options such as folder settings to show or hide file name extensions for known file types, show or hide hidden files and folders, show or hide protected operating system files, and show pop-up descriptions of folders and desktop items. If you don't like the options you set, you can restore the settings to Windows default settings. ■■■■ You're finding it hard to view files with extensions on the end, so you want to hide file extensions and customize folder settings to suit your needs.

STEPS

1. **In the Marketing folder, click the Views button arrow on the toolbar, then click Details, if necessary**

   The files and folders in the Marketing folder appear in Details view.

   QUICK TIP
   You can restore the Folder Options dialog box settings to the Windows default settings by clicking Restore Defaults.

2. **Click the Organize button on the toolbar, then click Folder and search options**

   The Folder Options dialog box opens, displaying the General tab, as shown in Figure D-3. In this case, the default options are selected.

3. **Click the Open each folder in its own window option button to select it**

   This option enables each folder to open in a separate window. Up to this point, each folder has opened in the current window.

4. **Click the View tab**

   The View tab options display, as shown in Figure D-4.

   QUICK TIP
   To restore all folders to the original Windows settings, click Reset Folders.

5. **Click Apply to Folders, then click Yes in the Folder Views dialog box that opens to accept the folder views change**

   The Apply to Folders feature sets all the folders of this type on your computer to match the current folder's view settings, which is currently Details view. The Advanced settings section at the bottom of the dialog box lists additional options relating to the way files and folders appear in the Computer and Windows Explorer windows.

6. **In the Advanced settings list box, click the Hide extensions for known file types check box to select it, if necessary**

   This option hides the file name extension, such as .rtf.

7. **In the Advanced settings list box, click the Always show menus check box to select it**

   This option shows menus in Explorer windows, which provides access to additional commands.

8. **Click OK**

   The dialog box closes and the Marketing window opens without extensions at the end of file names and with the menu bar displayed.

9. **Click Quest Travel in the Address bar, then double-click the Marketing folder**

   The Marketing folder opens in its own window, displaying the contents of the folder in Details view, as shown in Figure D-5. Based on the new folder option settings, all folders appear in Details view with the menu bar displayed and file name extensions hidden.

FIGURE D-3: Folder Options dialog box with the General tab displayed

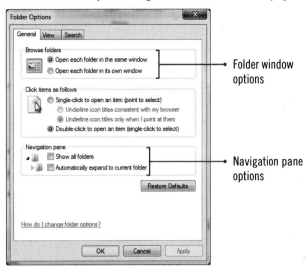

Folder window options

Navigation pane options

FIGURE D-4: Folder Options dialog box with the View tab displayed

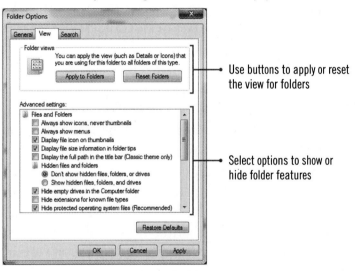

Use buttons to apply or reset the view for folders

Select options to show or hide folder features

FIGURE D-5: Marketing folder with new folder options applied

Menus show

File name extensions no longer appear

Folder opens in a separate window

Changing File Details to List

You can display files and folders in a variety of different ways, depending on what you want to see and do. When you view files and folders in an Explorer window with any view, a default list of file and folder information opens, which consists of Name, Date modified, Type, and Size. If the default list of file and folder details doesn't provide you with the information you need, you can add and remove the file and folder information you want, to and from the Details view. To do this, you use the Choose details command or right-click a column header to make changes to the details list. ▰▰▰▰ As you manage files, you find it easier to identify them by using more than the standard file details. You decide to add both the owner of a file and image size of picture files to the details list in Details view.

STEPS

1. **In the Marketing folder window, click View on the menu bar, then click Choose details**
   The Choose Details dialog box opens, as shown in Figure D-6. The selected check boxes indicate the current columns shown in the Explorer window. The unchecked items indicate items not used. The unchecked items are listed in alphabetical order.

QUICK TIP
When you set the default view to Details view, the items you add or remove from the Choose Details dialog box are not included in Details view.

2. **In the Details box, scroll down, then click the Owner check box to select it**
   This option adds a column to the Explorer window that lists the owner (the person who can make changes) of files.

3. **In the Details box, scroll up, then click the Dimensions check box to select it**
   This option adds a column to the Explorer window that lists the size of image files in pixels. A **pixel**, short for picture element, is a single point in a graphic image.

4. **Click OK, then click the Maximize button 🔲 in the Marketing folder window**
   The additional columns are displayed in Details view, as shown in Figure D-7.

QUICK TIP
From the shortcut menu, you can select More to open the Choose Details dialog box.

5. **Right-click any column header**
   A shortcut menu opens, as shown in Figure D-8. The columns that appear in the window have a check mark next to them.

6. **Click Date modified on the shortcut menu to deselect it, if necessary**
   The shortcut menu closes and the Date modified column is removed from Details view.

7. **Right-click any column header, then click Date modified on the shortcut menu to select it**
   The Date modified column is added back to Details view.

8. **Right-click any column header, click More on the shortcut menu, click the Dimensions check box to clear it, click the Owner check box to clear it, then click OK**
   The Dimensions and Owner columns are removed from the window.

9. **Click the Close button 🔲 in the Marketing window**
   The Marketing window closes and the Quest Travel window becomes active.

Moving columns in Details view

When you display files and folders in an Explorer window, you can change the order of the column details to make it easier to locate the information you need to find. You can change the order of columns by using the Choose Details dialog box or the mouse pointer. The easiest way to move a column detail a short distance on the screen is to drag the column indicator button between the two columns where you want to place the column. As you drag the column indicator button,

the column moves to display the new arrangement of the columns. If you need to move a column several columns across the screen, the best way to move it is to use the Choose Details dialog box. Open the Choose Details dialog box, click the column detail you want to move, then click Move Up or Move Down. When you're done, click OK to close the dialog box.

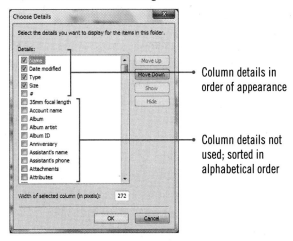
FIGURE D-6: Choose Details dialog box

Choose Details

Select the details you want to display for the items in this folder.

Details:
- ☑ Name
- ☑ Date modified
- ☑ Type
- ☑ Size
- ☐ #
- ☐ 35mm focal length
- ☐ Account name
- ☐ Album
- ☐ Album artist
- ☐ Album ID
- ☐ Anniversary
- ☐ Assistant's name
- ☐ Assistant's phone
- ☐ Attachments
- ☐ Attributes

Move Up
Move Down
Show
Hide

Width of selected column (in pixels): 272

OK   Cancel

● Column details in order of appearance

● Column details not used; sorted in alphabetical order

FIGURE D-7: Columns added in Details view

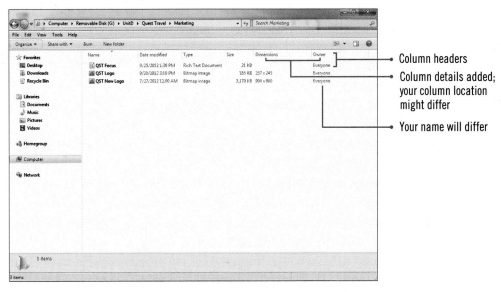

● Column headers

● Column details added; your column location might differ

● Your name will differ

FIGURE D-8: Columns modified in Details view

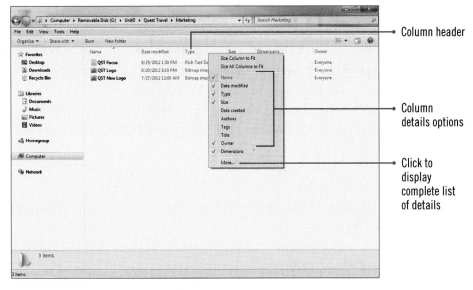

● Column header

● Column details options

● Click to display complete list of details

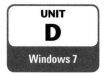

Changing Search Options

The Search box at the bottom of the Start menu and at the top of every Explorer window filters out items that don't match the text you type. The search includes text in the file name, text in the file, tags, and other file properties, such as the file type. You can also select options that appear below the list of results to search file contents or perform an advanced search. In the Search box, you can also perform advanced searches by specifying multiple keywords or properties connected by Boolean filters, such as AND, NOT, OR, Quotes, Parentheses, >, or <. For example, the advanced search kind: *(Rich Text Document OR Bitmap Image)* finds all files with the type Rich Text Document or Bitmap Image. Windows also provides an option to perform a **natural language search**, which allows you to perform the same property or Boolean search, using a more intuitive form. Instead of typing kind: *(Rich Text Document OR Bitmap Image)*, you can type *rich text or bitmap*. Before you can use natural language, you need to enable it on the Search tab in the Folder Options dialog box. On the Search tab, you can also set options to specify what searches to perform and how to perform them. You can specify whether to search indexed locations or everywhere, or to include subfolders or find partial matches. An **indexed location** is a file that Windows has kept track of and stored information about using an index to make locating files faster and easier. Your manager asks you to find a company document and logo file for a project, so you want to change search options to make it easier to find files using advanced search techniques.

STEPS

1. **Click the Organize button on the toolbar, then click Folder and search options**
   The Folder Options dialog box opens, displaying the General tab.

2. **Click the Search tab**
   The Folder Options dialog box reopens displaying the Search tab, as shown in Figure D-9. In this case, the default options are selected.

3. **Click the Always search file names and contents option button**
   This option expands the search to all folders on your computer.

4. **Click the Use natural language search check box to select it, then click the Find partial matches check box to select it, if necessary**
   This option turns on the Use natural language search feature and Find partial matches search option, which enables you to match text within text. For example, you can get a match with "rich text document" when you enter "rich."

5. **Click OK**
   The new search options are set.

TROUBLE
If you have Microsoft Office Word or another word processor installed on your computer, the file type for rich text files might be "Rich Text Format."

6. **Click in the Search box in the Quest Travel window, then type rich text or bitmap**
   The documents with the type Rich Text Document or Bitmap Image appear in the search results, as shown in Figure D-10. Because you changed default settings, you restore the computer to its default state.

7. **Click the Organize button on the toolbar, then click Folder and search options**
   The Folder Options dialog box opens, displaying the General tab.

8. **Click Restore Defaults, click the View tab, click Reset Folders, if available, click Yes in the warning dialog box to confirm the reset for all folder views, click Restore Defaults, click the Search tab, then click Restore Defaults**
   The folder and search options are restored to the Windows default settings. Because the figures in this book show file name extensions, you restore that option.

9. **Click the View tab, click the Hide extensions for known file types check box to deselect it, then click OK**

10. **Click the Close button [X] in the Search Results in Quest Travel window**
    The Search Results window closes and the desktop displays.

FIGURE D-9: Folder Options dialog box with the Search tab displayed

Default set to search locations and names only in nonindexed locations

Search file names and contents in all folder options

Find partial matches feature

Use natural language search method

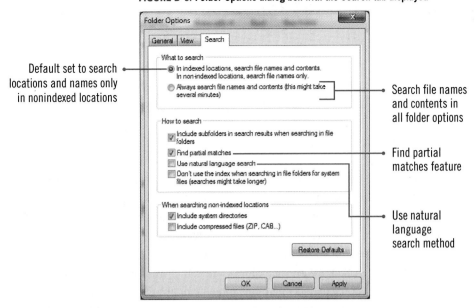

FIGURE D-10: Search results using a natural language search

Search box

Search results highlighted; your order might differ

Advanced search location options

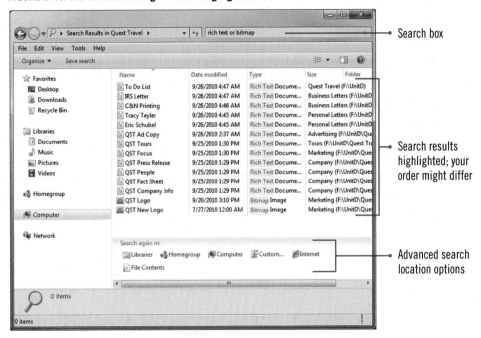

Modifying the index to improve searching

If you don't find the files you're looking for in an indexed location search, you can modify the index to customize and improve searching for your computer to make locating files faster and easier. By default, indexed locations include personal folder, e-mail, and offline files and exclude program files and system files. To change indexed locations, use Indexing Options in the Control Panel to view, add, remove, and modify indexed locations, indexed file types, and other advanced index settings. For example, if a file type is not recognized by the index, you can add it, or if you're having problems with the search index, you can rebuild or restore it. Click the Start button, click Control Panel, click in the Search box, type index, click Indexing Options, then click Modify. If you don't see all the locations, click Show all locations. If a folder location contains subfolders, you can double-click the folder to expand it. Select or clear the check box next to the folder locations you want to add or remove from the index. Click OK, then click Close.

Using Personal Folders

Windows 7 comes with a **personal folder** that stores your most frequently used folders in one location. The personal folder appears on the Start menu with the name of the person logged on to the computer. The personal folder only contains files and folders associated with the user account, and it is unique for each user. The personal folder includes a variety of subfolders, such as Contacts, Desktop, Downloads, Favorites, Links, My Documents, My Music, My Pictures, My Videos, Saved Games, and Searches. Depending on previous installations, devices installed, or other users, the names and types of personal folders might differ. The My Documents, My Music, My Pictures, and My Videos folder are included folders by default in their respective library folders, so when you save files into a library folder, they're actually stored in your personal folders. For example, when you save a file into the Documents library folder, it's actually saved in the My Documents folder. Windows 7 creates personal folders identified by each username on your computer to make sure the contents of personal folders remain private, unless you decide to share the contents with others who use your computer or network. If you and a friend use the same computer, there are two sets of personal folders, one with your name and another with your friend's name. When you log on to the computer, your personal folders open, but you cannot access your friend's personal folders. Your manager asks you to delete old files left over from the previous user of the computer, so you want to open the personal folders to see what's there.

STEPS

1. **Click the Start button ⊕ on the taskbar, then click the name at the top of the right column on the Start menu**

   The personal folder window opens, as shown in Figure D-11. The name displayed in the Address bar corresponds to the user account name when you logged on.

> **QUICK TIP**
> To view included folders in a library, display the library folder, then click the locations link under the library name.

2. **Double-click the My Pictures folder, then click the Pictures library folder in the Navigation pane**

   The My Pictures window opens and then the Pictures library window opens, displaying the contents of the folder. Because the My Pictures folder is included in the Pictures library folder, the same pictures that appear in the My Pictures folder appear in the Pictures library folder. The Sample Pictures folder is included in the Pictures library folder by default.

3. **Double-click the Sample Pictures folder, then click any of the images**

   Large Icons view displays each picture as a thumbnail miniature image of the contents of a file; thumbnails are often used to browse through multiple images quickly. If the folder doesn't contain images, icons representing the file type are displayed instead of thumbnails. Folders that contain pictures have buttons on the toolbar tailored specifically for working with pictures, such as Slide show, as shown in Figure D-12. Another button, the Preview button, becomes available after you select a picture file.

4. **Click the Slide show button on the toolbar, wait and watch the slide show or click the screen to view each slide, then press [Esc] to discontinue**

   The slide show closes and the Sample Pictures folder appears.

> **QUICK TIP**
> To change the save location for a library, display the library folder, click the Organize button on the toolbar, click Properties, select the folder you want, click Set save location, then click OK.

5. **Click the Videos library folder in the Navigation pane, then double-click the Sample Videos folder**

   The Sample Videos folder opens, displaying the contents of the folder as large icons. For videos, a frame, typically the first one, appears in the thumbnail.

6. **Click a video to select it, then click the Play button on the toolbar**

   Windows Media Player opens and plays the sample video.

7. **When the video is finished, click the Close button ⌐×⌐ in the Windows Media Player window, then click Computer in the Navigation pane**

   Windows Media Player closes and the Computer window becomes active.

FIGURE D-11: Personal folder

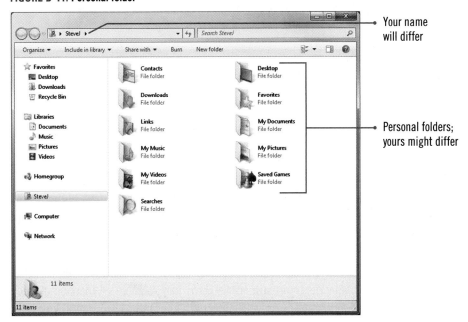

Your name will differ

Personal folders; yours might differ

FIGURE D-12: Sample Pictures folder

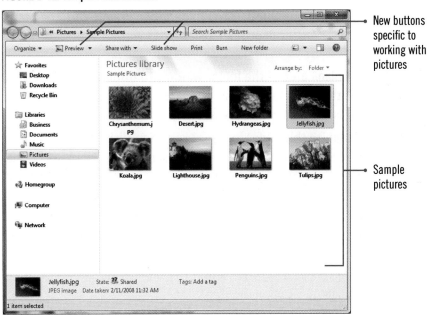

New buttons specific to working with pictures

Sample pictures

Using the Shared Documents folder

The contents of your personal folders are private, unless you decide to share the contents with others who use your computer. If you want the other users on your computer or network to have access to files, you can place those files in a shared folder called the Public folder. To access the Public folder, click Computer in the Navigation pane, double-click the main hard drive icon, double-click the Users folder, then double-click the Public folder. Like personal folders, the Public folder contains subfolders to help you organize the files you are sharing, including Public Documents, Public Downloads, Public Music, Public Pictures, Public Recorded TV, and Public Videos. If you're connected to a network, the files in the Public folder are available to network users. You can also designate any folder on your computer as a shared folder. When you specify a folder as a shared folder, you can set access permission levels for a person or group. Select the folder you want to share, click the Share with button on the toolbar, click Specific person, type a name or group, or select one from the list arrow, click Add, click the Permission Level list arrow, select a permission level, then click Share. To stop sharing, select the folder, click the Share with button on the toolbar, then click Nobody.

Customizing Personal Folders

The My Pictures, My Music, and My Videos folders located in your personal folder include specialized buttons on the toolbar for working with pictures, music, or videos. For example, the My Pictures folder includes a Slide show button to display the pictures in the folder as a full screen slide show. The My Music and My Videos folders include various Play buttons to play the music or videos in the folder. You can customize a new or existing folder for documents, pictures, music, and videos by applying a **folder template**, which is a collection of toolbar options for working with specialized content. Windows 7 comes with five folder templates: General Items, Documents, Music, Pictures, and Videos. After you apply a folder template to a folder and put related files in the folder, such as pictures in a folder with the Pictures template, the toolbar displays the specialized buttons, such as Slide show and Preview. Windows also comes with four libraries: Documents, Music, Pictures, and Videos. Each of these libraries applies the same type of folder template, which you can also change, to use a specialized toolbar. ▨▨▨ As a marketing specialist, you're going to be working with a lot of graphics, so you want to customize the Marketing folder for pictures.

STEPS

1. **Navigate to the drive and folder where you store your Data Files, double-click the** UnitD **folder, double-click the** Quest Travel folder, **then double-click the** Marketing folder
   The Marketing folder opens, displaying WordPad and Paint files. The toolbar displays the Organize, Share with, Burn, New folder, Views, Preview Pane, and Help buttons.

2. **Right-click a blank area of the folder window to display a shortcut menu, as shown in Figure D-13, then click** Customize this folder
   The Marketing Properties dialog box opens, displaying the Customize tab.

3. **Click the** Optimize this folder for list arrow, **then click** Pictures
   When you choose a template, you apply specific features to your folder, such as specialized task links and viewing options for working with pictures, music, or videos. The Pictures folder type is a good choice to select as a template for the Marketing folder.

4. **Click the** Also apply this template to all subfolders check box **to select it**
   The template now will be applied to all subfolders within the Marketing folder. See Figure D-14.

5. **Click** OK
   Notice that the Slide show button has been added to the toolbar. This command appears on the toolbar for folders based on the Pictures template.

6. **Click the** Close button ▨▨▨ **in the Marketing window**
   The Marketing window closes.

Customizing File and Folder Management

FIGURE D-13: Customize this folder command on the Shortcut menu

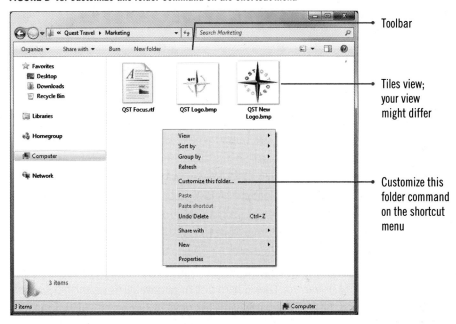

Toolbar

Tiles view; your view might differ

Customize this folder command on the shortcut menu

FIGURE D-14: Marketing Properties dialog box with the Customize tab displayed

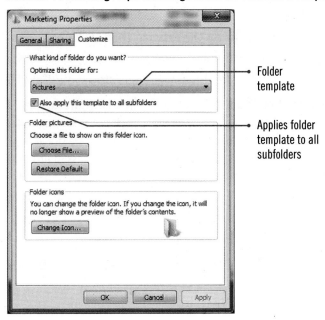

Folder template

Applies folder template to all subfolders

Customizing a library

Windows 7 comes with four default libraries: Documents, Music, Pictures, and Videos. Libraries are special folders that catalog files and folders in a central location, regardless of where you actually store them on your hard drive. A library can contain links to files, other folders, and other subfolders anywhere on your system. You can customize a library folder by using the Properties dialog box where you can include or re-move folders and set options to optimize, share, and display the library.

The Optimize this library command in the Properties dialog box works just like the Optimize this folder command and lets you customize the library window to include specialized buttons on the toolbar. You can also set the save folder location where you want to save a file when a library is selected. To change the location, open the library, select a linked folder location at the top of the Properties dialog box, then click Set save location. A check mark appears next to the new saved location.

Displaying Disk and Folder Information

When you create a file, it takes up space on a disk. Files that contain only text are smaller than files that contain only graphics. The size of a file is measured in bytes. A **byte** is a unit of storage capable of holding a single character or pixel. It's the base measurement for all other incremental units, which are kilobyte, megabyte, gigabyte, and terabyte. A **kilobyte** (KB) is 1,024 bytes of information while a **megabyte** (MB) is 1,048,576 bytes, which is equal to 1,024 kilobytes. A **gigabyte** (GB) is equal to 1,024 megabytes, and a **terabyte** (TB) is equal to 1,024 gigabytes. A disk that can store 1.44 megabytes of data, for example, is capable of storing approximately 1.4 million characters, or about 3,000 pages of information. As you work with files, folders, and programs, it's important to know the size of the disk and how much space remains available. A disk can store only a limited amount of data. You can use the Properties command on a disk to display the disk size, used and free space, and change a **disk label**, which is a name you can assign to a hard or removable disk. When you label a hard disk or removable drive, the label appears in the Computer and Explorer windows. Besides checking hard disk drive or removable disk information, you can also use the Properties command on a folder to find out the size of its contents. ▨▨▨ You have been adding Quest Specialty Travel files to your removable disk and want to find out how much space is available. You also want to determine the size of a folder's contents to see if it will fit on your removable disk.

STEPS

1. **Click the Start button** ⊕ **on the taskbar, then click Computer**
   The Computer window opens, displaying the disk drives available on your computer.

> **TROUBLE**
> If your Data Files are not stored on an external drive, right-click the icon for the drive where they are stored.

2. **Right-click the icon for the drive where you store your Data Files**

3. **Click Properties on the shortcut menu, then click the General tab, if necessary**
   A Properties dialog box opens, displaying the General tab, as shown in Figure D-15. Your dialog box will differ depending on the drive or disk where your Data Files are stored. A pie chart indicates the amount of space being used relative to the amount available for the disk or drive that you are using. In the example shown in Figure D-15, 693 megabytes are used and 3.05 gigabytes are free.

> **TROUBLE**
> If you are working in a lab and your Data Files are located on a hard or network disk, skip Step 4.

4. **Click in or select all the text in the text box if necessary, then type DataDisk**
   A disk label cannot contain any spaces, but can be up to 11 characters long.

5. **Click OK to close the Properties dialog box**

6. **Double-click the DataDisk icon or the drive where your Data Files are stored**
   The DataDisk window (or corresponding window where your Data Files are stored) opens displaying the contents of your drive.

7. **Navigate to the folder where you store your Data Files, then double-click the UnitD folder**
   The contents of the UnitD folder open in the Computer window.

8. **Right-click the Quest Travel folder, click Properties on the shortcut menu, then click the General tab, if necessary**
   The Quest Travel Properties dialog box opens, displaying the General tab, as shown in Figure D-16. The Properties dialog box displays the size of the folder (Size) and the actual amount of disk space used by the folder (Size on disk). The actual amount of disk space used is either the cluster size or compressed size of the selected folder. A **cluster** is a group of sectors on a disk. A **sector** is the smallest unit that can be accessed on a disk. A sector on a disk cannot always be filled, so the amount is generally higher. If the file or folder is compressed, the Size on disk amount is the compressed size.

9. **Click OK to close the Properties dialog box**

Customizing File and Folder Management

FIGURE D-15: Disk Properties dialog box with the General tab displayed

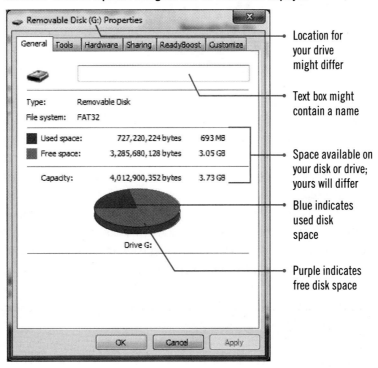

Location for your drive might differ

Text box might contain a name

Space available on your disk or drive; yours will differ

Blue indicates used disk space

Purple indicates free disk space

FIGURE D-16: Quest Travel Properties dialog box with the General tab displayed

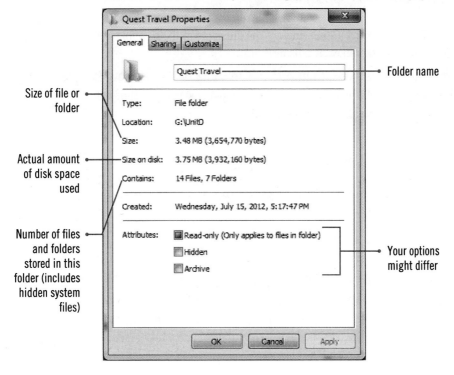

Folder name

Size of file or folder

Actual amount of disk space used

Number of files and folders stored in this folder (includes hidden system files)

Your options might differ

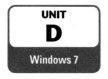
Compressing Files and Folders

You can **compress** files and folders in special folders that use software to decrease the size of the files they contain. Compressed folders are useful for reducing the file size of one or more large files, which frees disk space and reduces the time it takes to transfer files to another computer over a network or the Internet. A compressed folder is denoted by a zippered folder icon. When a file is compressed, a copy is used in the compression, and the original file remains intact in its original location. You can compress one or more files in a compressed folder by simply dragging them onto the compressed folder icon. You can uncompress, or **extract**, a file from the compressed folder and open it as you normally would, or open a file directly from the compressed folder by double-clicking the compressed file icon. When you open a file directly, Windows extracts the file when it opens and compresses it again when it closes. ▨▨▨ You want to compress the files in the Quest Travel folder as a backup copy.

STEPS

1. **Point to the Quest Travel folder**
   A ScreenTip appears, displaying information about the folder, including its size, 3.48 MB.

2. **Right-click the Quest Travel folder, then point to Send to on the shortcut menu**
   The Send to submenu opens, displaying the Compressed (zipped) folder command, as shown in Figure D-17.

3. **Click Compressed (zipped) folder**
   A dialog box briefly opens showing an animation of the compression progress, and then a new folder named Quest Travel.zip opens in the window. The file name of the new folder is selected (the extension is not selected) so that you can easily rename it.

4. **Type Compressed QST, then click a blank area of the window to deselect the folder**
   The Compressed QST.zip folder appears in the Explorer window, as shown in Figure D-18.

5. **Point to the Compressed QST.zip folder**
   A ScreenTip opens. Note that the compressed size of the folder is 116 KB.

6. **Double-click the Compressed QST.zip folder**
   The Compressed QST.zip folder opens and functions as a normal folder. The contents of the compressed folder are located in the Quest Travel folder. Note that a new button, Extract all files, appears on the toolbar in the window.

QUICK TIP
To extract individual files, click the file, then drag it from the compressed folder to another noncompressed folder or cut the file from the compressed folder and then paste it into a noncompressed folder.

7. **Click the Extract all files button on the toolbar**
   The Extract Compressed (Zipped) Folders dialog box opens, as shown in Figure D-19.

8. **In the text box that lists the path, select Compressed, type Extracted, click the Show extracted files when complete check box to deselect it, if necessary, then click Extract**
   A dialog box opens showing an animation of the extraction progress, and then closes when the extraction process is finished. The files and folders are extracted into a folder named Extracted QST in the drive and folder where you store your Data Files.

9. **Click UnitD in the Address bar**
   The folder Extracted QST appears in the UnitD folder. You can treat a compressed folder as an ordinary folder; for example, you can delete a file from a compressed folder without extracting it first.

10. **Double-click the Compressed QST.zip folder, double-click the Quest Travel folder, click To Do List.rtf, press [Delete], then click Yes to confirm the deletion**
    The file To Do List.rtf is deleted from the compressed Quest Travel folder.

Customizing File and Folder Management

FIGURE D-17: Creating a compressed folder

Select to compress the selected folder

FIGURE D-18: A compressed folder in an Explorer window

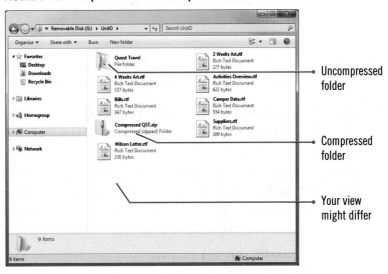

Uncompressed folder

Compressed folder

Your view might differ

FIGURE D-19: Extract Compressed (Zipped) Folders dialog box

Path to location where you store your Data Files; yours might differ

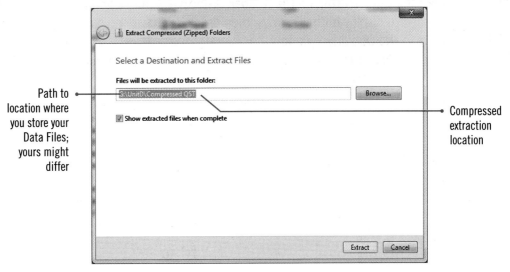

Compressed extraction location

Customizing File and Folder Management

Managing Files and Folders on a CD or DVD

A **compact disc** (**CD**) and **digital video disc** (**DVD**) are optical discs used to store large amounts of information. Typically, CDs hold 700 MB, while DVDs hold 4.7 GB. The low cost and convenient size of CD/DVDs and the popularity of disc recording hardware make them an effective media for file management. You can copy, or **burn**, files and folders to a **CD** or **DVD recordable** (**CD-R** or **DVD-R**) or a **CD** or **DVD rewritable** (**CD-RW** or **DVD-RW**). With CD or DVD-Rs, typically you can write files and folders only once, read them many times, but can't erase them. With CD or DVD-RWs, you can read, write, and erase files and folders many times. To create a CD or DVD, you must have a CD or DVD recorder and blank CDs or DVDs. You can burn a disc using two formats. The **Live File System** format (like a USB flash drive) allows you to copy files to a disc at any time, while the **Mastered** format (with a CD/DVD player) needs to copy them all at once. If the disc you are creating will be used only by computers running Windows XP or later, the Live File System is the best choice. When you need a disc compatible for use on older computers, the Mastered format is the better choice. You have to send out marketing materials on CD or DVD, so you want to burn the Quest Travel folder to a disc to practice performing this procedure.

STEPS

🛑 **If you don't have a CD-RW or DVD+/-RW drive and a blank recordable CD or DVD, close the UnitD window, then read the steps but do not perform any actions.**

> **QUICK TIP**
> Do not copy more files and folders to the disc than it will hold; anything beyond the limit will not be copied to the disc. Use the Properties dialog box to compare sizes.

1. **Click UnitD in the Address bar, click the Minimize button [—] in the UnitD folder window, then insert a blank CD or DVD into the CD or DVD drive**
   The AutoPlay dialog box opens by default unless the feature is turned off.

2. **If the AutoPlay dialog box opens, click Burn files to disc; otherwise, click the UnitD button on the taskbar, click the Quest Travel folder, then click the Burn button on the toolbar**
   The Burn a Disc dialog box opens with the current date listed as the default disc title. Before you burn a disc, it's important to give it a title, which is limited to 17 characters.

3. **Type QST Backup in the Disc title text box, click the With a CD/DVD player option button, as shown in Figure D-20, then click Next**
   The CD or DVD disc drive window opens showing a temporary area where files are held before they are burned to the CD or DVD.

> **QUICK TIP**
> If a pop-up notification opens, pointing to an icon in the notification area and indicating you have files waiting to be written to the disc, you can click the pop-up to open the disc recording drive.

4. **Click the UnitD button on the taskbar, if necessary, move and resize the two windows as needed to display both windows, then drag the Quest Travel folder from the Navigation pane to the Disc drive window**
   The Quest Travel folder opens in the CD or DVD window where you intend to burn the folders and files, as shown in Figure D-21.

5. **Click the Burn to disc button on the toolbar**
   The Burn to Disc dialog box opens, asking you to specify the disc title and recording speed. You already named the disc, and the default speed for recording is fine.

6. **Click Next to continue**
   A progress meter opens while the wizard writes the data files to the CD. When the process of writing folders and files to a CD or DVD finishes, the disc is ejected from the drive and the Burn to Disc dialog box opens again.

7. **Click Finish to close the Burn to Disc dialog box**

8. **Click the Close button [X] in the UnitD window**

Customizing File and Folder Management

FIGURE D-20: Burn a Disc dialog box

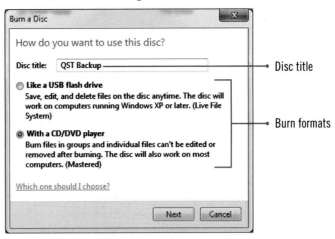

Disc title

Burn formats

FIGURE D-21: Contents of burned DVD disc

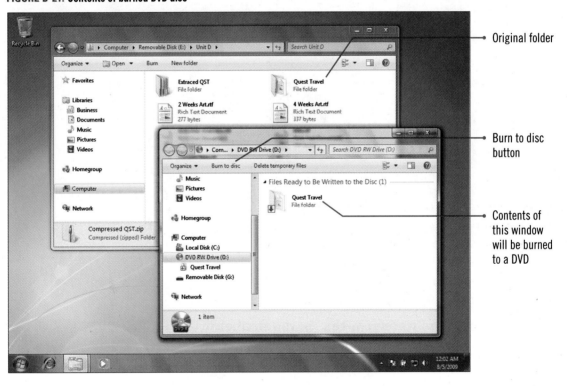

Original folder

Burn to disc button

Contents of this window will be burned to a DVD

Creating music CDs or DVDs

With Windows Media Player, you can create your own CDs or DVDs from music tracks you have stored in Media Library. To create a music disc, you must have a disc recorder and blank recordable CDs or DVDs. You can copy music files in the Windows Media (.wma), .mp3, and .wav formats from a media library to a disc. If you want to copy music from a CD to your computer, insert the CD into the CD disc drive,

select the files you want, then click the Rip CD button on the toolbar. To burn a music disc, insert a blank recordable disc in the CD or DVD disc drive, then click Burn tab. Songs in the library appear in the center pane, and a blank burn list appears in the right pane. Drag the music tracks or playlist you want to copy from the library to the burn list. When you're done, click Start burn.

Practice

Concepts Review

For current SAM information including versions and content details, visit SAM Central (http://samcentral.course.com). If you have a SAM user profile, you may have access to hands-on instruction, practice, and assessment of the skills covered in this unit. Since we support various versions of SAM throughout the life of this text, you will want to check with your instructor for instructions and the correct URL/Web site to access those assignments.

Match the statements below with the elements labeled in the screen shown in Figure D-22.

FIGURE D-22

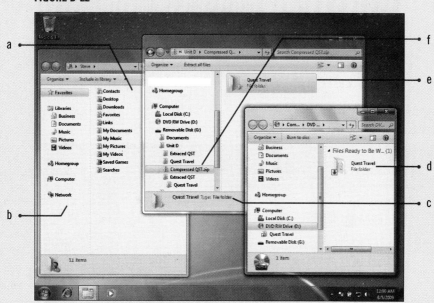

1. Which element is *not* a compressed file or folder?
2. Which element points to the Details pane?
3. Which element points to the Navigation pane?
4. Which element contains compressed folders or files?
5. Which element is a compressed file or folder?
6. Which element contains personal folders or files?

Match each term with the statement that best describes it.

7. Compressed folder   a. A place to store files
8. Pixel   b. A point in an image
9. Byte   c. A place to decrease file sizes
10. Extract   d. A term for uncompressing files
11. Personal folder   e. A unit of storage

Select the best answer from the list of choices.

12. Which of the following is a default element of an Explorer window layout?
    a. Menu bar   c. Default pane
    b. Preview pane   d. Search pane

Concepts Review (Continued)

13. **Which of the following is *not* a personal folder?**

    a. My Documents

    b. Programs

    c. My Pictures

    d. My Music

14. **Which of the following is a folder template?**

    a. General

    b. Videos

    c. Music icons

    d. Music Details

15. **Which of the following folder sizes is the largest?**

    a. 1 megabyte

    b. 2,000 kilobytes

    c. 1 gigabyte

    d. 1,248,896 bytes

16. **Which of the following is equal to 1,024 megabytes?**

    a. 1 kilobyte

    b. 1 megabyte

    c. 1 gigabyte

    d. 1 terabyte

17. **A cluster is a group of:**

    a. Sectors.

    b. Files.

    c. Folders.

    d. Bytes.

18. **Extract is another name for:**

    a. Uncompress.

    b. Expand.

    c. Compress.

    d. Zipped.

19. **Which of the following can read, write, and erase files and folders?**

    a. CD-ROM

    b. CD-R

    c. CD-RW

    d. DVD

Skills Review

1. **Change the layout of Explorer windows.**

   a. Open the Computer window.

   b. Navigate to the drive and folder where you store your Data Files.

   c. Open the UnitD folder, open the Quest Travel folder, then open the Company folder.

   d. Display the Preview pane.

   e. Preview the QST People.rtf file in the Preview pane.

   f. Hide the Preview pane, then display the contents of the Quest Travel folder.

2. **Change folder options.**

   a. Change the view to Details, if necessary.

   b. Change the folder option to open each folder in its own window.

   c. Change the folder option to hide extensions for known file types.

   d. Open the Company folder to verify the new folder options.

3. **Change file details to list.**

   a. Change the Company folder to Details view, if necessary.

   b. Add Date accessed and Folder path to Details view.

   c. Remove the Date accessed and Folder path columns from Details view.

4. **Change search options.**

   a. Change the search options to Always search file names and contents and Use a natural language search.

   b. Display the Quest Travel folder.

   c. Perform a natural language search for **ceo** or **vice** in the file contents.

   d. Restore all folder and search option defaults and reset all folders.

   e. Show file extensions for known file types.

   f. Close the Search results window.

Skills Review (Continued)

5. Use personal folders.

   a. Open your personal folder, then open the My Pictures folder, the Pictures library folder, and the Sample Pictures folder.

   b. View the graphics in the folder as a slide show.

   c. Display your personal folder, open the My Music folder, open the Music library folder, then open the Sample Music folder.

   d. Click the Play all button on the toolbar to start Windows Media Player and play all the music in the folder.

   e. Close Windows Media Player.

6. Customize a personal folder.

   a. Open the Quest Travel folder window, create a new folder named Travel Music, then open it.

   b. Copy three songs from the Sample Music folder to the Travel Music folder.

   c. Customize the Travel Music folder with the Music folder template.

   d. Verify that the Play all button opens on the toolbar in the Travel Music folder.

   e. Display the Quest Travel folder.

7. Display disk and folder information.

   a. In the window displaying the contents of the Sample Music folder, open the Computer folder, then display disk size information for any drive on your computer.

   b. Start WordPad, and in the document, note the disk capacity, how much is in use, and how much is available for further use.

   c. Display folder size information for the Quest Travel folder.

   d. Note the size and actual size on disk in the WordPad document.

   e. Add your name to the document, print it, then save the WordPad file as **Disk Info.rtf** to the drive and folder where you store your Data Files.

   f. Close the WordPad window.

8. Compress files and folders.

   a. In the current window, open the Quest Travel folder, then compress the Company folder and name it **Compressed Company.zip**.

   b. Open the compressed folder, then open the Company folder.

   c. Drag the QST Press Release.rtf file from the Compressed Company.zip folder to the Marketing folder in the Quest Travel folder using the Folders list.

   d. Open the Marketing folder to verify that the QST Press Release.rtf file was placed there.

   e. Extract the Compressed Company.zip folder into the Quest Travel folder with the name **Extracted Company.zip**.

   f. Close the Compressed Company.zip folder window.

9. Manage files and folders on a CD or DVD.

   a. Insert a blank recordable CD or DVD into the disc drive, then burn the Advertising and Letters folders located in the Quest Travel folder to the disc using the Mastered option. Name the disk **Advertising and Letters**.

   b. Verify that the folders appear on the disc.

   c. Close all open windows.

Independent Challenge 1

As manager of the summer program at a day camp, you need to keep your files and folders organized.

   a. Open the Computer folder, navigate to the UnitD folder in the drive and folder where you store your Data Files, then create three folders named **Day Camp**, **Campers**, and **Activities**.

   b. Move the file named **Camper Data.rtf** from the UnitD folder into the folder named Campers.

   c. Move the file named **Activities Overview.rtf** from the UnitD folder into the folder named Activities.

   d. Move the Activities folder and the Campers folder into the Day Camp folder.

   e. Apply the following settings to all folders of this type: Details view and hide extensions for known file types.

Independent Challenge 1 (Continued)

f. Open the Campers folder, then copy the Camper Data.rtf file into the Activities folder.

g. Open the Day Camp folder.

h. Perform a natural language search to find the files used in this independent challenge.

i. Restore search options to default settings.

j. Restore folder options to default settings, then show extensions for known file types.

k. Close the Computer window.

Independent Challenge 2

You own a sewing machine repair business, and you want to use Windows to organize your documents.

a. Open the Computer folder, navigate to the UnitD folder in the drive and folder where you store your Data Files, then create a new folder named **Sewing Works**.

b. In the Sewing Works folder, create three new folders: **Letters**, **Contacts**, and **Accounts**.

c. Expand the Sewing Works folder in the Folders list in the Navigation pane.

d. Move the file named **Wilson Letter.rtf** from the UnitD folder to the Letters folder, the file named **Suppliers.rtf** to the Contacts folder, and the file named **Bills.rtf** to the Accounts folder, then display the files named Wilson Letter and Suppliers in the Preview pane.

e. Display the file size in the Details pane for the files named Wilson Letter and Suppliers.

f. Close the Computer window.

Independent Challenge 3

The summer fine arts program you manage has different categories of participation for young adults, including two- and four-week programs. To keep track of who participates in each program, you must organize two lists into folders. When you're done, burn the information to a recordable disc to take the files with you to the program.

a. Open the Computer folder, navigate to the UnitD folder in the drive and folder where you store your Data Files, then create a folder named **Summer Program**.

b. In the Summer Program folder, create a folder named **Fine Arts**.

c. In the Fine Arts folder, create two other folders named **2 Weeks** and **4 Weeks**.

d. Move the files 2 Weeks Art.rtf and 4 Weeks Art.rtf from the UnitD folder into their respective folders: 2 Weeks and 4 Weeks.

e. Change folder options to Details view and open each folder in its own window. Apply to all folders, then display the contents of the 4 Weeks folder.

f. Compress the Summer Program folder, and name the compressed file **Compressed Summer Program.zip**.

g. Burn the compressed folder onto the recordable disc.

h. Restore the folder setting defaults, then show file extensions for known file types.

Advanced Challenge Exercise

- Copy two music files to a new folder named Camp Music in the UnitD folder, then add them to your Library. (Use two of the sample music files if you don't have any of your own.)
- Burn a music disc.
- Play the music from the disc.

i. Close the Computer window.

Real Life Independent Challenge

Organizing digital photographs on a computer is important if you want to be able to locate specific photos in the future. Organize your photographs into folders that you create to describe categories. Use descriptive names for the folders, and then move your photographs into the appropriate folders. When you're done, compress the folders and files.

a. In the UnitD folder in the drive and folder where you store your Data Files, create a folder called **Photographs**, then copy at least six photographs into the folder.

b. Open the Computer window, navigate to the drive and folder where you store your Data Files, then create at least three different folders with descriptive category names in the Photographs folder.

c. Move the photograph files in the Photographs folder into the appropriate folders to organize them.

d. Customize the folders for Pictures, if necessary.

e. Display a slide show for each of the folders.

f. Compress the Photographs folder with the name **My Photographs.zip**.

Advanced Challenge Exercise

■ Share the Photographs folder with specific people on your network.

■ Add a specific person to share with.

■ Add the Read/Write permission to the shared folder.

■ When you're done, set the folder sharing to Nobody.

g. Close the Computer window.

Visual Workshop

Re-create the screen shown in Figure D-23, which displays the desktop and a compressed folder with all the pictures from the Sample Pictures folder in the personal folder on the hard disk. Store the compressed file in the UnitD folder in the drive and folder where you store your Data Files. (Make sure you delete the compressed file from the personal folder after you copy it.)

FIGURE D-23

Customizing File and Folder Management

Customizing Windows Using the Control Panel

 If you are concerned about changing the aspects of Windows 7 and do not want to customize, simply read through this unit without completing the steps, or in any dialog box where you make a change, click the Cancel button instead of clicking the Apply button when instructed.

Files You Will Need:

No files needed.

In this unit, you customize Windows 7 to suit your personal needs and preferences. You can adjust most Windows features through the **Control Panel**, a central location for changing Windows settings. The Control Panel contains several links, each of which opens a dialog box or window for changing the **properties**, or characteristics, of a specific element of your computer, such as the desktop, the taskbar, or the Start menu. Before you can run Windows Aero, you need to set the proper settings in the Control Panel. Your computer at Quest Specialty Travel runs Windows Aero. You recently bought a new home computer with the capability to run Windows Aero so you can seamlessly work from home. You want to view and customize your settings in order to use them to enable Windows Aero.

OBJECTIVES
Change the desktop background
Change the desktop screen saver
Change desktop screen settings
Change the desktop appearance
Work with fonts
Customize the taskbar
Customize the Start menu
Work with desktop gadgets
Set the date and time

Changing the Desktop Background

The desktop **background**, or **wallpaper**, is a picture that serves as your desktop's backdrop, the surface on which icons and windows appear. You can select a background picture and change how it looks using the Desktop Background window. You can select one or more background pictures provided by Windows 7 or use ones stored in the Pictures Library folder or one you select on your computer. If you select more than one, you can display a slide show and shuffle the pictures. You can also display the desktop background on the screen several ways, including Fill, which displays the picture to fill the screen; Fit, which resizes the picture and displays it to fit the size of the screen; Stretch, which resizes the picture to fill the screen; Tile, which displays the picture in small boxes that fill the screen; and Center, which displays the picture in the center of the screen. Instead of selecting a background picture, which can sometimes make icons on the desktop difficult to see, you can also change the background to a color. ▓▓▓▓ You don't like the current background on your new home computer, so you want to choose a different background for your desktop.

STEPS

QUICK TIP
To quickly find a Control Panel option, type the name of the option in the Search Control Panel box.

1. **Click the Start button ⊕ on the taskbar, then click Control Panel**

   The Control Panel window opens, as shown in Figure E-1. Each option represents an aspect of Windows that you can change to fit your own working habits and personal needs.

2. **Click the Restore Down button 🗗 in the Control Panel window, if necessary, then resize the Control Panel window so you can see the desktop behind it**

3. **Click the Appearance and Personalization link**

   The Appearance and Personalization window opens, displaying Windows customization options. The name of the current window, Appearance and Personalization, appears as the rightmost label in the Address bar.

QUICK TIP
To open the Personalization window from the desktop, right-click an empty area on the desktop, then click Personalize.

4. **Click the Change desktop background link under Personalization**

   The Desktop Background window opens with the currently selected background highlighted.

5. **Scroll through the Background list, point to one of the available backgrounds, click the background image, then click the background image check box to select it, as shown in Figure E-2**

   This selects the background check box and displays a preview of the background on the desktop to show how the background will look on your screen. When you select multiple background pictures, additional options appear to specify a time interval to change the picture, shuffle the pictures, and save power.

6. **Click the Picture position list arrow, then click Center**

   The background picture appears centered on the desktop. Depending on the original size of the image and your screen size, the background might be larger than your screen, which is the case with all the background images installed by Windows 7 on a 1280 by 800 pixel screen. The Picture location list arrow allows you to select pictures from other locations, such as the Sample Pictures folder, or select a solid color from a list. Windows Desktop Backgrounds is the default folder.

QUICK TIP
To display the next background, right-click a blank area of the desktop, then click Next desktop background.

7. **Click the Picture location list arrow, then click Solid Colors**

   A list of available colors appears in the Desktop Background window.

8. **Click any color in the list**

   The color you selected appears on the desktop.

9. **Click Cancel**

   The changes to the desktop background do not take effect, the Desktop Background window closes, and the Appearance and Personalization window reopens.

FIGURE E-1: Control Panel window

Control
Panel links

FIGURE E-2: Desktop Background window

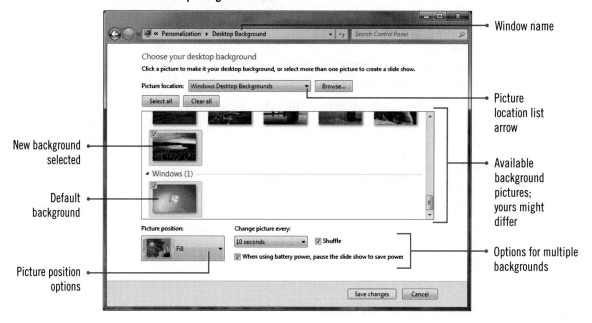

Window name

Picture
location list
arrow

New background
selected

Default
background

Available
background
pictures;
yours might
differ

Options for multiple
backgrounds

Picture position
options

Setting a picture as the desktop background

Instead of using one of the pictures in the Background list in the Desktop Background window, you can select a picture on your hard drive or from a Web page as the desktop background. To set a picture as the background, right-click the picture you want to use in a Windows Explorer window or a Web page, then click Set as desktop background or Set as Background on the shortcut menu. Acceptable formats for background files include bitmaps (the format of a Paint file) and JPEGs (the format of an Internet graphic file). You can use

Paint or any graphics program to create new background designs or change existing ones. After you set a specific picture as the desktop background, it is added to the list of available backgrounds in the Desktop Background window. To manage the files in the list of backgrounds, display the contents of your hard drive in a Windows Explorer window, open the Windows folder, the Web folder, then, finally, the Wallpaper folder, where you can remove, rename, or modify the wallpaper files.

Changing the Desktop Screen Saver

If you frequently leave your computer idle, with no movement on your screen for a long time, you should select a screen saver. A **screen saver**, a continually moving display, protects your monitor from **burn-in**, a condition that occurs when the same display remains on the screen for extended periods of time and becomes part of the screen. In addition to protecting your computer monitor, screen savers can also be used as a security measure. You can set an option in the Screen Saver Settings dialog box to resume computer usage with the Windows 7 logon screen, which can require users to specify a username and password. ▓▓▓▓ You want to set a screen saver to start when your computer remains idle for more than five minutes to keep company information confidential.

STEPS

QUICK TIP

When (None) is the selected screen saver, a screen saver will not appear, no matter how long your computer remains idle.

1. **Under Personalization, click the** Change screen saver link **in the Appearance and Personalization window**

   The Screen Saver Settings dialog box opens, displaying various screen saver options.

2. **Click the** Screen saver list arrow, **then click** 3D Text

   The 3D screen saver appears in the preview window of the Screen Saver Settings dialog box, as shown in Figure E-3.

QUICK TIP

To create your own screen saver slide show, click Photos in the Screen saver list, then click Settings to specify the location for the pictures.

3. **Click** Settings

   The 3D Text Settings dialog box opens, as shown in Figure E-4, displaying the 3D screen saver options. Not all screen savers have settings. Some screen savers require settings whereas others don't.

4. **Click the** Rotation Type list arrow, **then click** Wobble

   The Rotation Type option for the 3D Text screen saver is set to Wobble, which makes the 3D text move back and forth on the screen.

5. **Click** OK

   The 3D Text Settings dialog box closes and the Screen Saver Settings dialog box reappears.

6. **In the Wait box, click the** up arrow **or** down arrow **until it reads** 5

   The Wait box option is set so that your computer will begin the screen saver if it doesn't detect any mouse or keyboard activity for five minutes.

7. **Click** Preview

   The 3D Text screen saver previews on the screen.

QUICK TIP

To display the logon screen when you resume using your computer after the screen saver is activated, click the On resume, display logon screen check box to select it.

8. **Move the mouse or press any key to stop the preview**

   The preview ends and the Screen Saver Settings dialog box reappears.

9. **Open the 3D Text Settings dialog box, change the Rotation Type back to** Spin, **click** OK **to close that dialog box, then click** Cancel **in the Screen Saver Settings dialog box**

   The Screen Saver Settings dialog box closes and the changes to the screen saver settings do not take effect. The Appearance and Personalization window reopens.

FIGURE E-3: Screen Saver Settings dialog box

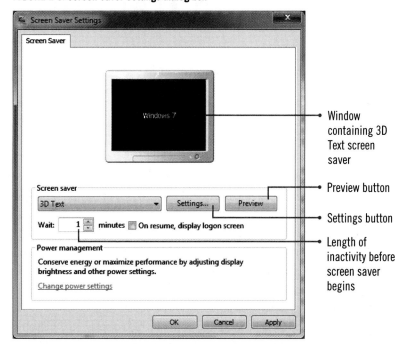

- Window containing 3D Text screen saver
- Preview button
- Settings button
- Length of inactivity before screen saver begins

FIGURE E-4: 3D Text Settings dialog box

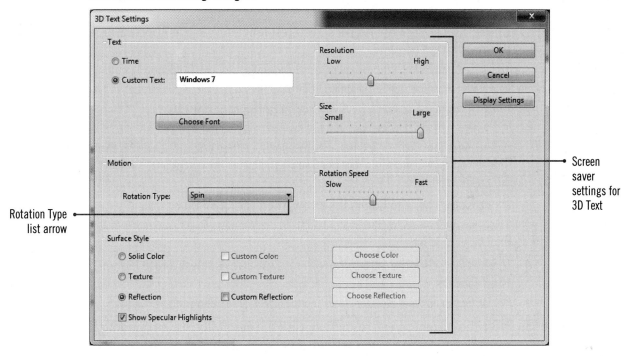

- Rotation Type list arrow
- Screen saver settings for 3D Text

Changing power settings

From the Screen Saver Settings dialog box, you can change power options properties for a portable or laptop computer to reduce power consumption and maximize battery life. For example, if you often leave your computer for a short time while working, you can set your computer to **sleep**, or **standby**, a state in which your monitor and hard disks turn off after being idle for a set time. If you are often away from your computer for an extended time, you can set it to go into **hibernation**, a state in which your computer first saves everything in memory on your hard disk and then shuts down. To set power options, you can choose one of the power plans included with Windows or modify one to suit your needs. A **power plan** is a predefined collection of power usage settings. In addition, you can set power options for how you want the computer power button and closing a laptop lid to work, whether to require a password on wake up, and screen brightness settings. Windows detects and makes available your power options based on your computer's hardware configuration.

Changing Desktop Screen Settings

If you find yourself frequently scrolling within windows as you work or squinting to read small text, you might want to change the size of the desktop on your monitor. A monitor displays pictures by dividing the display screen into thousands or millions of pixels, arranged in rows and columns. The pixels are so close together that they appear connected, forming the image you see on the monitor. The **screen resolution** refers to the number of pixels on the screen, which determines the amount of information your monitor displays. A low screen resolution setting, such as 640 by 480 pixels (width by height), displays less information on the screen, but the items appear relatively large, while a higher setting, such as 1024 by 768 pixels, displays more information, but the items on the screen appear smaller. Many monitors have different shapes and sizes, so you can adjust the screen orientation to suit your needs. Landscape, the default, appears as 1024 by 768 pixels, which would be 768 by 1024 in Portrait. Another factor in making text and graphics easy to read on screen is the color quality. The higher the color quality, the more colors are displayed, but this requires greater system memory. The most common color quality settings are 16-bit, which displays 768 colors, and 24-bit and 32-bit, both of which display 16.7 million colors. ▚▚▚ You want to view color and monitor settings and change the resolution of the desktop so the screen is easier to read.

STEPS

1. **Under Display, click the Adjust screen resolution link in the Appearance and Personalization window**

    The Screen Resolution window opens, as shown in Figure E-5. This dialog box allows you to change the appearance of several desktop elements at once.

2. **Click the Advanced settings link, then click the Monitor tab**

    The Properties dialog box for your monitor opens. See Figure E-6. The Monitor tab allows you to change the screen refresh rate. To use Windows Aero, the monitor refresh rate must be higher than 10 Hertz. **Hertz** is a unit of frequency to measure a monitor display. The higher the refresh rate, the better the display. A typical refresh rate is 60 Hertz.

3. **If necessary, click the Colors list arrow, then click a 32-bit option**

    The color quality is set to True Color (32-bit). To use Windows Aero, the number of colors for your monitor must be set to 32-bit.

4. **If necessary, click the Screen refresh rate list arrow, select a rate higher than 10 Hertz, then click OK**

    The dialog box for your monitor closes and the Screen Resolution window reappears.

5. **Note the current screen resolution, click the Resolution list arrow, drag the screen resolution slider to a lower setting, if possible, then click off the menu to close it**

    The preview at the top of the dialog box increases in size based on your new screen resolution setting.

6. **Click Apply**

    The resolution of your screen changes to the new setting, and a warning dialog box opens asking you to confirm the change and warning you that the resolution will revert to its original setting in 15 seconds. Use the Apply button when you want to test your changes and keep the dialog box open, and the Keep changes button when you want to keep your changes and close the dialog box.

7. **Click Revert in the warning dialog box to disregard the change**

    The warning dialog box closes. The screen resolution setting returns to its original setting.

8. **Click Cancel**

    The Screen Resolution window closes, and the Appearance and Personalization window reopens.

Customizing Windows Using the Control Panel

FIGURE E-5: Screen Resolution window

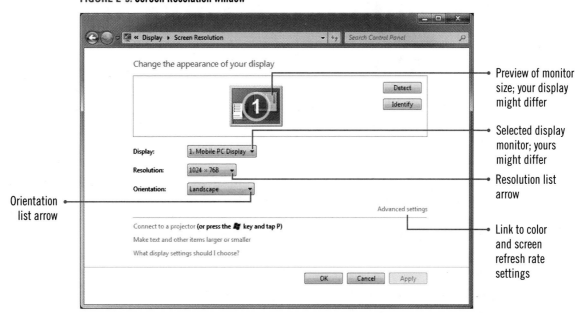

Preview of monitor size; your display might differ

Selected display monitor; yours might differ

Resolution list arrow

Orientation list arrow

Link to color and screen refresh rate settings

FIGURE E-6: Properties dialog box with the Monitor tab displayed

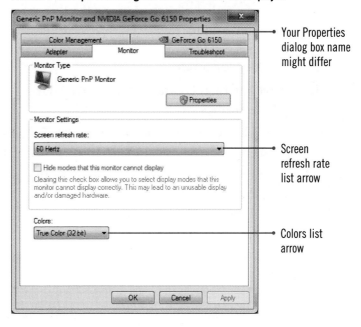

Your Properties dialog box name might differ

Screen refresh rate list arrow

Colors list arrow

Using more than one monitor

You can increase the size of your workspace on the desktop by adding another monitor to your computer. With two monitors, you can work on a document in WordPad while you search for Web content in your Web browser. One monitor functions as the primary monitor, which displays the dialog boxes that appear when you start your computer and most programs, while the other is the secondary monitor, which displays windows, icons, and programs you drag to it from the primary monitor. To use a second monitor, you need to install another **display adapter**, a hardware device that allows a computer to communicate with its monitor, on your computer that supports multiple monitors. Many laptops already have this capability built into the computer; check your documentation for more information. After you install the display adapter according to the manufacturer's instructions and restart the computer, Windows detects the new device and installs the related software. In the Control Panel, click the Adjust screen resolution link under Display, click the monitor icon that represents the secondary monitor that you want to use, click the Multiple displays list arrow, click Extend these displays or another display option, then click Apply to use the secondary monitor options. To make the secondary monitor your primary monitor, click the Make this my main display check box to select it. To arrange multiple monitors, click the monitor icons and drag them in the preview window to the positions you want. You can set different display, screen resolution, orientation, and advanced settings for each monitor.

Changing the Desktop Appearance

You can change the entire appearance of the desktop by using themes. A **theme** changes the desktop background, screen saver, mouse pointers, sounds, icons, and fonts to coordinating colors and designs. You can use one of the predefined desktop themes, either an Aero Theme or Basic and High Contrast Theme, or create your own. If a theme isn't exactly what you want, you can change the appearance of colors, fonts, and sizes used for major window elements such as title bars, icons, menus, borders, and the desktop itself. To do this, you use a **scheme**, which is a predefined combination of settings that ensures visual coordination of all items. Windows includes many predefined schemes, or you can create your own. The predefined schemes allow you to switch between Windows 7 Basic and Windows Aero, the two user experiences provided by Microsoft Windows 7. When you create a custom scheme or modify an existing scheme, you save your changes with a unique name. ▰▰▰ You want to set theme, color scheme, and transparency settings to use Windows Aero and change the desktop appearance to a more casual look.

STEPS

1. **Under Personalization, click the** Change the theme link **in the Appearance and Personalization window**

   The Personalization window opens, as shown in Figure E-7. With a theme, you can change the appearance of several desktop elements at once.

2. **Under Basic and High Contrast Themes, scroll down if necessary, then click** Windows Classic **in the Themes list**

3. **Wait while Windows applies the Windows Classic theme**

   The Windows Classic theme is applied to the desktop. To use Windows Aero, the theme must be Windows 7.

4. **In the Themes list, click** Windows 7 **under Aero Themes, then wait while Windows applies the Windows 7 theme**

   The Windows 7 theme is applied to the desktop.

5. **Click the** Window Color link

   The Window Color and Appearance window opens, similar to the one shown in Figure E-8, displaying color variations for Windows Aero. Within this window, you can change the color of windows, the Start menu, and the taskbar. Other options allow you to enable transparency and change color intensity.

6. **If necessary, click the** Enable transparency **check box to select it**

   Enabling the transparency option allows you to achieve the Windows Aero transparent look.

7. **Click any color square, then drag the** Color intensity slider **left and right**

   The color of the window border changes to reflect the new color you selected, and it grows lighter and darker as you drag the slider. In the Figure E-8 example, the Sky blue color square is selected and the slider was dragged to the right to intensify the color.

8. **Click** Cancel, **then click the** Back button ◉ **in the Personalization window**

   The color settings do not take effect and the Window Color and Appearance window closes. The Appearance and Personalization window reappears.

TROUBLE
If the Window Color and Appearance dialog box opens with a window color scheme, Aero is not enabled. Click Cancel. To enable Aero, click a theme under Aero Themes, then repeat Step 6. If your machine is not capable of using Aero, read, but do not perform, the rest of the steps in this lesson.

QUICK TIP
If Aero is enabled and you want to turn the Aero interface off, click a theme under Basic and High Contrast Themes in the Personalization window.

FIGURE E-7: Personalization window

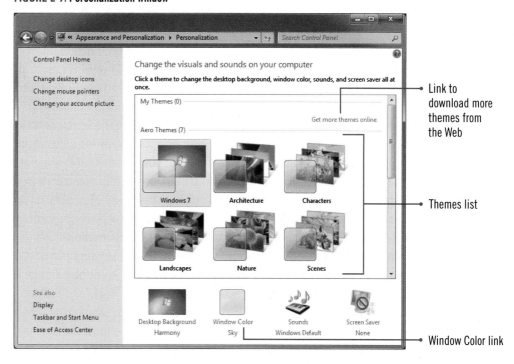

Link to download more themes from the Web

Themes list

Window Color link

FIGURE E-8: Window Color and Appearance window

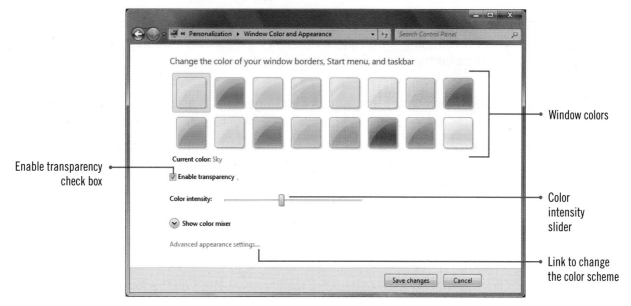

Enable transparency check box

Window colors

Color intensity slider

Link to change the color scheme

Adding sound effects

Besides customizing the desktop appearance of Windows 7, you can also add sound effects to common Windows commands and functions, such as starting and exiting Windows, printing complete, opening and closing folders, or emptying the Recycle Bin. To add sound effects, click the Appearance and Personalization link in the Control Panel, then click the Change sound effects link. The events that happen in Windows to which sounds can be attached are listed in the Program Events list. Windows comes with sound schemes, which contain related sounds for the events. To apply a new sound to an event, in the Program Events list, click the event to which you want to apply a sound, such as System Notification. Click the Sounds list arrow, then click the sound you want to link to the event. To hear the sound, click Test to the right of the Sounds list arrow. To save your settings as a sound scheme, click Save As, type a name, then click OK. When you're done, click OK to apply the sound effect changes to Windows.

Working with Fonts

Everything you type appears in a **font**, or typeface, a particular design set of letters, numbers, and other characters. The height of characters in a font is measured in **points**, each point being approximately 1/72 inch. You might have heard common font names, such as Times New Roman, Arial, Courier, or Symbol. Windows has a variety of fonts for displaying text and printing documents created with programs that are part of Windows, such as WordPad and Paint. Using the Fonts window, you can view these fonts, compare them to each other, see a sample of how a font appears when printed, and even install new fonts. The Fonts window lists the fonts available on your system and indicates whether each is a TrueType, OpenType, or screen font. **TrueType** and **OpenType** fonts are **outline** (sometimes called **vector** or **scalable**) **fonts** based on a mathematical equation that creates resizable, or scalable, letters with smooth curves and sharp corners. OpenType is a newer technology and an extension of TrueType, and it provides features such as multiplatform support and support for international characters. A **screen font**, also known as **raster**, consists of **bitmapped characters**, which are small dots organized to form a letter. TrueType and OpenType fonts are designed for quality screen display and desktop printer output at any size, whereas screen fonts are designed for quality screen display and desktop printer output at only the font sizes installed on the computer. Besides the scalability, the main advantage of outline fonts is that they look better at high resolutions. The disadvantage of outline fonts is that small outline fonts do not look very good on low-resolution devices, such as display monitors. If you're having problems seeing the text on your monitor, **ClearType** makes on-screen text clearer, smoother, and more detailed. 🔩🔩🔩 You want to examine the fonts on your computer to make sure the ones you like to use in your reports are installed.

STEPS

QUICK TIP

To enable ClearType, click the Adjust ClearType text link in the Fonts window, click the Turn on ClearType check box to select it, click Next, then follow the on-screen instructions.

1. **Click the Fonts link in the Appearance and Personalization window, then click the Maximize button 🔲 in the Fonts window, if necessary**
   The Fonts window opens.

2. **Click the Views button arrow, then click Large Icons, if necessary**
   The Fonts window displays the different types of fonts listed alphabetically, as shown in Figure E-9.

3. **Right-click a blank area in the Fonts window, point to Group by, click More, click the Font type check box to select it, click OK, right-click a blank area again, point to Group by, then click Font type**
   The Fonts window groups the fonts by type, including OpenType and Raster. Your font types might differ depending on what fonts are installed on your computer.

4. **Double-click the Arial font icon**
   The Arial window opens, displaying font family details for the Arial font.

5. **Click the Arial Black icon, then click the Preview button on the toolbar**
   The Arial Black (OpenType) window opens, displaying information about this font and showing samples of it in different sizes, as shown in Figure E-10.

6. **Click Print in the Arial Black (OpenType) window, then click Print in the Print dialog box**
   The Print dialog box closes and the samples for the Arial Black font print.

QUICK TIP

To show and hide fonts based on language settings, click the Font settings link in the Fonts window, select the options you want, then click OK.

7. **Click the Close button 🗙 in the Arial Black (OpenType) window, then click the Back button 🔙**
   The Arial Black (OpenType) window closes and the Fonts window reappears.

8. **Right-click a blank area in the Fonts window, point to Group by, then click (None)**

9. **Click 🔙, click the Restore Down button 🗗, then click the Minimize button ➖ in the Appearance and Personalization window**
   The Appearance and Personalization window minimizes to the taskbar.

FIGURE E-9: Fonts window

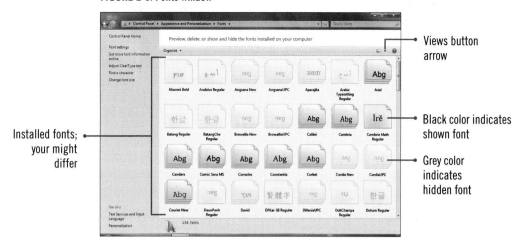

Views button arrow

Black color indicates shown font

Grey color indicates hidden font

Installed fonts; your might differ

FIGURE E-10: Arial Black (Open Type) window

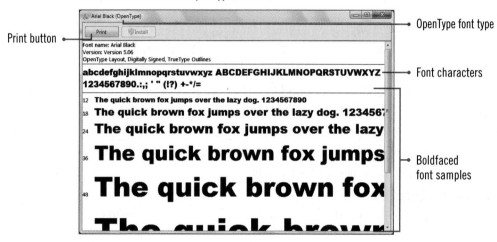

Print button

OpenType font type

Font characters

Boldfaced font samples

Installing, removing, or hiding a font

Although many fonts come with Windows, you can purchase and install additional fonts. To install a new font, drag the font into the Fonts window or right-click the font in a Windows Explorer window, then click Install. This installs the new font so that it's available in the Fonts window and to all your Windows programs. To remove a font, select the font in the Fonts window, then click the Delete button on the toolbar. You can also hide/show a font in your programs; select the font (grayed out are hidden) in the Fonts window, then click the Hide or Show button on the toolbar.

Changing the screen text size

If text and other items, such as icons, on the screen are not large enough for you to comfortably view, you can customize the screen to display items larger. Windows 7 allows you to increase the screen scaling option, known as the **dots per inch (dpi)** scale, which is the number of dots that a device can display or print per linear inch. The greater number of dots per inch, the better the resolution. To change the screen size, click the Change font size link in the Fonts window. To set a custom DPI setting, click the Set custom text size (DPI) link in the Display window.

Customizing the Taskbar

The taskbar is located at the bottom of the Windows desktop by default, and is most often used to switch from one open program or window to another. As with other Windows elements, you can customize the taskbar; for example, you can change its size and location, customize its display, or add or remove toolbars, such as the Address bar toolbar, to help you perform the tasks you need to do. If you need more room on the screen to display a window, the **Auto-hide** feature can be used to hide the taskbar automatically when it's not in use. You can also customize the notification area. If icons in the notification area are hidden when you want to see them, you can customize the notification area to always show the icons you want to use. When you hide an icon, you can choose to hide or show any notification alerts that go with it. In addition, you can lock and unlock the taskbar, keep the taskbar visible, use small icons, change the taskbar desktop location, combine similar task-bar buttons together in one button, and use or not use Aero Peek to preview the desktop with the Show desk-top button. You want to customize your taskbar on the desktop so you can work more efficiently.

STEPS

QUICK TIP

To open the Taskbar and Start Menu Properties dialog box from the desk-top, right-click an empty area of the taskbar, then click Properties.

1. **Position the pointer in an empty area of the taskbar, right-click the taskbar, then point to Toolbars**

   The Toolbars submenu opens, as shown in Figure E-11.

2. **Click a blank area of the desktop to close the menu**

   The Address toolbar appears on the taskbar to the right of the Start button.

3. **Click the Appearance and Personalization taskbar button, then click the Taskbar and Start Menu link in the Appearance and Personalization window**

   The Taskbar and Start Menu Properties dialog box opens, displaying the Taskbar tab, as shown in Figure E-12.

4. **Click the Auto-hide the taskbar check box to select it, then click Apply**

   The taskbar scrolls down out of sight.

QUICK TIP

To hide system icons in the notification area, click the Turn system icons on or off link in the Notifi-cation Area Icons dialog box, set the icons to Off, then click OK twice.

5. **Click Customize**

   The Notification Area Icons dialog box opens, which allows you to specify the behavior you want for a task-bar icon. For example, you can always show or hide icons and notifications, or only show notifications to display the amount of information you want.

6. **Under Behaviors, click the Volume list arrow, as shown in Figure E-13, click Hide icon and notifications if necessary, then click OK**

   The Notification Area Icons dialog box closes and the Taskbar and Start Menu Properties dialog box reap-pears. The Volume icon you selected will now be hidden in the notification area.

7. **Move the mouse pointer to the bottom of the screen to display the taskbar, then click the Show hidden icons button ▲ in the notification area**

   The taskbar scrolls up into view, and the Volume icon you set to hide no longer appears in the notification area. While the mouse pointer is at the bottom of the screen, the taskbar appears. When you move the mouse pointer up, the taskbar is hidden. The Show hidden icons button provides access to hidden icons.

8. **Click Customize in the Notification window, click the Volume list arrow, click Show icon and notifications, then click OK**

   The Volume icon reappears in the notification area and any related notifications will appear.

QUICK TIP

To view transparent windows in Aero with Aero Peek, point to the Show desktop button at the end of the taskbar.

9. **Click the Auto-hide the taskbar check box to deselect it, then click OK**

   The Taskbar and Start Menu Properties dialog box closes and the Appearance and Personalization window reappears.

10. **Click the Minimize button ▭ in the Appearance and Personalization window**

FIGURE E-11: Taskbar with the Toolbars submenu displayed

Shortcut menu

Your add or remove a toolbar options might differ

Show hidden icons button

Notification icons

FIGURE E-12: Taskbar and Start Menu Properties dialog box with the Taskbar tab displayed

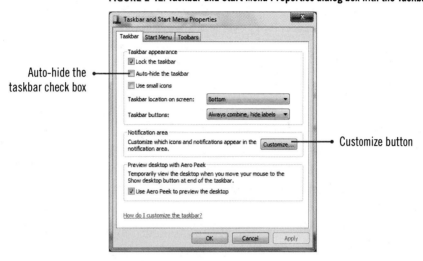

Auto-hide the taskbar check box

Customize button

FIGURE E-13: Notification Area Icons dialog box

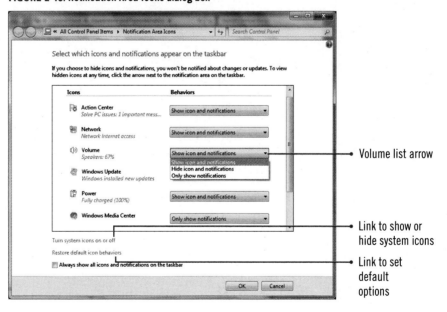

Volume list arrow

Link to show or hide system icons

Link to set default options

Pinning and unpinning items to the taskbar

The taskbar allows you to start programs, and open files and windows. The taskbar comes with three pinned default programs: Internet Explorer, Windows Explorer, and Windows Media Player. The pinned items remain on the taskbar, like a push pin holds paper on a bulletin board, until you unpin them. To pin a program to the taskbar, open the program, right-click the icon on the taskbar, then click Pin this program to taskbar. To unpin it, right-click the pinned icon, then click Unpin this program from taskbar.

Customizing the Start Menu

The Start menu is the beginning point for accessing most programs and features in Windows 7. Customizing the Start menu can save you time and effort. You can add shortcuts to programs, files, or folders to the Start menu or customize the way the Start menu looks and functions. The left column of the Start menu is separated into two lists: pinned items above the separator line and most frequently used programs below. The **pinned items** remain on the Start menu, like a push pin holds paper on a bulletin board, until you unpin them. The right column of the Start menu provides easy access to folders, Windows settings, devices and printers, help information, and shutdown options. You can customize the right column on the Start menu to display additional menu items or extend a submenu from the Control Panel, Documents, or Personal folder menu items for easy access. ⬛⬛⬛⬛ Because you work often with the Windows Media Center program, you decide to add it to the Start menu for easy access.

STEPS

1. **Click the Start button 🔘 on the taskbar, point to All Programs, then point to Windows Media Center, but do not click it**

   The Start menu appears with the Windows Media Center program highlighted.

QUICK TIP
To remove an un-pinned item from the Start menu, right-click the item, then click Remove from this list.

2. **Right-click Windows Media Center, as shown in Figure E-14, click Pin to Start Menu on the shortcut menu, then point to Back at the bottom of the Start menu**

   The Windows Media Center program appears above the separator line on the Start menu in the pinned items section. The Windows Media Center menu item will now always appear at the top of the Start menu until you unpin it.

3. **Click outside the Start menu to close it, click the Appearance and Personalization taskbar button, then, under Taskbar and Start Menu, click the Customize the Start menu link**

   The Taskbar and Start Menu Properties dialog box opens, displaying the Start Menu tab, which allows you to choose the Start menu style you want.

4. **Click Customize**

   The Customize Start Menu dialog box opens, as shown in Figure E-15. The Customize Start Menu dialog box allows you to modify the way links, icons, and menus appear on the Start menu. You can also indicate the number of recently used programs you want to appear on the Start list.

5. **Under Control Panel, click the Display as a menu option button, click OK, then click Apply in the Taskbar and Start Menu Properties dialog box**

   The customized Control Panel option is applied to the Start menu; the Taskbar and Start Menu Properties dialog box remains open.

6. **Click 🔘 on the taskbar, then point to Control Panel**

   A submenu listing the various Control Panel options displays. These options correspond to the items in the Control Panel window.

QUICK TIP
To change the function of the Power button, right-click the Start button, click Properties, click the Power button action list arrow, click a power option, then click OK.

7. **Right-click Windows Media Center on the Start menu, then click Unpin from Start Menu**

   The Windows Media Center program is unpinned from the Start menu.

8. **Click outside the Start menu to close it, click Customize in the Taskbar and Start Menu Properties dialog box, click the Display as a link option button under Control Panel, then click OK twice**

   Both dialog boxes close, and the Start menu is restored to its original settings. The Appearance and Personalization window reappears.

FIGURE E-14: Adding a program to the Start menu

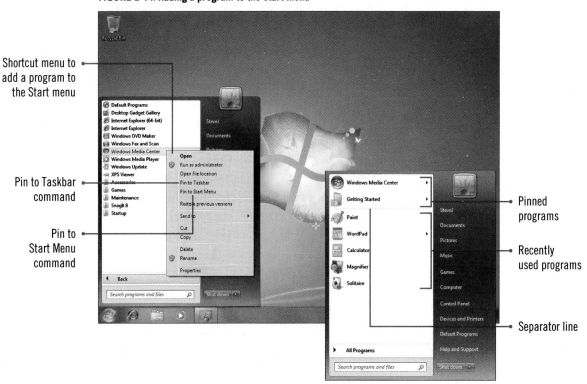

Shortcut menu to add a program to the Start menu

Pin to Taskbar command

Pin to Start Menu command

Pinned programs

Recently used programs

Separator line

FIGURE E-15: Customize Start Menu dialog box

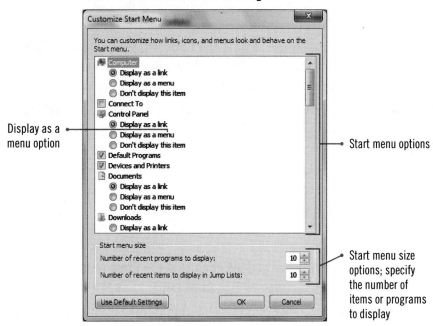

Display as a menu option

Start menu options

Start menu size options; specify the number of items or programs to display

Working with Start menu items

In addition to tracking frequently used programs, Windows also tracks recently opened files, known as **jump lists**. When you point to a program on the Start menu with an arrow next to it, a list of recently opened files or folders and related tasks appear for easy access. You can also pin recently opened files to the Start menu that you want to use on a regular basis. When you display a list of recently opened files, you can point to a file to display a pin icon, which you can click the icon to pin the file to the top of the submenu. You can also point to a pinned item, then click the icon to unpin the file. If you want to clear all recently opened documents from the Start menu, clear the Store and display recently opened items in the Start menu and the taskbar check box on the Start Menu tab in the Taskbar and Start Menu Properties dialog box.

UNIT
E
Windows 7

Working with Desktop Gadgets

Instead of opening a program, such as your Web browser, to get information, you can use your Windows 7 desktop to get quick access to gadgets such as news headlines and updates, weather information, traffic maps, Internet radio streams, and slide shows of online photo albums. **Gadgets** are miniapplications that can connect to Web services, such as an **RSS (Really Simple Syndication) feed** (which automatically delivers Web content, such as headline news, to your desktop), or integrate with many of your applications, such as viewing your calendar or e-mail and browsing the Web. You can move gadgets anywhere on your desktop to suit the way you work—for example, whether you want them to appear above or below maximized windows. Windows 7 comes with a set of gadgets to get you started, including one for Windows Media Center. However, you can easily download more gadgets from an online gadget gallery. See Table E-1 for specific ways to work with desktop gadgets. Because you frequently travel, you want to add the Weather gadget to the desktop so you can easily check the weather.

STEPS

QUICK TIP
To quickly open the Gadget Gallery window, right-click a blank area of the desktop, then click Gadgets.

QUICK TIP
To download more gadgets, click the Get more gadgets online link in the Gadget Gallery window, find the gadget you want, then download it.

1. **Under Desktop Gadgets, click the Add gadgets to the desktop link in the Appearance and Personalization window**
   The Gadget Gallery window opens, as shown in Figure E-16.
2. **Double-click the Weather gadget icon or drag it to the upper-right corner of the desktop**
   The Weather gadget is added to upper-right corner of the desktop. After a moment, the gadget accesses the Internet for weather-related information.
3. **Click the Close button in the Gadget Gallery window, then click the Minimize button in the Appearance and Personalization window**
   The Gadget Gallery window closes and the Appearance and Personalization window minimizes to the taskbar.
4. **Point to the Weather gadget, click the Larger size button to the right of the gadget, then click the Options button**
   The Weather dialog box opens, as shown in Figure E-17, displaying options to customize the gadget.
5. **Click in the Select current location text box, type your city followed by a comma, press [Spacebar], type your state, click the Search button, select the nearest location, if necessary, then click OK**
   The Weather dialog box closes and the Weather gadget displays the current temperature for the specified city, as shown in Figure E-18.
6. **Point to the Weather gadget, then click the Close button**
   The Weather gadget is removed from the desktop.
7. **Click the Appearance and Personalization taskbar button on the taskbar**
   The Appearance and Personalization window reopens.

FIGURE E-16: Gadget Gallery window

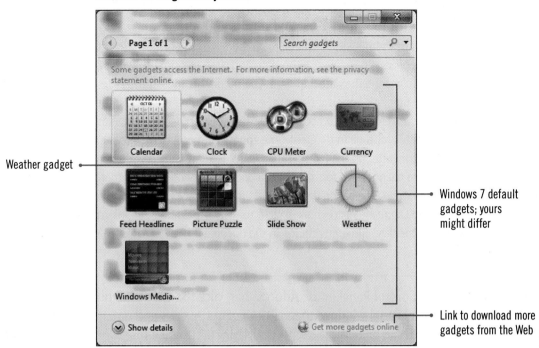

Weather gadget

Windows 7 default gadgets; yours might differ

Link to download more gadgets from the Web

FIGURE E-17: Weather dialog box

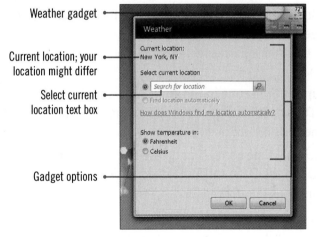

Weather gadget

Current location; your location might differ

Select current location text box

Gadget options

FIGURE E-18: Weather gadget

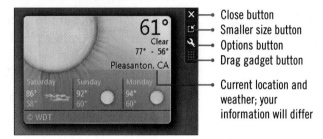

Close button

Smaller size button

Options button

Drag gadget button

Current location and weather; your information will differ

TABLE E-1: Working with desktop gadgets

to:	do the following:
Close a gadget	Point to the gadget you want to close, click the Close button ✖ in the small bar that appears to the right of the gadget, then click Close Gadget if a dialog box opens.
Change gadget options	Point to the gadget you want to change, click the Options button 🔧 in the small bar that appears to the right of the gadget, select the options you want, then click OK.
Move a gadget	Point to the gadget, then drag it or ▦ to another location on the desktop.
Resize a gadget	Point to the gadget, then click the Smaller size button ◰ or Larger size button ◳ in the small bar that appears to the right of the gadget.

Setting the Date and Time

The time appears in the notification area. When you click or hover over the clock in the notification area, the date appears. Programs use the date and time to establish when files and folders are created and modified. To change the date and time, you modify settings in the Date and Time dialog box. When you modify the time, it's important also to verify or update the time zone setting in the Time Zone Settings dialog box, which is used to accurately display creation and modification dates and send e-mail with the accurate date and time in different time zones. With an Internet connection, you can synchronize your clock to a computer on the Internet that keeps accurate time. In addition to changing the date and time, you can also change their format. This is handy if you work on documents from a different country or region of the world. To change the date and time display, you modify the settings on the Formats tab in the Region and Language dialog box. ░▒▓ You want to work on an international document so you decide to change the date and time settings so the document is easier for them to read.

STEPS

QUICK TIP

To open the Date and Time dialog box quickly, click the time in the notification area on the taskbar, then click the Change date and time settings link.

1. **Click Control Panel in the Address bar, click the Clock, Language, and Region link in the Control Panel window, then click the Set the time and date link under Date and Time**

   The Date and Time dialog box opens, displaying the Date and Time tab, as shown in Figure E-19.

2. **Click Change date and time, then click Continue in the security dialog box, if necessary, to get permission to make changes**

   The Date and Time Settings dialog box opens, displaying a calendar and clock. You can use the calendar to select a month using the left and right arrows, or select a day by clicking a date, and use the clock to change the time in hours, minutes, or seconds.

3. **Click another date in the calendar, double-click the current minute in the text box in the Time section, click the up arrow three times, then click OK**

   The new date that you clicked and the new time—three minutes later—appear in the clock in the Date and Time dialog box and in the notification area.

QUICK TIP

If you have a connection to the Internet, you can click Change settings on the Internet Time tab and then click Update now to update the time on your computer with an accurate time on the Internet.

4. **Click Change time zone, note the current time zone in the Time Zone Settings dialog box, click the list arrow, click (UTC) Dublin, Edinburgh, Lisbon, London, then click OK**

   The adjusted time appears in the clock in the dialog box and in the notification area.

5. **Change the time zone back to the original time zone, change the current time and date back to the correct time, then click OK in the Date and Time dialog box**

   The Date and Time dialog box closes, and the Clock, Language, and Region window is visible again.

QUICK TIP

To change the regional format by language and country, click the Format list arrow, then click a language.

6. **Click the Change the date, time, or number format link under Region and Language**

   The Region and Language dialog box opens, displaying the Formats tab, which shows the language format, short and long date, short and long time, first day of the week, and examples of each.. See Figure E-20.

7. **Click the Short date format list arrow, then click dd-MMM-yy**

   The short date format is changed and appears as 06-Mar-12, for example, in the Short date text box on the Formats tab.

8. **Click Cancel, then click the Close button ▬x▬ in the Clock, Language, and Region window**

   The Region and Language dialog box and the Control Panel window close.

9. **Point to the time and date in the notification area to display a ScreenTip of the date and time, click the time and date in the notification area to display a calendar and clock, then click a blank area of the desktop**

   The Calendar and clock window closes.

Customizing Windows Using the Control Panel

FIGURE E-19: Date and Time dialog box with the Date and Time tab displayed

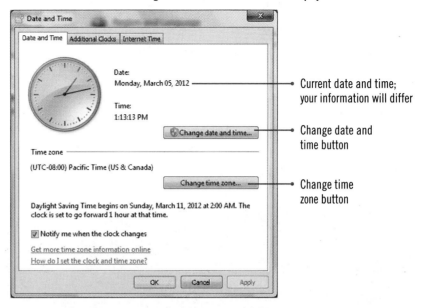

Current date and time; your information will differ

Change date and time button

Change time zone button

FIGURE E-20: Region and Language dialog box

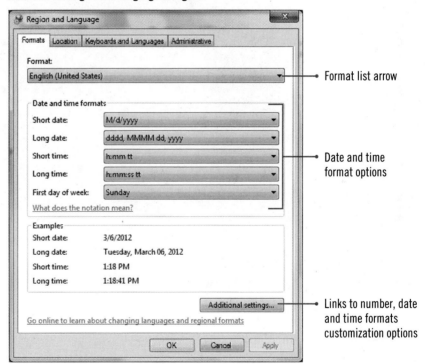

Format list arrow

Date and time format options

Links to number, date and time formats customization options

Adding and displaying another clock

If you need to know the time in other time zones, you can add one or two additional clocks using the Additional Clocks tab in the Date and Time dialog box. After you add a clock, you can display both clocks by clicking or hovering over the taskbar clock. See Figure E-21. To add a clock, click the taskbar clock, click the Change date and time settings link, click the Additional Clocks tab, select the Show this clock check box, select a time zone, enter a display name, then click OK.

FIGURE E-21: Added clock display from the taskbar

Practice

Concepts Review

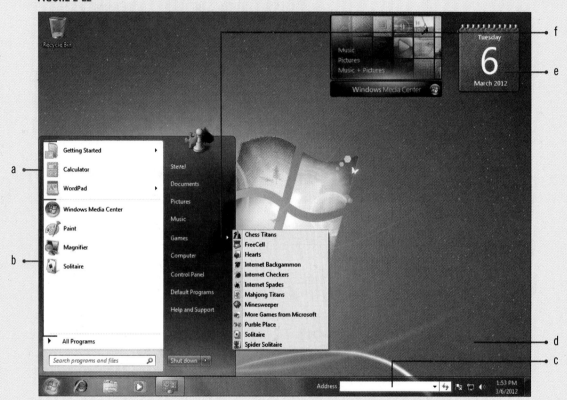

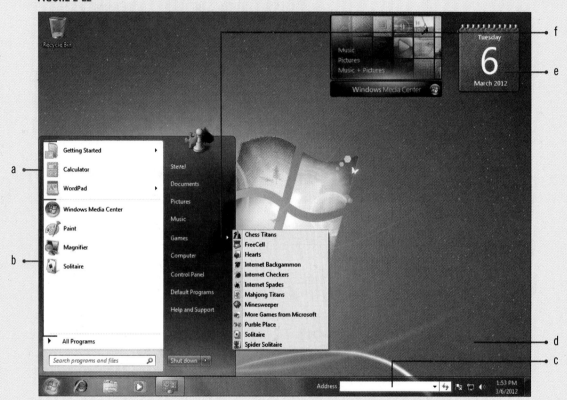

For current SAM information including versions and content details, visit SAM Central (http://samcentral.course.com). If you have a SAM user profile, you may have access to hands-on instruction, practice, and assessment of the skills covered in this unit. Since we support various versions of SAM throughout the life of this text, you will want to check with your instructor for instructions and the correct URL/Web site to access those assignments.

Match the statements below with the elements labeled in the screen shown in Figure E-22.

FIGURE E-22

1. Which element points to an expanded menu?
2. Which element points to a gadget?
3. Which element points to the desktop background?
4. Which element points to pinned programs?
5. Which element points to a toolbar?
6. Which element points to recently used programs?

Match each term with the statement that best describes it.

7. **Start menu**
8. **Screen saver**
9. **Control Panel**
10. **Color schemes**
11. **Wallpaper**

a. Preset designs for the desktop
b. Used to start programs and open documents
c. Used to change properties of various elements of a computer
d. Preset combinations of desktop colors
e. Used to prevent damage to the monitor

Concepts Review (Continued)

Select the best answer from the list of choices.

12. **Which of the following is NOT an acceptable format for a desktop background?**
    a. JPEG
    b. TIF
    c. PNG
    d. RTF

13. **To customize the appearance of the desktop, you need to open the:**
    a. Desktop Settings window.
    b. Appearance and Personalization window.
    c. Personalization window.
    d. Appearance window.

14. **A Paint file used as a background is called (a):**
    a. Display.
    b. Shortcut.
    c. Picture.
    d. Wallpaper.

15. **Which of the following screen resolutions displays screen elements the largest?**
    a. 640 by 480 pixels
    b. 1024 by 768 pixels
    c. 1280 by 1024 pixels
    d. 1600 by 1200 pixels

16. **Which of the following color quality values displays the smallest number of colors?**
    a. 16-bit
    b. 24-bit
    c. 32-bit
    d. The same number of colors is displayed with all three values.

17. **Which of the following changes the background, screen saver, mouse pointers, sounds, icons, and fonts?**
    a. Theme
    b. Scheme
    c. Desktop
    d. Gadget

18. **Which of the following fonts consists of bitmapped characters?**
    a. TrueType
    b. Screen
    c. OpenType
    d. Outline

19. **Where does a gadget appear?**
    a. Control Panel
    b. Desktop
    c. Start menu
    d. Taskbar

20. **A gadget is a:**
    a. Miniapplication.
    b. Full application.
    c. Utility.
    d. Program.

Skills Review

1. **Change the desktop background.**
    a. Open the Control Panel window.
    b. Open the Desktop Background window.
    c. Add the Penguins background in the Pictures Library to the list, minimize the Desktop Background window to view the desktop slide show, display the Desktop Background window, then cancel the change. (*Hint*: Click the Picture location list arrow to locate the Pictures Library folder.)
    d. Close the Desktop Background window.

2. **Change the desktop screen saver.**
    a. Open the Screen Saver Settings dialog box.
    b. Select the Bubbles screen saver, then preview it.
    c. Close the Screen Saver Settings dialog box without saving the change.

3. **Change desktop screen settings.**
    a. Open the Screen Resolution window.
    b. Open the Advanced Settings dialog box for your monitor.
    c. Display the Monitor tab, note the screen refresh rate.
    d. Make sure the Colors option is set to True Color (32-bit), then close the dialog box.
    e. Change the Screen resolution to a different setting, then apply the change.
    f. Restore the resolution to its original setting, then close the Screen Resolution window.

Skills Review (Continued)

4. Change the desktop appearance.

   a. Open the Personalization dialog box.

   b. Change the theme to Windows Classic.

   c. Change the theme to Windows 7, then close the window.

   d. Open the Window Color and Appearance window.

   e. Select a color, then change the color intensity.

   f. Cancel the changes you made and close the Window Color and Appearance window.

5. Work with fonts.

   a. Open the Fonts window.

   b. Display the size and style samples for a Times New Roman font.

   c. Print the Times New Roman font information.

   d. Close the Times New Roman and Fonts windows.

6. Customize the taskbar.

   a. Open the Taskbar and Start Menu Properties dialog box.

   b. Set the option to Auto-hide taskbar.

   c. Set any notification icon in the list to Hide icon and notifications, then apply the changes.

   d. Display the hidden taskbar, then show the hidden icons.

   e. Deselect the Auto-hide feature, then restore the notification icon to its default setting to Show icon and notifications.

   f. Apply the changes, then close the Taskbar and Start Menu Properties dialog box.

7. Customize the Start menu.

   a. Point to the Paint program on the Accessories submenu on the Start menu.

   b. Pin the Paint program to the Start menu.

   c. Open the Taskbar and Start Menu Properties dialog box, then display the Customize Start Menu dialog box. Show Pictures as a menu on the Start menu, then apply the change.

   d. Display the Start menu with the changes.

   e. Unpin the Paint program from the Start menu, then change the Pictures menu to display as a link.

   f. Close the Taskbar and Start Menu Properties dialog box.

8. Work with desktop gadgets.

   a. Open the Gadget Gallery window, then add the Slide Show gadget to the desktop.

   b. Close the Gadget Gallery window.

   c. Open the Slide Show Options dialog box.

   d. Change the Show each picture time to 10 seconds.

   e. Select a transition between pictures, then click OK.

   f. Watch the slide show in the gadget, then close the gadget.

9. Set the date and time.

   a. Open the Date and Time dialog box.

   b. Change the time to three hours ahead, then apply the change.

   c. Change the time zone to International Date Line West time.

   d. Change the time zone back to the original time zone.

   e. Change the current time back to the correct time.

   f. Close the Date and Time dialog box.

   g. Close the Control Panel, if necessary.

Independent Challenge 1

You just got a new computer for your birthday, and you want to set up Windows Aero and customize the desktop. Before you can run Windows Aero, you need to make sure Windows 7 contains the proper settings. Make sure the color is set to 32-bit, the monitor refresh rate is higher than 10 Hertz, the theme is set to the Windows 7 Aero theme, and the window transparency is turned on.

Independent Challenge 1 (Continued)

a. Open the Appearance and Personalization window from the Control Panel.

b. Open the Screen Resolution window.

c. Make sure the color is set to 32-bit.

d. Make sure the monitor refresh rate is set to higher than 10 Hertz.

e. Close the Screen Resolution window.

f. Change the theme to Windows Classic.

g. Change the theme to Windows 7.

h. Enable transparency, if necessary.

i. Change the color used for your window borders, Start menu, and taskbar.

Advanced Challenge Exercise

- Select a picture of your own to use as the desktop background.
- Select Photos as the screen saver, and specify the picture location you want to use.
- Select a slide show speed and select to shuffle contents.
- Display the screen saver.
- Restore the desktop background and screen saver back to their original state.

j. Restore the original settings, then close the Control Panel.

Independent Challenge 2

As a reporter for a local newspaper, you are continually looking for possible news stories that affect local readers and keep notes you can refer to later. To accomplish this task, you need to add the Feed Headlines gadget and display headlines (if necessary), add the Large Notes gadget (available online) to the desktop, and type new notes in the Large Notes gadget.

a. Open the Desktop Gadget Gallery window.

b. Add the Feed Headlines gadget if necessary, then, if necessary, click View Headlines in the gadget on the desktop to display feeds.

c. Go online to the Personalization Gallery, then click the Desktop gadgets tab.

d. Download and add the Large Notes gadget to the desktop. If the gadget is not available, select another online gadget to download and install.

e. Type the title of a current news feed in the Large Notes gadget.

f. Click the plus sign to create a new note pad page, then type another news feed title.

g. Remove the Feed Headlines and Large Notes gadgets from the desktop.

Independent Challenge 3

You accepted a temporary consulting job in Rome, Italy. After moving into your new home and unpacking your stuff, you decide to set up your computer. Once you set up and turn on the computer, you decide to change the date and time settings and other region and language options to reflect Rome, Italy.

a. Open the Control Panel, then open the Date and Time dialog box.

b. Open the Time Zone Settings dialog box.

c. Change the time zone to (UTC 101:00) Amsterdam, Berlin, Bern, Rome, Stockholm, Vienna.

d. In the Date and Time dialog box, change the month and year to June 2010, then click OK.

e. Display the Internet Time tab, then update the time if you have an Internet connection. Otherwise, change the time back three hours manually.

Independent Challenge 3 (Continued)

Advanced Challenge Exercise

- ■ Display the Additional Clocks tab, enable a clock, select the time zone from your previous location, then enter a name for the clock.
- ■ Apply the changes, then point to the time in the Notification area to display both clocks.
- ■ Disable the secondary clock.

f. Close the Date and Time dialog box.

g. Open the Region and Language dialog box.

h. On the Formats tab, set the language formats to Italian (Italy).

i. Restore the original date and time zone settings and the regional and language options to English (United States).

j. Close the Control Panel window.

Real Life Independent Challenge

People often work on specific projects for a length of time. You can make it easier to work on your project if you customize your desktop for the specific needs of the project. For instance, you can pin the programs you use on a regular basis on the Start menu, rearrange them in the order you want, and display any toolbars you need.

a. Pin at least two programs to the Start menu.

b. Rearrange the order of the pinned programs.

c. Customize the Start menu to display the Control Panel as a menu.

d. Change the taskbar to auto-hide.

e. Add the Address (bar) toolbar to the taskbar.

f. Restore the Start menu and taskbar to their original states.

Visual Workshop

Re-create the screen shown in Figure E-23, which displays the Windows desktop. Your username on the Start menu and the list of games on the submenu might differ.

FIGURE E-23

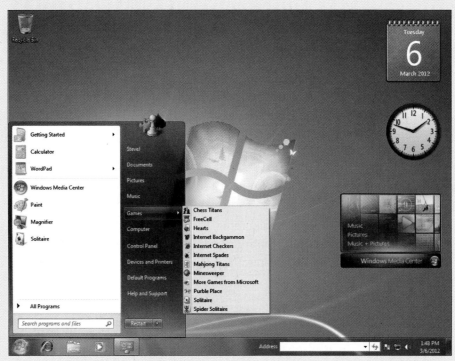

Customizing Windows Using the Control Panel

Securing Your Computer

 To perform some of the lessons in this unit, you need to use the administrator password or use an administrator account. See your instructor or technical support person for more information.

Windows 7 makes communicating with other computers over the Internet more secure and easier than ever. The **Action Center** enables you to manage computer security by providing a single place to view alerts and take actions about security and maintenance issues with your computer. The Action Center makes it easy to find information about the latest virus or security threat, check the status of essential security settings, quickly get support from Microsoft for a security-related issue, and access the Control Panel utilities that allow you to set additional security and privacy settings.  You are an IT computer specialist at Quest Specialty Travel. As part of your job, you need to make sure company computers are protected from outside threats, so you want to make sure computer security settings are properly set.

OBJECTIVES
Explore the Action Center
Manage Windows Firewall
Get Automatic Updates
Defend against malicious software
Set up Internet security
Protect your Internet identity
Protect your Internet privacy
Delete Internet information
Set Parental Controls

Exploring the Action Center

The Action Center is divided into two main areas: Security and Maintenance. In the Security area, you can view settings relating to network firewall, Windows Update, virus protection, spyware and unwanted software protection, Internet security settings, User Account Control, and Network Access Protection. In the Maintenance area, you can view and change settings relating to Windows Update, Windows Backup, and system maintenance. The Action Center displays important and recommended alerts to help protect your computer and keep Windows running smoothly. As you work, Windows 7 displays security alerts and icons in the notification area on the taskbar to make you aware of potential security risks, such as a new virus, out-of-date antivirus software, if an important security option is turned off, or other security-related issues from Microsoft. To open the Action Center, you can click on an alert, access it from the Control Panel or click the Action Center icon in the notification area on the taskbar. When you click the Action Center icon, a small window with a list of alert messages appears that you can click to address the issue. In the Action Center, you can also find links to troubleshooters and system restore tools. ⬛⬛⬛ As the IT specialist, you want to check out the current security settings on your computer to make sure Quest Specialty Travel company information is safe.

STEPS

1. **If available, click the Action Center icon ⬛ in the notification area on the taskbar**

   A message window appears with links to important and recommended alerts. In the window, some options have a security icon ⬛ next to it, as shown in Figure F-1. When you see the security icon next to any option within Windows 7, it means that you need permission to access the settings. To access the settings, you need to enter an administrator password. This adds an additional level of security on your computer.

   > **QUICK TIP**
   > To change User Account Control settings, click the Change User Account Control settings link in the task pane, drag the slider for the notification level you want, then click OK.

2. **Click the Open Action Center link if available, or click the Start button ⬤ on the taskbar, click Control Panel, then click Review your computer's status link under System and Security**

   The Action Center window opens, displaying the essential security areas and their current status, as shown in Figure F-2. In this case, there are two important issues for no virus protection software and a problem with Windows Update and two recommended issues for unreported problems and no backup. You can click the Expand button ⬇ or anywhere on the bar to show information about that security area; click the Collapse button ⬇ or the bar again to hide it. You can use the options available to install and update any needed protection software.

3. **Click the Expand button ⬇ for Security**

   A list of security information and links to specific security options appear.

4. **In the task pane, click the Change Action Center settings link**

   The Change Action Center settings dialog box opens, displaying security and maintenance message options. You can turn alert messages on or off.

5. **Click Cancel**

   The current alert message settings remain the same. The Action Center window reopens.

   > **QUICK TIP**
   > To view archived messages to past solutions, click the View archived messages link in the task pane. Double-click a manually archived message to view information.

6. **In the task pane, click the Change User Account Control settings link**

   The User Account Control Settings dialog box opens, displaying a notification slider option you can set to help prevent potentially harmful programs from making changes to your computer.

7. **Click Cancel**

   The current User Account Control settings remain the same. The Action Center window reopens.

8. **Click System and Security in the Address bar**

   The System and Security window opens, displaying system-, security-, and maintenance-related options, such as Action Center, Windows Firewall, System, Windows Update, Power Options, and Backup and Restore.

FIGURE F-1: Alert messages from the Action Center

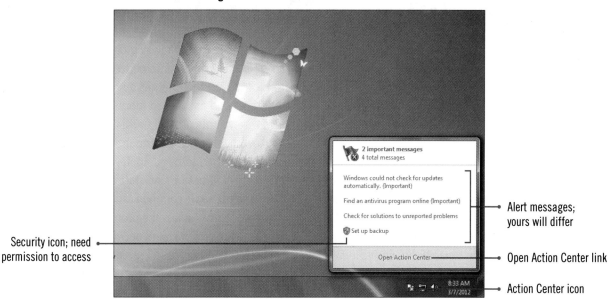

Security icon; need permission to access

Alert messages; yours will differ

Open Action Center link

Action Center icon

FIGURE F-2: Action Center window

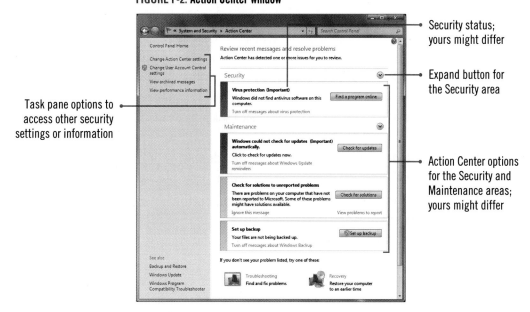

Task pane options to access other security settings or information

Security status; yours might differ

Expand button for the Security area

Action Center options for the Security and Maintenance areas; yours might differ

Protecting against malware

A **computer virus** is a program that attaches itself to a file, reproduces itself, and then spreads to other files. A virus is typically "caught" from programs and files downloaded from the Internet, electronic mail attachments, or shareware discs containing free or inexpensive software or illegally obtained pirated software. When you open a program or file with the computer virus, the computer becomes infected with the virus and can corrupt or destroy data, or disrupt program or Windows functionality. Many viruses stay dormant on a computer before doing any damage, so catching and destroying these viruses before they cause damage can prevent computer disaster. A **worm** is like a virus, but it can spread without human action across networks. For example, a worm might send e-mail copies of itself to everyone in your e-mail

Address Book. A worm can consume memory, causing your computer to stop responding or even take it over. A **Trojan horse**, like its mythological counterpart, is a program that appears to be useful and come from a legitimate source, but actually causes problems, such as gathering personal information or deleting files. **Antivirus software**, or virus detection software, examines the files stored on a disk to determine whether they are infected with a virus, then destroys or disinfects them. Antivirus software provides protection when you start Windows and checks for viruses whenever your computer is on. Popular antivirus software, which needs to be purchased from a software retailer, includes Norton AntiVirus and McAfee VirusScan. New viruses appear all the time, so it is important that your antivirus software be kept up to date.

Managing Windows Firewall

If your computer is directly connected to the Internet, you need a firewall program. A **firewall** is a protective barrier between your computer or network and others on the Internet. **Windows Firewall** protects your computer from unauthorized access from others on the Internet by monitoring communication between your computer and the Internet and preventing unsolicited inbound traffic from the Internet from entering your private computer. Windows Firewall discards all unsolicited communications from reaching your computer unless you specifically allow them to come through. Windows Firewall is enabled by default for all Internet and network connections. However, some computer manufacturers and network administrators might turn it off, so you need to check it before you start using the computer. When Windows Firewall is enabled, you might not be able to use some communication features, such as sending files with a messaging program or playing an Internet game, unless the program is listed in the Allowed Programs window in Windows Firewall. If you use multiple Internet and networking connections, you can enable or disable the specific individual connections or modify firewall settings for each type of network location you use.  Because firewall protection is an essential aspect of computer protection, you want to make sure your Windows Firewall is running so Quest Specialty Travel company information is safe.

STEPS

1. **In the System and Security window, click Windows Firewall**

   The Windows Firewall window opens, as shown in Figure F-3, displaying the current firewall settings. In this case, for the Home or work networks, Windows Firewall is turned on, inbound connections are blocked, and display notification when a program is blocked is enabled.

> **QUICK TIP**
>
> To restore default settings, click the Restore defaults link in the task pane, click Restore defaults, then click Yes to confirm.

2. **In the left pane, click the Turn Windows Firewall on or off link**

   The User Account Control window might open, asking you for permission to make changes to the security or personal settings.

3. **If prompted, click Continue, or type the administrator password and click OK**

   The Customize Settings window opens, as shown in Figure F-4.

4. **Click the Turn on Windows Firewall option button if necessary under Home or work (private) network location settings**

   This enables Windows Firewall to prevent hackers or malicious software from accessing your computer.

5. **Click Cancel**

   The current firewall settings remain the same and the Windows Firewall window opens. Some programs, such as Remote Assistance (a program that allows you to control another computer over the Internet), need to communicate through the firewall, so you can create an exception to allow them to work, yet still maintain a secure computer.

> **QUICK TIP**
>
> If you're having connection problems, click the Troubleshoot my network link in the task pane to access troubleshooting wizards.

6. **In the task pane, click the Allow a program or feature through Windows Firewall**

   The Allowed Programs window opens, displaying the current programs or connection ports allowed to communicate through the firewall. A **port** is the actual connection on your computer that links to devices, such as a printer.

7. **Scroll down the list, then click the Windows Media Player Network Sharing Service (Internet) check box to select it**

   Selecting this option enables the Windows Media Player program to freely communicate over the Internet for network-sharing purposes through the firewall.

8. **Click OK**

   The change that you made to the firewall is applied and the Windows Firewall window reopens.

9. **Click System and Security in the Address bar**

   The System and Security window reopens.

FIGURE F-3: Windows Firewall window

Turn Windows Firewall on or off link

Help button

Collapse button for Public networks

Current firewall settings; yours might differ

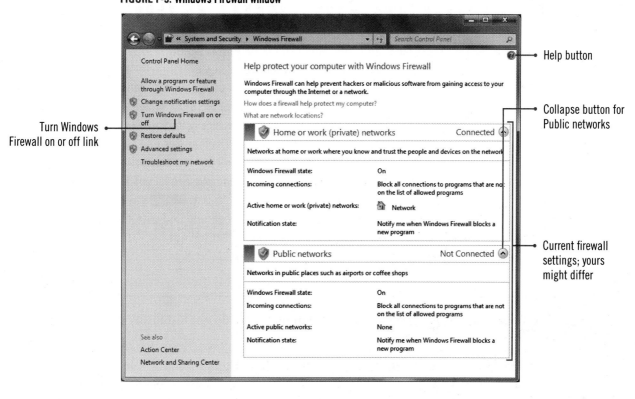

FIGURE F-4: Customize Settings window

Turn on Windows Firewall option button

Block all incoming connections, including those in the list of allowed programs check box

Firewall settings for your Public network

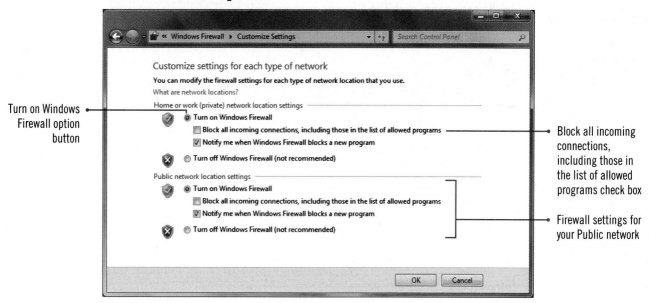

Adding additional security at start-up

For added security, you can require users to press [Ctrl][Alt][Delete] before they can select a user account and enter a password when they turn on the computer. This prevents programs, such as spyware or a virus, from stealing your username and password when you enter it on your computer. When you lock your computer or switch users, this security option also requires users to press [Ctrl][Alt][Delete] to log back on. To set the Ctrl+Alt+Delete option, click the Start button, point to All Programs, click Accessories, click Run, type *NetplWiz.exe*, then click OK. In the User Accounts dialog box, click the Advanced tab, click the Require users to press Ctrl+Alt+Delete check box to select it, then click OK. You can also access the User Accounts dialog box from the "Enable or disable secure logon (CTRL + ALT + DELETE)" help topic in Windows Help and Support.

Getting Automatic Updates

Automatic updating provides protection when you update your Windows software to make sure it's up-to-date and safe. It provides a central location where you can view currently installed updates and install new Windows features, system and security updates, and device drivers. Windows Update can review device drivers and system software on your computer, compare those findings with a master database on the Web, and then recommend and install updates specifically for your computer. You can also restore a previous device driver or system file using the uninstall option. Because Microsoft provides updates on a regular basis over the Internet, it is important to check for new content and other updates. If you want to be notified when updates occur, you can set up Windows 7 to let you know as soon as they happen. The default setting is to have Windows check the site every day.  You're not sure how long it's been since your computer at Quest Specialty Travel has been updated with the latest Windows 7 software. You want to check your computer for updates and current settings.

STEPS

 If you're working on a network run by an administrator, do not install any software without permission.

1. **In the System and Security window, click Windows Update**

   The Windows Update window opens, as shown in Figure F-5, displaying information and the current settings for Windows Update. Windows Update is turned on by default and set to automatically check for and install updates at a regular time every day.

2. **In the task pane, click the Change settings link**

   The Change settings window opens, displaying the Windows Update notification settings, as shown in Figure F-6. These settings allow you to automatically check for important updates and install them.

3. **Click Cancel**

   The current Windows Update notification settings remain the same and the Windows Update window reopens.

4. **In the task pane, click the View update history link**

   The View update history window opens, displaying a list of your computer's complete update history. The history includes the update name, installation status and date, and importance to your system, either Important, Recommended, or Optional.

> **QUICK TIP**
> To remove an installed update, click Installed Updates in the task pane in the Windows Update window, select the update, then click Uninstall.

5. **Click OK**

   The Windows Update window reopens.

6. **Click the Installed Updates link at the bottom of the task pane**

   The Installed Updates window opens, displaying a list of the currently installed Windows Updates on your computer that you can uninstall.

7. **Click the Back button ⊙ to the left of the Address bar, then click the Check for updates link in the task pane**

   The Installed Updates window closes and the Windows Update window reopens. Windows Update checks your computer to see if it needs any updates. If it detects that updates are necessary, Windows Update indicates how many updates are available and the importance of each.

> **QUICK TIP**
> If you want to install any updates during future use, click the check boxes next to the updates you want to install, click OK, then click Install updates.

8. **In the task pane, click the link for important or optional updates, if available**

   The Select updates to install window opens.

9. **Click OK, then if necessary, click System and Security in the Address bar**

   The System and Security window reopens.

Securing Your Computer

FIGURE F-5: Windows Update window

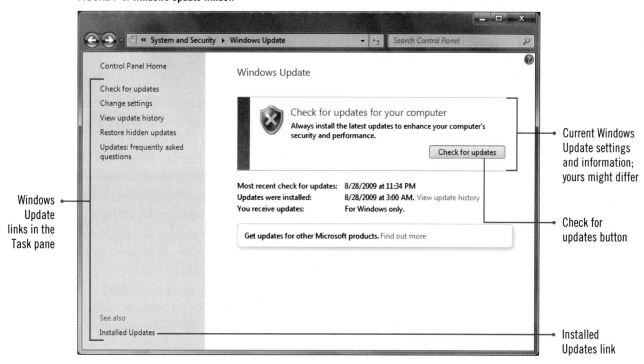

Windows Update links in the Task pane

Current Windows Update settings and information; yours might differ

Check for updates button

Installed Updates link

FIGURE F-6: Change settings window

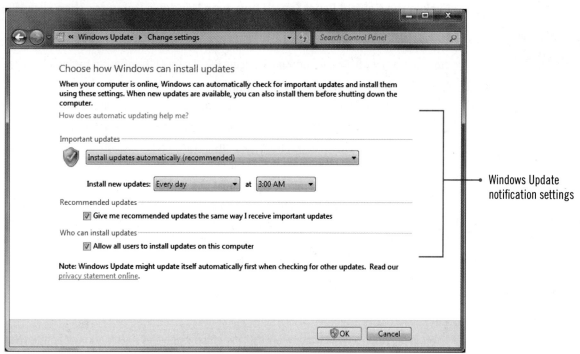

Windows Update notification settings

Locking the computer

If you are working on sensitive material and need to leave your computer unattended, you can lock it so that no one can use it without your permission. While your computer is locked, all your programs continue to run, as opposed to shutting down, but it is password protected. When you return to your computer, you can access it in the same way you normally start Windows. If the Ctrl+Alt+Del option is enabled, you need to press [Ctrl][Alt][Delete] before you can enter a password. To lock your computer, click the Start button, point to the arrow next to the Power button, then click Lock or press [⊞] + L to lock the computer. At the Welcome screen, click your name (if prompted), type your password, and then press [Enter].

Defending Against Malicious Software

Malware protection provides information and security against **malware**, which is malicious software, such as viruses and spyware that can delete or corrupt files and steal personal information. **Spyware** is software that attempts to collect your personal information or change computer settings without your consent. Typically, spyware is downloaded without your knowledge and installed on your computer along with free software you willingly accept, such as freeware, games, or music file-sharing programs. Spyware is often associated with ad-ware software that displays advertisements, such as a pop-up ad. Windows Defender uses alerts to protect your computer from malware, spyware, and any other potentially harmful software that attempts to install itself or run on your computer. When you receive an alert of a potential problem, you can use the Microsoft SpyNet community to help you determine if the software is alright to run. Windows Defender determines if there are potential problems by using definitions. A **definition** provides instructions on how to defend against malware software. Because software dangers continually change, it's important to have up-to-date definitions, which you can get online. If Windows Defender finds a problem, it quarantines the software, which prevents it from running. You can then decide if it is software you indeed want to run. ▰▰▰ You want to continue checking security settings on Quest Specialty Travel computers to make sure company information is safe.

STEPS

1. **Click in the Control Panel Search box, type** Windows Defender, **then click** Windows Defender **in the System and Security window**

   The Windows Defender window opens, displaying status and information about your computer's current protection against malicious software. In Figure F-7, the user is being asked to check for new definitions.

   > **TROUBLE**
   > If Check for Updates Now is not available, click the Help button arrow, then click Check for updates to check for Windows Defender and definition updates.

2. **Click** Check for Updates Now **if available**

   The User Account Control window opens, asking you for permission to make security changes.

3. **Click** Continue, **or type the administrator password, then click** OK

   Windows Defender checks for definitions and installs any updates. Upon completion, status information at the bottom of the window is updated with the definition version and date and time.

   > **QUICK TIP**
   > You can click the Scan button to start a quick scan.

4. **Click the** Scan button arrow **at the top of the window, then click** Quick scan

   Windows Defender scans the essential files on your computer, as shown in Figure F-8. Upon completion, scan statistics appear, including start time, elapsed time, and number of objects scanned. Status information at the bottom of the window is also updated. The status information includes scan schedule, which you can modify.

5. **Click the** Tools button **at the top of the window**

   The Tools and Settings window opens, displaying links for Options, Microsoft SpyNet, Quarantined items, Allowed items, Windows Defender website, and the Microsoft Malware Protection Center website.

6. **Click** Microsoft SpyNet

   The Join Microsoft SpyNet window opens. This window provides a description of how SpyNet works. SpyNet allows Windows Defender to send Microsoft information to help identify and stop spyware infections.

7. **Click** Cancel

   The Join Microsoft SpyNet window closes and the main Windows Defender window reopens.

8. **Click** Quarantined items

   The Quarantined items window opens, displaying any items identified as potential problems.

9. **Click the** Close button ⊠ **in the Windows Defender window, then click the** Close button ⊠ **in the Control Panel Search box**

   The System and Security window reopens.

FIGURE F-7: Windows Defender window

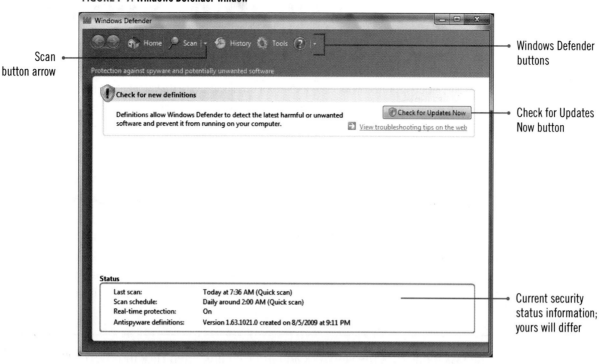

Scan button arrow

Windows Defender buttons

Check for Updates Now button

Current security status information; yours will differ

FIGURE F-8: Scanning for malware

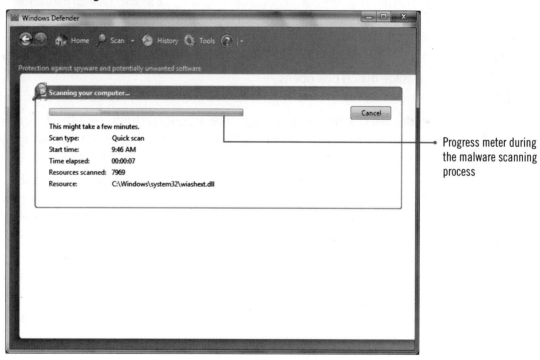

Progress meter during the malware scanning process

Monitoring and managing programs using Windows Defender

You can use Windows Defender to monitor all the programs on your computer or just specific ones. In the Windows Defender window, click the Tools button to open the Tools and Settings window. To remove or restore quarantined programs, click the Quarantined items link, select a program, then click Remove or Restore. To remove a program from the allowed items (not monitored) list, click the Allowed items link, select a program, then click Remove from list.

Setting Up Internet Security

Windows provides Internet security options to prevent users on the Internet from gaining access to personal information without your permission, such as credit card information, while you shop online. In addition, Windows security options protect your computer from unsafe software downloaded or run from the Internet. Internet security is divided into **zones**, or Web site areas, to which you can assign different levels of security. There are four security zones: Internet, Local intranet, Trusted sites, and Restricted sites. See Table F-1 for a description of each security zone. When you access a Web page or download content from a site, Internet Explorer checks its security settings and determines the Web site's zone, which displays on the right side of the Internet Explorer status bar. All Internet Web sites are by default assigned to the Internet zone until you assign individual Web sites to other zones. In addition to security zones, you can also control the Web content that appears on your computer with the Content Advisor. The **Content Advisor** allows you to prevent access to Web sites that contain material you deem inappropriate, due to elements such as language or violence. This is a helpful feature for protecting children from inappropriate content. You can create a supervisor password to prevent other users from making changes to the Content Advisor settings. ░░░░░ Your manager has asked you to check Internet security settings to make sure company computers are secure for Internet use.

STEPS

QUICK TIP
To customize a security level for a selected zone, click Custom level on the Security tab, select the settings you want, then click OK.

1. **In the task pane, click the** Network and Internet link, **then click** Internet Options

   The Internet Properties dialog box opens, displaying the General tab.

2. **Click the** Security tab

   The Internet Properties dialog box reopens, displaying the Security tab with the Internet zone and its current security level, as shown in Figure F-9. The security levels are High, Medium-high, and Medium. You can move the slider up for a higher level of security or down for a lower level of security.

TROUBLE
If the slider is not available, click Default level to change the security level to Medium and display the slider.

3. **Drag the slider up or down to adjust the security level, then click** Yes **if a Warning message dialog box opens**

   A detailed description appears next to the security level, which changes as you adjust the security level.

4. **Under Select a zone to view or change security settings, click the** Trusted sites icon

   The security-level information for Trusted sites appears, where you can add and remove trusted sites or change the security-level settings. The security levels are Low, Medium-low, Medium, Medium-high, and High.

5. **With the Internet Properties dialog box still open, click the** Content tab

   The Content tab opens, displaying settings to control Internet content. You can set parental controls and content ratings for viewing Internet content, protect your Internet identity using certificates, suggest content entries using AutoComplete, and access Web site content using feeds.

6. **Under Content Advisor, click** Enable

   The Content Advisor dialog box opens, as shown in Figure F-10. This dialog box allows you to make changes to security or personal settings.

QUICK TIP
To create a password to change Content Advisor settings, click the General tab in the Content Advisor dialog box, click Create password, type and confirm a password and related hint as indicated, then click OK.

7. **If prompted, click** Continue, **or type the administrator password and click** OK

   The Content Advisor dialog box opens, displaying the Ratings tab with current rating levels for the ICRA3 (Internet Content Rating Association) service, as shown in Figure F-10. You can select any of the categories to change their rating levels independently of the others. The rating levels specify what users are allowed to see and range from None to Unrestricted.

8. **Drag the slider to adjust the content rating level for the selected category**

   When you change the rating level, the detailed description below the rating level changes.

9. **Click** Cancel **in the Content Advisor dialog box, then click** Cancel **in the Internet Properties dialog box**

   The Network and Internet window opens.

FIGURE F-9: Internet Properties dialog box with the Security tab displayed

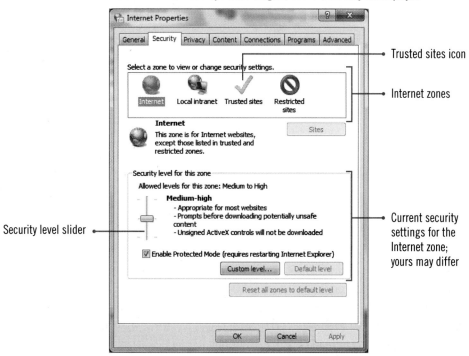

Trusted sites icon

Internet zones

Security level slider

Current security settings for the Internet zone; yours may differ

FIGURE F-10: Content Advisor dialog box

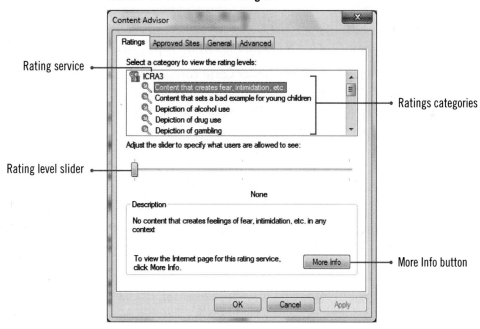

Rating service

Rating level slider

Ratings categories

More Info button

TABLE F-1: Security zones in Internet Explorer

zone	description	default setting
Internet	Contains all Web sites that are not assigned to any other zone	Medium-high
Local intranet	Contains all Web sites that are on your organization's intranet and don't require a proxy server	Medium-low
Trusted sites	Contains Web sites that you trust not to threaten the security of your computer	Medium
Restricted sites	Contains Web sites that you believe threaten the security of your computer	High (blocks all cookies)

Protecting Your Internet Identity

To further protect your privacy, you can use certificates to verify your identity and protect important information, such as your credit card number, on the Internet. A **certificate** is a digitally signed statement verifying the identity of a person or the security of a Web site. A certificate is also known as a **Digital ID** in other programs, such as Microsoft Outlook. For normal transactions over the Internet in which you provide personal information, you won't have to think about certificates. When you visit a secure Web site (one whose address often starts with "https" instead of "http"), it automatically sends you its certificate. When Internet Explorer receives the certificate, it displays a lock icon on the status bar, which you can click to view a report, and validates the certificate information, which includes the Web site address, expiration date, and certifying authority. If any of the information in the certificate is invalid, Internet Explorer blocks access to the site. If you need to provide a certificate by request of a Web site, you can obtain a personal security certification from an independent Certification Authority (CA). There are two types of certificates: personal and Web site. A **personal certificate** verifies your identity to a secure Web site that requires a certificate, whereas a **Web site certificate** verifies its security to you before you send them information. To transfer information and files on the Internet, you want to learn more about using certificates and import a certificate issued by John Casey, a coworker at Quest Specialty Travel, to see how it works.

STEPS

1. **Click** Internet Options

   The Internet Properties dialog box opens, displaying the General tab.

2. **Click the** Content tab, **then under Certificates, click** Certificates

   The Certificates dialog box opens, displaying the Personal tab. The Personal tab stores your individual ("personal") certificates, while the other tabs in this dialog box, such as Other People, store certificates based on the purpose described by the tab name. The subsequent tabs are identified as trusted or untrusted, which indicates whether you should use them or not. Because the certificate example is not yours and not issued by a CA, you want to import and store it under the Other People tab.

   > **QUICK TIP**
   > To obtain a personal certificate, find a certification authority on the Trusted Root Certification Authorities tab in the Certificates dialog box or search for one on the Internet. The certification authority works with you to create the certificate file and import it to your computer.

3. **Click the** Other People tab, **click** Import **to start the Certificate Import Wizard, then click** Next

   The next Certificate Import Wizard dialog box opens, asking you to select a certificate file.

4. **Click** Browse **to display the Open dialog box, navigate to the drive and folder where you store your Data Files, double-click the file** WIN F-1.cer, **then click** Next

   The next Certificate Import Wizard dialog box opens, asking you to select a certificate location.

5. **Click** Next **to display a summary of your choices in the wizard, click** Finish, **then click** OK **in the dialog box that opens telling you the import was successful**

   The John Casey certificate appears in the Certificates dialog box, as shown in Figure F-11.

6. **Double-click the** John Casey certificate

   The Certificate dialog box opens, as shown in Figure F-12, displaying information about the specific certificate, including its trustworthiness and the dates between which it's valid.

   > **TROUBLE**
   > If the Remove button is not available, press [Delete] instead. See your network administrator for permission, if necessary.

7. **Click** OK **to close the Certificate dialog box, click the** John Casey certificate **to select it, if necessary, click** Remove, **then click** Yes **in the message box to confirm the deletion**

8. **Click** Close **to close the Certificates dialog box, then click** Cancel **to close the Internet Properties dialog box**

   The Internet Properties dialog box closes and the Network and Internet window reopens.

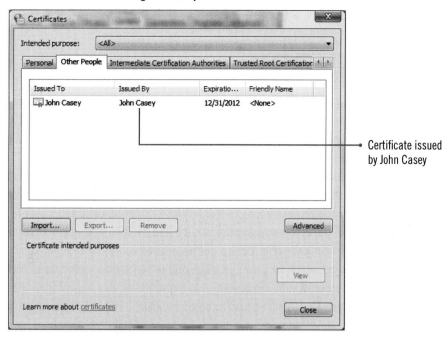
FIGURE F-11: Certificates dialog box with a personal certificate

Certificate issued
by John Casey

FIGURE F-12: General tab in the Certificate dialog box

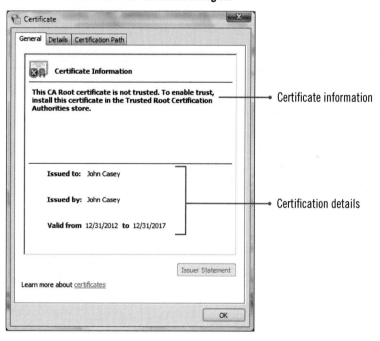

Certificate information

Certification details

Sending secure information using Windows CardSpace

With Windows CardSpace, you can securely send information in the form of online cards to Web sites or online services. Windows CardSpace is a system for creating relationships with Web sites and online services that provides a consistent way for you to review the identity of a site, manage your information, review information before sending it to a site, and for sites to request information from you. Windows CardSpace can replace the usernames and passwords that you use to register and log on to Web sites and online services.

You can create a personal card or have a business or organization issue you a managed card. To start Windows CardSpace, click the Start button, click Control Panel, click User Accounts and Family Safety, then click Windows CardSpace. To add a card, click the Add a card button, select a card type, enter the requested information, and then click Save. In the main screen, you can use commands to edit, duplicate, delete, back up, and restore cards. When you're done, click Close.

Protecting Your Internet Privacy

When you browse the Internet, you can access and gather information from Web sites, but Web sites can also gather information about you without your knowledge. You can set Internet privacy options to protect your personal identity from unauthorized access. When you visit a Web site, the site creates a **cookie** file, known as a **first-party cookie**, which stores information on your computer, such as your Web site preferences or personal identifiable information, including your name and e-mail address. The next time you visit that site, it can access the cookie to collect this information. Not all cookies are harmful; many first-party cookies save you time reentering information on a return visit to a Web site. However, there are also **third-party cookies**, which are created by Web sites using advertising banners, for example, you are not currently viewing. Once a cookie is saved on your computer, only the Web site that created it can read it. Windows privacy options allow you to block or permit cookies for Web sites in the Internet zone; however, when you block cookies, you might not be able to access all the features of a Web site. If a Web site that you have blocked tries to place a cookie, a red icon appears on the status bar. To find out if the Web site you are viewing in Internet Explorer contains third-party cookies or if any cookies have been restricted, you can get a privacy report from the site. The privacy report lists all the Web sites with content on the current Web page and shows how each site handles cookies. As you continue to check the current security settings on your computer, you want to check the privacy settings and get a privacy report for a Web page.

STEPS

1. **Click Internet Options**

   The Internet Properties dialog box opens, displaying the General tab.

2. **Click the Privacy tab**

   The Privacy tab dialog box opens, as shown in Figure F-13, displaying a slider, which you use to select a privacy setting to block cookies for the Internet zone. You move the slider up for a higher level of privacy or down for a lower level of privacy.

3. **Drag the slider to adjust the privacy setting**

   When you change your privacy settings, a detailed description appears next to the level. When you apply the privacy changes, they might not affect cookies that are already on your computer, but they will affect any new ones. Whether you set the privacy level to a high setting, which blocks most or all cookies, or a low setting, which blocks only a few or no cookies, you can click Sites in the section below to override cookie handling for individual Web sites.

TROUBLE
If a blank page appears in Internet Explorer, see "Opening a Web Page and Following Links" in Unit G for information to visit a Web site.

4. **Click Cancel**

   The Internet Properties dialog box closes without making any changes and the Network and Internet window reopens.

5. **Click the Internet Explorer button ⊚ on the taskbar**

   Internet Explorer opens, displaying your home page.

QUICK TIP
To view a Web site's privacy policy summary, select a Web site in the Privacy Report dialog box, then click Summary.

6. **Click the Safety button on the toolbar, then click Webpage Privacy Policy**

   The Privacy Report dialog box opens, as shown in Figure F-14, displaying all the Web sites associated with the current Web page and how your computer handled their cookies.

7. **Click Close to close the Privacy Report dialog box, then click the Close button ✖ in the Internet Explorer window**

   Internet Explorer closes and the Network and Internet window reopens.

FIGURE F-13: Internet Properties dialog box with the Privacy tab displayed

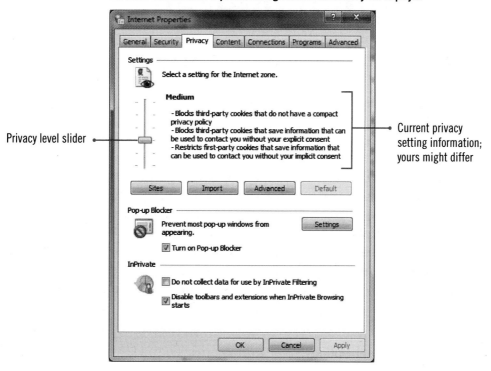

Privacy level slider •

Current privacy setting information; yours might differ

FIGURE F-14: Privacy Report dialog box

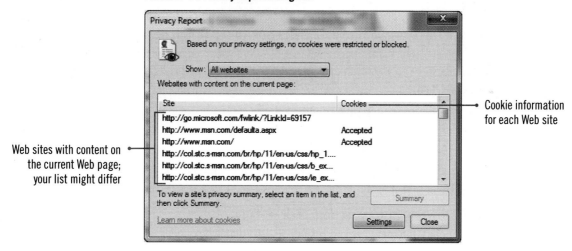

Web sites with content on the current Web page; your list might differ

Cookie information for each Web site

Providing security with the Information Bar

The Information Bar in Internet Explorer makes it easy for you to make informed decisions about potentially harmful content entering your computer. By default, Internet Explorer blocks pop-ups, certain programs, downloads, security risks, and other harmful threats. If the default settings in Internet Explorer are turned on, the Information Bar appears under the Address bar when a Web site tries to open a pop-up window, install an add-on, such as an ActiveX control, or download a file to your computer. Pop-up windows typically display annoying ads.

ActiveX controls provide added functionality to Internet Explorer, which makes using the Internet more enjoyable. However, it also opens the door for spyware and adware to invade your computer and privacy. When the Information Bar appears, you can click it to display options for dealing with the program or pop-up or to get more information. You can also ignore the Information Bar and continue viewing the Web site, although all the features on the site might not function properly if you choose not to allow the blocked content or program.

Deleting Internet Information

As you browse the Web, Internet Explorer stores information about your activities, including the information you have provided to Web sites when you log on (passwords) or fill out a form, the location of Web sites you have visited (history), and preference information used by Web sites (cookies). Internet Explorer also saves Web pages, images, and media (temporary Internet files) for faster viewing in the future. If you frequently browse the Web, Internet Explorer can gather and store a large amount of Internet-related data (including normal and InPrivate browsing), which can fill up your hard drive and slow down your computer. To help prevent computer performance problems, you need to periodically delete the Internet files and information; yet you can still preserve the files and information for your trusted sites in your Favorites. You can delete the Internet files and information individually or all at once.  Your computer at Quest Specialty Travel seems to be slowing down, so you decide to clean up the temporary Internet files on the computer and check related settings to reduce the amount stored in the future.

STEPS

QUICK TIP

To delete browsing history upon exiting Internet Explorer, select the Delete browsing history on exit check box to select it on the General tab in the Internet Explorer Properties dialog box.

1. **Click** Internet Options

   The Internet Properties dialog box opens, displaying the General tab.

2. **In the Browsing history section, click** Delete

   The Delete Browsing History dialog box opens, as shown in Figure F-15, displaying the different types of files and data stored when you browse the Web.

3. **Click the** Temporary Internet files check box **to select it, if necessary, then click the** Preserve Favorites website data check box **to select it, if necessary**

   These options delete the temporary Internet files from your computer, except for the ones in your Favorites, freeing disk space on your computer. The files are not placed in the Recycle Bin, so you need to be sure you want to delete them.

4. **Click the** History check box **to select it**

   This option deletes the list of Web sites you have recently visited and no longer need.

5. **Click** Delete

   The Delete Browsing History dialog box closes and the Internet Properties dialog box reopens with the General tab displayed.

6. **In the Browsing history section, click** Settings

   The Temporary Internet Files and History Settings dialog box opens, as shown in Figure F-16, displaying settings to customize the way temporary Internet files and history items are deleted.

7. **In the Temporary Internet Files section, click the** arrows **in the Disk space to use (8 – 1024MB) box as necessary until you reach 40 MB**

   Changing this amount decreases the space allocated to store temporary Internet files.

8. **In the History section, click the** arrows **in the Days to keep pages in history box as necessary until you reach 25**

   Changing this amount increases the number of days Internet Explorer builds the History list.

9. **Click** Cancel, **then click** OK

   The Temporary Internet Files and History Settings and Internet Properties dialog boxes close without saving changes, and the Network and Internet window reopens.

Securing Your Computer

FIGURE F-15: Delete Browsing History dialog box

Preserve Favorites website data check box

Temporary Internet files check box

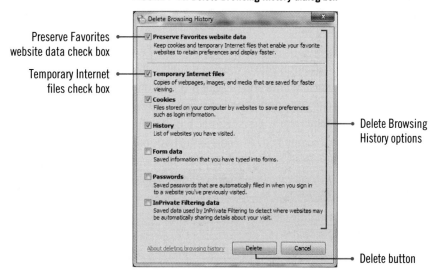

Delete Browsing History options

Delete button

FIGURE F-16: Temporary Internet Files and History Settings dialog box

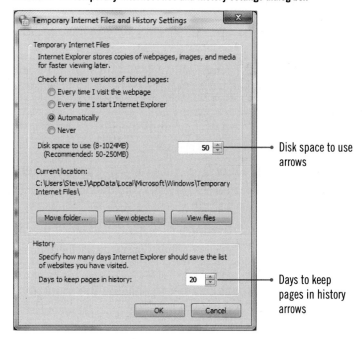

Disk space to use arrows

Days to keep pages in history arrows

Encrypting files using BitLocker

If you have an internal or external hard drive, or removable drive, you can use BitLocker to encrypt the entire system drive, including the Windows system files needed to start up and log on to Windows 7. A **partition** is a section of a disk drive that behaves like a separate drive. Partitioning is particularly useful if you run more than one operating system. BitLocker helps protect your system and blocks hackers from accessing sensitive information. When you add files to your computer, BitLocker automatically encrypts them. When you copy files to another location, the files are decrypted. After you turn on BitLocker, it's critical that you create a recovery password, because BitLocker locks up the entire drive if it detects a problem during start-up. To use BitLocker, click the Start button, click Control Panel, click System and Security, click BitLocker Drive Encryption, click Turn On BitLocker for the drive you want to encrypt, follow the BitLocker setup wizard, then click the Close button. If the Turn On BitLocker button is not available, your drive configuration is not suitable for BitLocker. Click the Help button for more information.

Setting Parental Controls

The Parental Controls feature helps you manage your child's access to the Internet, programs, and files on your computer. Parental Controls allows you to set limits on Web access, the amount of time spent logged on the computer, and which games and programs can be used. You can specify different settings for each user account on your computer, so the level of access you want for each individual can be set accordingly. You can also review activity reports on a periodic basis to check what your children are specifically doing during their time on the computer. In addition to the basic parental controls, you can download and install additional online Web site filters and activity reports. With Windows Live Family Safety from Microsoft, you can limit searches, monitor and block or allow Web sites, and limit communication in Windows Live Spaces, Messenger, or Hotmail. During a visit to your Quest Specialty Travel office, your child wants to use your computer so you want to set up Parental Controls.

STEPS

Before you complete the steps in this lesson, you need to have access to a standard user account on your computer. See your instructor or technical support person.

1. **In the task pane, click the User Accounts and Family Safety link, then click Parental Controls**

    The User Account Control window may open, asking you for permission to make changes to the security or personal settings.

2. **If prompted, click Continue, or type the administrator password, then click OK**

    The Parental Controls window opens. See Table F-2 for a description of the different type of controls you can set.

3. **Click the standard user account specified by your instructor or administrator**

    The User Controls window opens.

4. **Under Parental Controls, click the On, enforce current settings option button**

    Selecting this option enables Parental Controls and collects information about computer usage by the user, as shown in Figure F-17.

5. **Under Windows Settings, click Allow and block specific programs**

    The Application Restrictions window opens, displaying options to allow all programs or only the ones you want to allow.

6. **Click the <account name> can only use the programs I allow option button**

    The Application Restrictions window opens, as shown in Figure F-18, displaying options to block specific programs.

7. **Click Cancel, click OK, then click the Close button** [x] **in the Parental Controls window**

    The Parental Controls window closes without saving changes.

TABLE F-2: Parental Control settings

settings	description
Time limits	Click and drag the hours you want to block or allow.
Games	Select options to block or allow games based on ratings or content.
Allow and block specific programs	Select an option to use all programs or only approved programs.
Windows Live Family Safety	Select options to block or allow Web sites or communications with contacts and get reports for online activity; available when Family Safety is downloaded and installed from Windows Live Essentials.

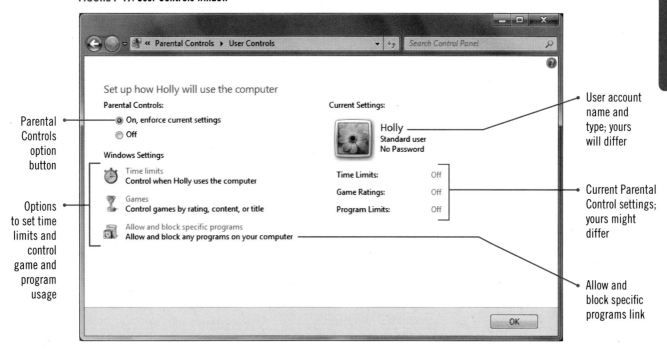

FIGURE F-17: User Controls window

Parental Controls option button

Options to set time limits and control game and program usage

User account name and type; yours will differ

Current Parental Control settings; yours might differ

Allow and block specific programs link

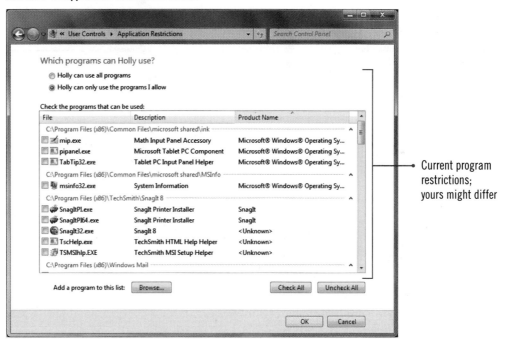

FIGURE F-18: Application Restrictions window

Current program restrictions; yours might differ

Creating a new user account

There are two main types of user accounts: administrator and standard. The **administrator** account is for the person who needs to make changes to anything on the computer as well as manage user accounts. A **standard** account is for people who need to manage personal files and run programs. If you have an administrator account, you can create a new user account or delete an existing one. When you add a new user to your computer, Windows creates a separate identity, allowing the user to keep files completely private and customize the operating system with personal preferences. The name you assign to the user appears on the Welcome screen and on the Start menu when the user is logged on. The steps to add and delete user accounts differ, depending on whether your computer is part of a company or personal network. To create a new user account on a personal network, click the Start button, click Control Panel, click Add or remove user accounts, grant permission to continue, click Create a new account, type a username, select an account type, click Create Account, then click Close.

Practice

Concepts Review

For current SAM information including versions and content details, visit SAM Central (http://samcentral.course.com). If you have a SAM user profile, you may have access to hands-on instruction, practice, and assessment of the skills covered in this unit. Since we support various versions of SAM throughout the life of this text, you will want to check with your instructor for instructions and the correct URL/Web site to access those assignments.

Match the statements below with the elements labeled in the screen shown in Figure F-19.

FIGURE F-19

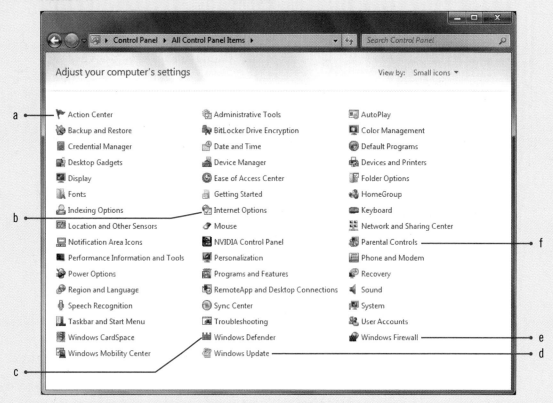

1. Which element allows you to view essential protection settings?
2. Which element allows you to limit computer time?
3. Which element protects your privacy?
4. Which element prevents access to your computer?
5. Which element provides malware protection?
6. Which element allows you to install Windows updates?

Match each term with the statement that best describes it.

7. **Spyware**
8. **Virus**
9. **Worm**
10. **Certificate**
11. **Firewall**

   a. A program that tries to collect information about you
   b. A security system that creates a protective barrier between your computer and others on the Internet
   c. A program you open that infects your computer
   d. A program you don't need to open for it to infect your computer
   e. A statement that verifies the identity of a person or the security of a Web site

   Securing Your Computer

Concepts Review (Continued)

Select the best answer from the list of choices.

12. **Which of the following is NOT considered malware?**

    a. Virus

    b. SpyNet

    c. Worm

    d. Trojan horse

13. **Which of the following programs protects you from viruses?**

    a. Antivirus

    b. SpyNet

    c. Windows Defender

    d. Windows Update

14. **Which of the following creates a protective barrier between your computer and the Internet?**

    a. Definition

    b. Firewall

    c. Content Advisor

    d. Digital ID

15. **Which of the following is NOT a security zone?**

    a. Internet

    b. Intranet

    c. Trusted sites

    d. Restricted sites

16. **Which of the following are types of certificates?**

    a. Personal and Web site

    b. Trusted and approved

    c. Trusted and personal

    d. Personal and approved

17. **Which of the following is also known as a certificate?**

    a. Definition

    b. Digital ID

    c. Cookie

    d. Port

18. **Which of the following is NOT an Internet file cleanup operation?**

    a. Cookies

    b. History

    c. Favorites

    d. Passwords

19. **Which of the following is NOT a parental control?**

    a. Web restrictions

    b. Games

    c. Time limits

    d. Definitions

Skills Review

1. **Explore the Action Center.**

   a. Open the Control Panel.

   b. Open the System and Security window.

   c. Open the Action Center window.

   d. Expand each of the Action Center areas.

   e. Go back to the System and Security window.

2. **Manage Windows Firewall.**

   a. Open the Windows Firewall window.

   b. Open the Allowed Programs dialog box.

   c. Change program exceptions to deselect Windows Media Player Network Sharing Service (Internet).

   d. Go back to the System and Security window.

3. **Get Automatic Updates.**

   a. Open the Windows Update window.

   b. View the update history.

   c. Open the Change settings window.

   d. Check for updates. (Stop: Don't install any updates without permission.)

   e. Go back to the System and Security window.

Skills Review (Continued)

4. **Defend against malicious software.**
   a. Open the Windows Defender window. (*Hint*: Use the Search Control Panel box.)
   b. Check for new definitions if necessary.
   c. If prompted, grant permission to make security changes.
   d. Perform a full scan.
   e. Display Windows Defender tools.
   f. View Allowed items and options.
   g. Close the Windows Defender window.

5. **Set up Internet security.**
   a. Open the Network and Internet window.
   b. Open the Internet Properties dialog box and display security settings.
   c. Change the security level.
   d. Display content settings, then open the Content Advisor dialog box.
   e. If prompted, grant permission to make security changes.
   f. Change the content rating for Violence.
   g. Close the Content Advisor dialog box without applying any changes.

6. **Protect your Internet identity.**
   a. Display content settings in the Internet Properties dialog box.
   b. Open the Certificates dialog box.
   c. Import the file **WIN F-2.cer** from the drive and folder where you store your Data Files into the Other People tab.
   d. Remove the certificate.
   e. Close the Certificates dialog box.

7. **Protect your Internet privacy.**
   a. Display privacy settings in the Internet Properties dialog box.
   b. Change the privacy level to Low.
   c. Close the Internet Properties dialog box without accepting any changes.
   d. Start Internet Explorer.
   e. Visit a Web page other than your home page and get a Web page privacy report.
   f. Close the report and Internet Explorer.

8. **Delete Internet information.**
   a. Open the Internet Properties dialog box and display the Delete Browsing History dialog box.
   b. Delete temporary Internet files, yet preserve Favorites website data.
   c. Delete cookies.
   d. Close the Delete Browsing History dialog box.
   e. Open the Settings dialog box for Browsing history, review the settings, then close it without making any changes.
   f. Close the Internet Properties dialog box.

9. **Set Parental Controls.**
   a. Open the Parental Controls window.
   b. If prompted, grant permission to make security changes.
   c. Select a user account to change parental controls.
   d. Set time restrictions.
   e. View the Application Restrictions window, then close it without making any changes.
   f. Close the Parental Controls window.

Independent Challenge 1

You work at a small pet shop supply company called PetStop. Because you have some experience with computers and the Internet, your manager asks you to set Internet security and privacy settings for the company computers.

a. Open the Internet Properties dialog box from the Control Panel.

b. Display the security settings, then change the security level for the Internet to High.

c. Display privacy settings, then change the privacy level to High.

d. Delete cookies and temporary Internet files, yet preserve Favorites.

e. Close the Internet Properties dialog box and the Control Panel without accepting any changes.

Independent Challenge 2

You are the network administrator at Robotz, Inc., a toy company that specializes in the production and distribution of robots. You want employees to update their computer systems with the latest Windows 7 system updates. You access Windows Update and determine which components you want the employees to install.

a. Open the Windows Update window from the Control Panel.

b. Check for updates.

c. View Installed Updates.

d. View the update history.

e. Check Windows Update settings for your computer.

f. Close the Windows Update window and the Control Panel.

Advanced Challenge Exercise

- Enable the option to require users to press [Ctrl][Alt][Delete] at the Welcome screen.
- Lock the computer.
- Press [Ctrl][Alt][Delete] and log on to the computer.
- Disable the option to require users to press [Ctrl][Alt][Delete].

Independent Challenge 3

You manage an international computer security company called Secure-One International. You want to test out your security system with noncertified certificates. Gary O'Neal, an employee, was asked to create his own certificate and try to pass it off as an authorized certificate from a trusted Certification Authority.

a. Open the Internet Properties dialog box from the Control Panel.

b. Display the content settings, then open the Certificates dialog box.

c. Import the file **WIN F-3.cer** from the drive and folder where you store your Data Files into the Other People tab.

d. Remove the Gary O'Neal certificate, then close the Certificates dialog box.

e. Close the Internet Properties dialog box and the Control Panel without accepting any changes.

Real Life Independent Challenge

Even if you don't have children of your own, you might have visitors one day with children who want to play games on your computer. Rather than just letting them have access to your entire system, it would be better to set up a standard user account with Parental Controls.

a. Open the User Accounts and Family Safety window from the Control Panel.

b. Set up Parental Controls for a standard user.

c. Turn on Parental Controls.

d. Open the Application Restrictions window, select the wordpad.exe check box, then close the window.

Real Life Independent Challenge (Continued)

Advanced Challenge Exercise

- Open the Time Restrictions window.
- Block 6 to 12 Monday through Friday, then close the window.
- Open the Game Controls window.
- Allow the user to play games.
- Set the Hearts game to Always Block, then close the window.

e. With permission from your network administrator, switch to the standard user, if necessary, open the WordPad and Hearts programs to view the parental controls in place, then switch back to the administrator.

f. Restore the parental controls for the standard user.

g. Turn off Parental Controls.

h. Close the Parental Controls window.

Visual Workshop

Re-create the screen shown in Figure F-20, which shows an Application Restrictions window for a user account; your specific result will differ.

FIGURE F-20

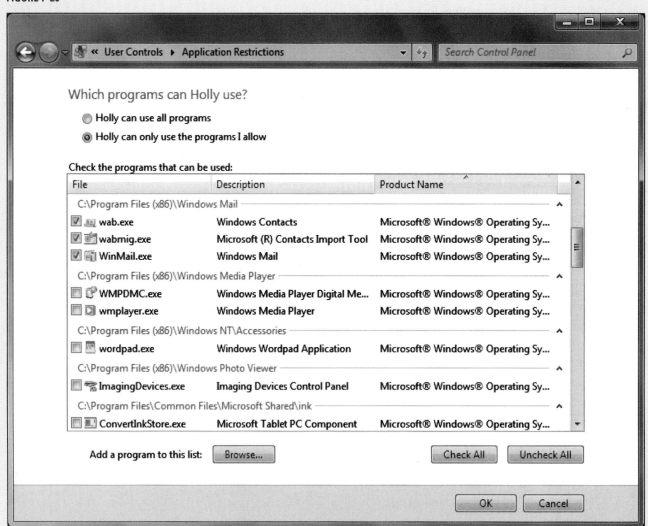

UNIT G
Windows 7

Exploring the Internet with Microsoft Internet Explorer

Files You Will Need:

No file needed.

The **Internet** is a global collection of millions of computers linked together to share information. Using the Internet, computer users can share many types of information, including text, graphics, sounds, videos, and computer programs. The **Web** (also known as the **World Wide Web** or **WWW**) is a part of the Internet that consists of Web sites located on different computers around the world. A **Web site** contains Web pages linked together to make searching for information on the Internet easier. **Web pages** are specially formatted documents that contain highlighted words, phrases, and graphics called **hyperlinks** (or simply **links**) that open other Web pages when you click them. Some Web pages contain **frames**, which are windows within a Web page to display other Web pages or content. **Web browsers** are software programs that you use to "surf the Web," or display and navigate Web pages. This unit features **Microsoft Internet Explorer 8**, a popular browser from Microsoft that comes with Windows 7. Keisha Lane, Vice President of Operations for Quest Specialty Travel, asked you to use the Web to evaluate the company Web site. You want to find Web sites for other travel companies to see if there are any elements on those sites that Quest Specialty Travel should consider adding to its own site.

OBJECTIVES

Connect to the Internet

Open a Web page and follow links

Use tabs to browse Web pages

Change your home page

Search the Web

Add a Web page and Slices to Favorites

View and subscribe to a feed

Get and use Accelerators

Block pop-ups and filter phishing

Connecting to the Internet

The Internet's physical structure includes telephone lines, cables, satellites, and other telecommunications media, as depicted in Figure G-1. Universities and large companies are most likely connected to the Internet via high-speed cable wiring that transmits data very quickly. In many areas, **DSL (digital subscriber line)** provides a completely digital connection using telephone lines, whereas **cable modems** provide one using cable television lines. DSL and cable modems, also known as **broadband** connections, are continually connected to the Internet and use a network setup. In remote areas, or if you want a lower-cost alternative to a broadband connection, you can create a connection with a dial-up modem and telephone line, which needs to be established each time you connect to the Internet. You can avoid using physical telephone or cable lines by using a **wireless connection**, which uses radio waves or microwaves to maintain communications. Data travels more slowly over telephone wires than over digital lines and cable modems. Whether you use a telephone line, DSL line, cable modem, or wireless signal, Windows can help you establish a connection between your computer and the Internet. First, you need to select an **ISP (Internet service provider)**, which is a company that provides Internet access through servers connected directly to the Internet. Your ISP sets you up with an **Internet account** and connection information that provides you Internet access for a monthly rate. ▓▓▞▞▞ Quest Specialty Travel already has an ISP account. You want to set up an Internet connection so you can browse the Web.

STEPS

> **TROUBLE**
> If you connect to the Internet through a network, follow your instructor's or technical support person's directions.

1. **Click the** Network icon 🖳 **(for broadband) or** 📶 **(for wireless) on the taskbar, then click the** Open Network and Sharing Center link
   The Network and Sharing Center window opens.

2. **Under Change your networking settings, click the** Set up a new connection or network link, **click** Connect to the Internet, **if necessary, then click** Next
   The Connect to the Internet Wizard dialog box opens, displaying connection options.

> **TROUBLE**
> If not all the options are available, click the Show connection options that this computer is not set up to use check box to select it.

3. **Click** Set up a new connection, **or** Set up a new connection anyway **if you are already connected to the Internet**
   The next screen in the wizard asks you to choose how to connect to the Internet, as shown in Figure G-2, either wireless, broadband (cable or DSL), or dial-up.

4. **Click the option with the way you want to connect:** Broadband (PPPoE) **or** Dial-up
   The next screen in the Connect to the Internet Wizard asks you to type the information from your Internet service provider (ISP). Your ISP documentation provides you with a username and password.

5. **In the User name text box, type your username, press [Tab], then type your password in the Password text box**
   As you type the password, bullets appear to protect others from seeing it instead of characters unless the Show characters check box is selected.

6. **If you are creating a dial-up connection, type the area code and telephone number of your ISP in the Dial-up phone number text box**
   Your ISP documentation provides the numbers you should use.

7. **Click the** Remember this password check box **to clear it, if necessary**
   This option remembers your password, so you don't have to enter it to access the Internet when you connect. A default connection name appears in the Connection name text box. Keep the default name.

8. **Click the** Allow other people to use this connection check box **to clear it, if necessary**
   This option allows other users on your network to connect to the Internet using your Internet connection.

9. **Click** Connect **to complete and establish the Internet connection**

10. **If the connection is successful, click** Close; **otherwise click** Cancel

Exploring the Internet with Microsoft Internet Explorer

FIGURE G-1: Structure of the Internet

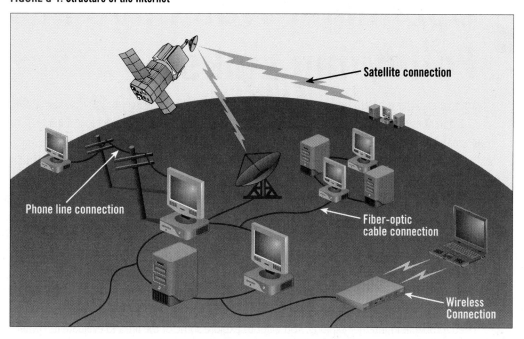

Satellite connection

Phone line connection

Fiber-optic cable connection

Wireless Connection

FIGURE G-2: Selecting an Internet connection option

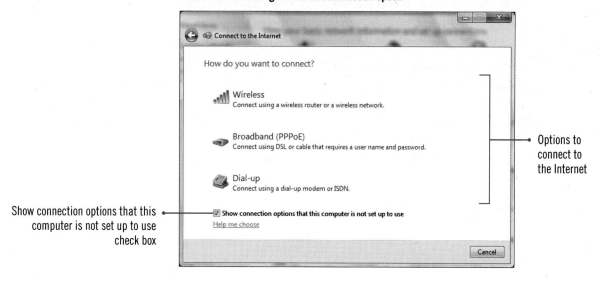

Show connection options that this computer is not set up to use check box

Options to connect to the Internet

Sharing an Internet connection

If you have a home or small office network using Windows, you can share an Internet connection with all the computers on the network using one connection. If you are setting up a connection, you can enable Internet connection sharing by selecting the Allow other people to use this connection check box during the Connect to the Internet Wizard process. If your connection to the Internet is already set up, open the Control Panel, click the Network and Internet link, then click the Network and Sharing Center link. Click the Change adapter settings link in the left pane, right-click your connection icon, click Properties, click Continue, if necessary, to gain access to the properties, click the Sharing tab, click the Allow other network users to connect through this computer's Internet connection check box to select it, then click OK.

Opening a Web Page and Following Links

Internet Explorer is a Web browser that you use to view, print, and search for information on the Internet. Table G-1 describes the various elements of the Internet Explorer window. In Internet Explorer, you can open a Web page quickly and easily by entering a Web address in the Address bar. A **Web address** is a unique place on the Internet where a Web page resides. A Web address is also called a **URL**, which stands for **Uniform Resource Locator**. Web pages connect to each other through links that you can follow to obtain more information about a topic, as shown in Figure G-3. A **link** is specially formatted text or a graphic that you can click to move to another location on the same Web page, or to a different Web page altogether. To follow a link, simply click the highlighted word, phrase, or graphic. The mouse pointer changes to 🖑 when it is over a link. If you change your mind, or if a Web page takes too long to **load**, or open on the screen, you can click the Stop button ✖ on the Address bar. If you stop a Web page while it is loading, and the page doesn't completely open, you can click the Refresh button 🔄 on the Address bar to update the screen. If an older Web page doesn't display correctly, you can click the Compatibility button 🖹 to fix it. ▰▰ To evaluate the Quest Specialty Travel Web site, you need to open it in Internet Explorer. You want to explore some of the links to evaluate its content.

STEPS

TROUBLE
If the Set Up Windows Internet Explorer 8 dialog box opens, click Next, enable Suggested Sites, click Next, enable Express settings, then click Finish.

1. **Click the Internet Explorer button 🅮 on the taskbar**
   Internet Explorer opens, displaying the default home page in a tab in the browser window. The **home page**, the main Web page around which a Web site is built, appears when you start Internet Explorer.

2. **Click anywhere in the Address bar at the top of the window**
   The current address is highlighted, and any text you type will replace the current address.

3. **Type www.questspecialtytravel.com, then press [Enter]**
   When you enter a Web address, Internet Explorer automatically inserts "http://" in the Address bar before the URL. The status bar displays the connection process. After downloading for a few seconds, the Web page appears in the document window. To make the site easier to identify, the domain name is highlighted in black while the remainder of the URL appears in gray in the Address bar.

QUICK TIP
To open a Web page in a new tab in the browser window, enter the URL in the Address bar, press and hold [Alt], then press Enter.

4. **Move the pointer over Destinations, as shown in Figure G-3**
   "Destinations" is a link. When you move the pointer over a link, the pointer changes to 🖑, and the address of the link appears in the status bar.

5. **Click Destinations**
   The Internet Explorer logo on the tab changes to the busy icon ⊙ as you access the Web page and then changes back when the new Web page appears. The Destinations page on the Quest Specialty Travel site opens in the document window.

6. **Move the pointer over the Quest Travel logo in the upper-left corner so that the pointer changes to 🖑, then click the Quest Travel logo**
   The Quest Specialty Travel home page opens in the document window.

7. **Click the Back button ⊙ next to the Address bar**
   The Web page you viewed immediately before the home page—the Destinations page—reopens in the document window.

8. **Click the Forward button ⊙ next to the Address bar**
   The Quest Specialty Travel home page reopens in the browser window.

9. **Click the Recent Pages list arrow ▾ next to the Address bar, then click Quest Specialty Travel :: Destinations**
   The Destinations page opens in the browser window again.

Title bar
Back and Forward buttons and Recent Pages list arrow
Internet Explorer logo
Favorites bar
Current tab
Status bar

Search box
Command bar
Web page address in the Address bar
Quest Travel logo
Pointer when positioned over a link

TABLE G-1: Elements of the Internet Explorer window

option	description
Title bar	Displays the name of the Web page and browser you are using at the top of the window
Navigation buttons	Provides buttons to view recently visited Web pages
Address bar	Opens or displays the address of the current Web page or the contents of a local or network computer drive
Search box	Displays link buttons to Web pages on the Internet or to documents on a local or network drive
Favorites bar	Provides buttons and links to view or add favorites, feeds, history, suggested sites, and get add-ons
Tabbed window	Displays Web page in a tabbed window; allows you to display many different Web pages at one time; you might need to scroll down the page to view its entire contents
Command bar	Provides buttons for easy access to the most commonly used commands in Internet Explorer
Status bar	Displays information about both your connection progress with new Web pages that you open and locations of the links in the document window as you move your mouse pointer over them; you can also change the view percentage to zoom in and out within a Web page and set security options

Understanding a URL

A Web site consists of a main Web page and a collection of related Web pages located on a computer with a connection to the Internet. Each Web site has a unique URL that is typically composed of four parts: the **protocol** (a set of rules that allows computers to exchange information), the location of the Web site, the name of the Web site, and a suffix that identifies the type of site. At the end of the Web site name and suffix, another slash may appear, followed by one or more folder names and a filename. A URL begins with a protocol, followed by a colon, two slashes, the location of the Web site, a dot, the name of the Web site, a dot, and a suffix. For example, in the address *http://www.questspecialtytravel.com/destination.html*, the protocol is *http* (Hypertext Transfer Protocol), the location of the Web site is *www* (World Wide Web), the name of the Web site is *questspecialtytravel*, the suffix is *com* (a commercial organization), and the Web page file is *destination.html*.

Using Tabs to Browse Web Pages

As you open Web sites, you can display each site in a separate tab, so you can view multiple Web sites in a single window. You can open Web pages in new tabs by using the redesigned New Tab page with links—use an Accelerator, browse the Web privately, reopen closed tabs, and reopen your last browsing session—to help you get started quickly. Once you open a tab, you can click to another one to quickly switch between tabs or click the Close button on the tab to exit it. If you prefer a visual way to switch between tabs, you can use **Quick Tabs**, which displays thumbnails of each page currently open in a tab, to open and close Web pages. When you open a new tab from another tab, the new tab is grouped together and color coded, which you can always change or ungroup later. You can right-click a tab to quickly perform a variety of operations, such as close a tab or tab group, ungroup a tab, refresh tabs, open a new tab, re-open the last tab closed, or see a list of all recently closed tabs and reopen any or all of them. ▟▟▟▟ You want to visit the Web site of another travel company so you can compare the functionality and content of the Quest Specialty Travel site with it.

STEPS

1. **Point to the New Tab button to the right of the Quest Specialty Travel:: Destinations tab**
   The New Tab icon ▢ appears on the New Tab button.

2. **Click ▢**
   A new tab appears, displaying information about using tabs in Internet Explorer. The URL "about:Tabs" is selected in the Address bar. The Destinations page on the Quest Specialty Travel site remains open in the other tab behind the new tab.

TROUBLE
If this travel Web page is not available or couldn't be found, type another Web page location and use it through-out this lesson.

3. **Type www.travel.com in the Address bar, then press [Enter]**
   The home page for Travel.com, a Web site that provides a service for making travel arrangements, opens in the new tab. When you type a Web address in the Address bar, a feature called **AutoComplete** displays a list of possible matches from history, Favorites, or addresses you've typed previously. If a suggestion in the list matches the Web address you're typing, a drop-down list appears with the items highlighted in blue. You can click the suggestion in the list you want to enter or continue to type.

4. **Click the Quest Specialty Travel:: Destinations tab**
   The Destinations page on the Quest Specialty Travel site reappears as the active tab, as shown in Figure G-4.

QUICK TIP
To open a Web page in a new tab without making it the active tab, press and hold [Ctrl], then click the link to the page you want to open.

5. **Press and hold [Ctrl][Shift], then click About Us**
   The About Us page for Quest Specialty Travel opens in a new colored tab grouped with the tab from which it was opened and becomes the active tab. When you have more than one tab open, the Quick Tabs button and the Tab list arrow become available to the left of the tabs. You can use these to switch between tabs quickly. Clicking the Quick Tabs button displays a thumbnail of each open Web page that you can click to switch among tabs, while the Tab list arrow provides a menu list of open tabs.

6. **Click the Quick Tabs button ▦**
   Quick Tabs displays a thumbnail of each open tab, as shown in Figure G-5.

QUICK TIP
To ungroup a tab, right-click the tab in a group, then click Ungroup This Tab.

7. **Click the Travel.com thumbnail to close Quick Tabs and switch to that tab, then click the Close button ⊠ on the Travel.com tab**
   The Travel.com tab closes, and the About Us page for Quest Specialty Travel appears in the active tab.

8. **Click ⊠ on the Quest Specialty Travel:: About Us tab**
   The About Us tab closes, and the Destinations page for Quest Specialty Travel reopens.

9. **Click the Quest Specialty Travel link**
   The Quest Specialty Travel home page reopens.

Exploring the Internet with Microsoft Internet Explorer

FIGURE G-4: Web page opened in a tabbed window

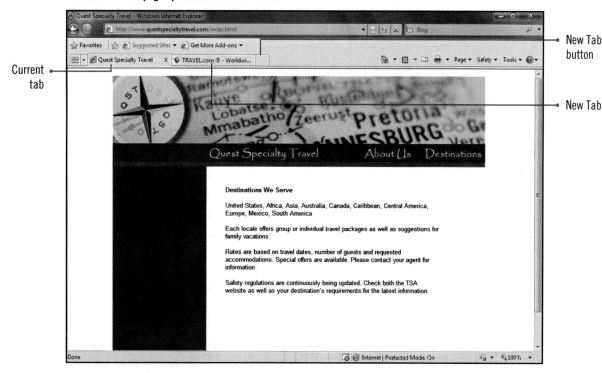

Current tab

New Tab button

New Tab

FIGURE G-5: Switch between tabs with Quick Tabs

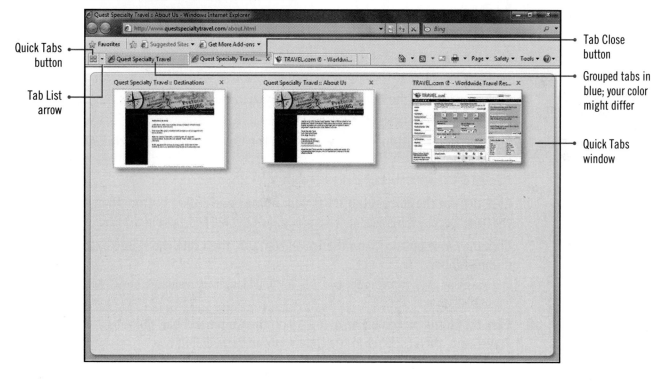

Quick Tabs button

Tab List arrow

Tab Close button

Grouped tabs in blue; your color might differ

Quick Tabs window

Using InPrivate browsing

If you're using a computer at a friend's house, another office, a hotel, or an Internet café and you don't want to leave any trace or evidence of your Web activity, you can use InPrivate browsing. **InPrivate browsing** doesn't retain or keep track of browsing history, searches, temporary Internet files, form data, cookies, or usernames and passwords. You can start InPrivate browsing from a new tab or use the Safety button on the Command bar. When you start InPrivate browsing, Internet Explorer opens a new browser window. An InPrivate indicator icon appears in the Address bar when the featured is turned on. When you're done, simply close the browser window to end the InPrivate browsing session.

Changing Your Home Page

A home page is referred to several different ways on the Web—one way in a browser and another way in a Web site. A **home page** in a browser is the page that opens when you start the program, whereas a home page in a Web site is the first page that appears when you open it. The home page also loads when you click the Home button 🏠 on the Command bar. When you start Internet Explorer for the first time, the default home page is the Microsoft Network (MSN) Web site, unless the standard Windows 7 installation was modified by a third party, such as your network administrator or the computer manufacturer. You can change your home page if you want a different page to appear when you start Internet Explorer. You can also display one or more pages in tabs as the home page. You can choose one of the millions of Web pages available through the Internet, or you can select a particular file on your hard drive. As you continue to research the design and features of other travel Web sites, you decide to change your home page to Quest Specialty Travel, and then add another travel Web page to display in a second tab as one of your home pages.

STEPS

1. **Click the Home button list arrow 🏠▾ on the Command bar, then click Add or Change Home Page**

   The Add or Change Home Page dialog box opens, displaying the address of the current Web page and options to use this page as your only home page or add this page to your home page tabs.

2. **Click the Use this webpage as your only home page option button, as shown in Figure G-6, then click Yes**

   The Quest Specialty Travel home page is set as the home page.

3. **Click the About Us link, then click the Home button 🏠 on the Command bar**

   The Quest Specialty Travel home page opens in the document window.

TROUBLE
If this travel Web page is not available or couldn't be found, type another Web page location and use it throughout this lesson.

4. **Click anywhere in the Address bar, type www.travel.com, then press [Alt][Enter]**

   The Travel.com home page opens in a new tab.

5. **Click the Home button list arrow 🏠▾ on the Command bar, then click Add or Change Home Page**

   The Add or Change Home Page dialog box opens again.

6. **Click the Use the current tab set as your home page option button, then click Yes**

   The Quest Specialty Travel and the Travel.com home pages will both open in two tabs.

7. **Click the Close button ⊠ on the Travel.com tab, then click the Home button 🏠 on the Command bar**

   The two home pages appear in the two tabs. If you no longer want multiple home pages, you can remove one or all of them.

8. **Click the Home button list arrow 🏠▾ on the Command bar, point to Remove, click Travel.com, then click Yes in the Delete Home Page dialog box**

   Travel.com is removed from the list of home pages.

9. **Click the Tools button Tools▾ on the Command bar, click Internet Options to open the Internet Options dialog box, as shown in Figure G-7, click Use default on the General tab or type the URL of your original home page, then click OK**

   The home page is restored to the default MSN Web page at *www.msn.com* or your original home page URL.

FIGURE G-6: Add or Change Home Page dialog box

Current Web page

Home page options

FIGURE G-7: Internet Options dialog box

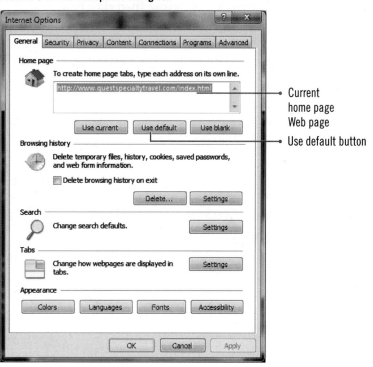

Current home page Web page

Use default button

Viewing and maintaining a History list

Sometimes you run across a great Web site and simply forget to add it to the Favorites Center. With Internet Explorer, there's no need to try to remember all the sites you visit. The History feature keeps track of where you've been by date, site, most visited, or order visited today. To view the History list, click the Favorites button on the Favorites bar, click the History tab, then click a day or week in the Favorites Center pane to expand the list of Web sites visited. You can click the History list arrow to search the list, or sort the list by date, site, most visited, or order visited today. Internet Explorer deletes the History list periodically based on the settings you specify on the General tab of the Internet Options dialog box. You can also use commands in the Internet Options dialog box to delete the History list. Click the Tools button, click Internet Options, then click the General tab. Select the Delete browsing history on exit check box to automatically delete the History list, or click Delete, select the History check box, then click Delete to delete the list manually.

Searching the Web

You can find all kinds of information on the Web. The best way to find information on the Web is to use a search engine. A **search engine** is a program provided by a **search provider** you access directly from Internet Explorer or through a Web site and use to search through a collection of Internet information to find what you want. Many search engines are available on the Web, such as Bing (default) by Microsoft, Wikipedia, Google, and Yahoo!, which you can add on to Internet Explorer. When you perform a search, you submit words or phrases, known as **keywords** that best describe what you want to retrieve to the search engine using the Search box to the right of the Address bar. As you type in the Search box, the search engine displays a menu list of text and visual suggestions for the matched sites. These matched sites are sometimes called **hits**. The search results of different search engines vary. If you're looking for information on a page, you can use the Find toolbar to help highlight the text you want to find. ▓▓▓▓ You decide to use Bing to search for and examine another travel-related Web site for your competitive review.

STEPS

QUICK TIP
To specify a default search provider, click the Search box list arrow, click Manage Search Providers, select a provider, click Set as default, then click Close.

1. **Click the Search box list arrow, then click Bing**

   Before you start a search, you should select the search engine you want to use for this session, or specify the default you want to use. Bing is selected as the search engine for this session. With the Search box, you can enter keywords to search for the information you want.

2. **Click in the Search box next to the Address bar or press [Ctrl][E]**

   The more specific your search criteria or keyword in the Search box, the better the list of matches you will receive from the search engine. Use specific words, eliminate common words, such as "a" or "the", and use quotation marks for specific phrases.

QUICK TIP
To add more search providers, click the Search box list arrow, click Find More Providers, then click Add to Internet Explorer for the provider you want.

3. **Type africa**

   A menu appears, as shown in Figure G-8, displaying suggestions based on your search criteria. With the keywords in the Search box, you can use the Search button 🔍 in the Search box or press [Enter] to display the results in the current tab, or press [Alt][Enter] to display the results in a new tab.

4. **Press [Alt][Enter]**

   The search engine, Bing, retrieves and displays a list of links to Web pages that contain your keywords in a new tab. The total number of Web sites found is listed at the top. The search results appear in order of decreasing relevance. If the search results return too many hits, you can narrow the search by adding more keywords. As you add more keywords, the search engine finds fewer, more specific Web pages that contain all of those words.

5. **Click the Search box list arrow 🔍▾, then click Find on this Page**

   The Find toolbar opens below the tabs, displaying find options, such as Previous, Next, and Highlight All Matches, Match Whole Word Only, and Match Case, and the number of matches. The search keyword is highlighted on the page, as shown in Figure G-9.

QUICK TIP
To use the Address bar to search, type go, find, or ? followed by a space and a word or phrase in the Address bar, and then press Enter.

6. **Click any link in the list of matches**

   The corresponding Web page appears in the tabbed window. You can click links on this Web site to jump to other related Web sites.

7. **Click the Close button ⊠ on the Find toolbar**

   The Find toolbar closes and the search text highlighting is turned off.

8. **Click the Back button ◔, then click the Quest Specialty Travel tab**

   You return to the Quest Specialty Travel home page and the Search results page remains open.

FIGURE G-8: Search box with keyword and visual suggestions

Search box with keyword

Search button

Search box list arrow

Visual suggestions; your list might differ

FIGURE G-9: Highlighted search results with the Find toolbar

Search results in a separate tabbed window

Close button on Find toolbar

Text to find and highlight on the page

Find toolbar

Search results with highlighted keyword; yours might differ

Previewing and printing a Web page

Web pages are designed for viewing on a computer screen, but you can also print all or part of one. Before you print, you should verify that the page looks the way you want. Print Preview shows you exactly how your Web page will look on the printed page. To preview a Web page, click the Print button arrow on the Command bar, then click Print

Preview. To print the current Web page with the current print settings, click the Print button on the Command bar. If you want to set print options using the Print dialog box, click the Print button arrow on the Command bar, then click Print.

Adding a Web Page and Slices to Favorites

Rather than memorizing URLs or keeping a handwritten list of Web pages you want to visit, you can use the **Favorites Center** to store and organize Web addresses. When you display a Web page in your browser window that you want to use at a later time, you can add the Web page to your list of Favorites in the Favorites Center. If you have opened a set of tabs, you can save them as a tab group to Favorites. If your list of Favorites grows long, you can delete Favorites you don't visit anymore or organize Favorites into folders. If you frequently visit a Web page for specific updates, such as sports scores or stock quotes, you can use Web Slices to have Internet Explorer let you know when updates are available. A **Web Slice** is a portion of a Web page that lets you know when an update is available. If a Web Slice is available on a page, a green Web Slice button appears in the Command bar, similar to an RSS feed. When you click the button, the Web Slice appears on the Favorites bar, where it becomes bold when an update is available. You want to add the Quest Specialty Travel Web page to your Favorites list.

STEPS

QUICK TIP

To add a Web page as a Favorite to a new or existing folder, click the Favorites button on the Favorites bar, click the Add to Favorites button, select an existing folder or click New Folder to create one, then click Add.

1. **Click the Add to Favorites Bar button on the Favorites bar**

   The Quest Specialty Travel Web page is added to the Favorites bar and stored in the Favorites Center.

2. **Click anywhere in the Address bar, type www.msn.com, then press [Enter]**

   The MSN home page replaces the Quest Specialty Travel home page in the tabbed window. When you display a Web page with a Web Slice, the Add Web Slice button appears on the Command bar. You can click the button arrow to display a list of available Web Slices as well as feeds.

3. **Click the Add Web Slices button list arrow on the Command bar, then click an available Web Slice on the menu**

   The Internet Explorer dialog box to add a Web Slice opens, as shown in Figure G-10.

4. **In the Internet Explorer dialog box, click Add to Favorites Bar**

   The Web Slice is added to the Favorites bar and the name appears bold to indicate an update is available.

QUICK TIP

To add a group of open tabs to the Favorites Center, click the Favorites button, click the Add to Favorites button arrow, click Add Current Tabs to Favorites, type a name in the Folder Name text box, then click Add.

5. **Click the Web Slice button you just added on the Favorites bar**

   A window opens, displaying a preview of the Web Slice, as shown in Figure G-10.

6. **Press [ESC] to close the preview window, then click the Favorites button on the Favorites bar**

   The Favorites Center pane opens on the left side of the tabbed window with your Favorites list. If you want to work with several Favorites at a time, you can pin the Favorites Center pane to the tabbed window.

7. **Click the Pin the Favorites Center button in the Favorites Center pane**

   The tabbed window resizes and the Favorites Center pane is pinned to the left of the tab. The Favorites list contains several folders, including the Favorites Bar folder that accompanies Internet Explorer.

QUICK TIP

You can also organize your Favorites in the Favorites Center by dragging a folder or site to a new location.

8. **Click the Favorites tab in the Favorites Center pane, click the Favorites Bar folder in the Favorites list, then point to the Quest Specialty Travel link**

   When you point to a Favorite or folder, a blue arrow appears to the right. Clicking the blue arrow rather than the link results in the Favorite opening in a new tabbed window.

9. **Click the Quest Specialty Travel link**

   The Quest Specialty Travel home page opens in the tabbed window, as shown in Figure G-11.

10. **Right-click the Quest Specialty Travel link in the Favorites list, click Delete, click Yes to delete it, right-click the Web Slice on the Favorites bar, click Delete, click Yes to delete it, then click the Close button in the Favorites Center pane**

    You return to the Quest Specialty Travel home page and the Search results page remains open.

Exploring the Internet with Microsoft Internet Explorer

FIGURE G-10: Adding a Web Slice to the Favorites bar

Add Web Slices button list arrow on Command bar

Web Slice on Favorites bar

Add Web Slices button on Web page

Add to Favorites Bar button

FIGURE G-11: Internet Explorer window with the Favorites Center pane displayed

Favorites Bar button

Favorites button

Favorites folder

Favorite link

Web Slice on Favorites bar

Blue arrow

Web site on Favorites bar

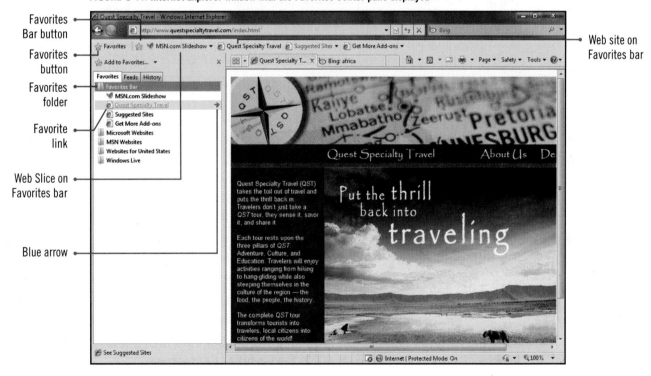

Using Suggested Sites

One way to find Web sites based on your browsing history is to use Suggested Sites, a free online service from Microsoft. To turn Suggested Sites on or off, click the Tools button on the Command bar, click Suggested Sites, then click Yes or No. When enabled, Microsoft uses your browsing history to give you suggestions. Simply click the Suggested Sites Web Slice on the Favorites bar to see a list of suggestions. The more places you visit, the better the suggested sites. You can also delete sites from your history. If you no longer want to use the service, you can choose to turn it off at any time.

Viewing and Subscribing to a Feed

A feed delivers frequently updated Web content to your browser on a continuous basis. A **feed**, also known as an RSS (Really Simple Syndication) feed, XML feed, syndicated content, or Web feed, is usually offered on a subscription basis and typically free of charge. A feed can deliver text content in the form of news headlines or blogs, or digital content in the form of pictures, audio, and video. When audio content is delivered (usually in the MP3 format), it's referred to as a **podcast**. When you visit a Web site, Internet Explorer checks for available feeds. If it locates a feed, the Feeds button changes color and plays a sound if an option is set in the Feed and Web Slice Settings dialog box. You can view an individual feed or subscribe to one to get content automatically. When you subscribe to a feed, Internet Explorer checks the Web site and downloads new content to keep you updated with the latest site content. You can also add an RSS feed to your Favorites bar, making it easy to view updates. Internet Explorer manages a common Feeds list, which allows other programs, such as e-mail, to access and use them. ░░░░░░ Because you are working with other travel-related Web sites, you want to subscribe to a travel feed, so you can always get the latest information.

STEPS

QUICK TIP
To check for feeds on a Web page, press [Alt][J].

1. **Click the tab with the Bing Search results**

   The Web page opens in the current tabbed window. The Feeds button on the Command bar changes to an orange color to indicate that there are feeds available on this page.

2. **Click the Feeds button 🔲 on the Command bar**

   A Web page opens, displaying a list of content you can read and subscribe to, similar to the one shown in Figure G-12. If multiple feeds are available, a list of feeds appears.

3. **Click the Subscribe to this feed link, then click the Add to Favorites Bar check box to select it in the Subscribe to this Feed dialog box**

   In the Subscribe to this Feed dialog box, as shown in Figure G-13, you can type a new name for the feed, create a folder to organize your feeds, which is similar to the way Favorites work, or add the feed to the Favorites bar.

4. **Click Subscribe**

   The Web page displays the message, "You've successfully subscribed to this feed!" The Web page feed appears on the Favorites bar and the feed name appears bold to indicate an update is available.

QUICK TIP
To change Feed options, click the Tools button on the Command bar, click Internet Options, click the Content tab, click Settings under Feeds and Web Slices, then select the options you want.

5. **Click the added feed button on the Favorites bar**

   A preview window appears, displaying a list of feeds, as shown in Figure G-13. An individual feed name appears bold to indicate an update is available. If you want to visit a feed, click the link on the menu.

6. **Press [ESC] to close the menu, then click the Close button 🔲 on the Bing Search results tab**

   The tabbed window closes and the Quest Specialty Travel home page opens in the current tabbed window.

7. **Click the Favorites button 🔲 on the Favorites bar, click the Pin the Favorites Center button 🔲, then click the Feeds tab in the Favorites Center pane**

   The current feeds appear in the Feeds list.

8. **Right-click the Bing Search results tab, click Delete, click Yes to confirm the deletion, then click the Close button 🔲 in the Favorites Center pane**

   The Favorites Center pane closes with the feed deleted from the Favorites Center.

9. **Right-click the added feed button on the Favorites bar, click Delete, then click Yes to delete it**

   The feed is deleted from the Favorites bar. The Quest Specialty Travel home page reappears.

Exploring the Internet with Microsoft Internet Explorer

FIGURE G-12: Displaying a Web page with a feed

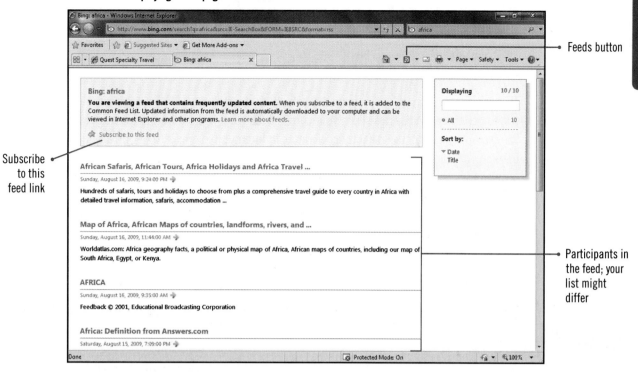

Feeds button

Subscribe to this feed link

Participants in the feed; your list might differ

FIGURE G-13: Subscribing to and viewing a feed

Stores feed in another folder in the Favorites Center

Name of feed; yours might differ

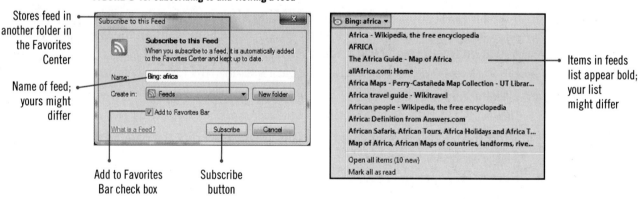

Items in feeds list appear bold; your list might differ

Add to Favorites Bar check box

Subscribe button

Saving a Web page and a Web graphic

If there is a Web page that contains content you don't want to update or cannot legally be changed, such as a published article, you can save the page on your computer. There are several ways to save a Web page ranging from just saving the text to saving all of the graphics and text needed to display that page as it appears on the Web. To save a Web page, click Page on the Command bar, then click Save As. In the Save Webpage dialog box, specify the location where you want to save the file, type the name you want for the file, click the Save as type list arrow, select the file format type you want, then click Save. When you

save a complete Web page, Internet Explorer saves all the graphic and text elements in a folder. If you want to save an individual graphic on a Web page, right-click the graphic, click Save Picture As, specify the location where you want to save the file, type the name you want for the file, click the Save as type list arrow, select the file format type you want, then click Save. If you want to send a Web page by e-mail, select the Send Page by E-mail command on the Page menu, then address and send the message using your e-mail program.

Getting and Using Accelerators

An **Accelerator** is an add-on program that extends the functionality of Internet Explorer. An Accelerator allows you to perform everyday tasks from your current Web page without having to navigate to other Web sites. For example, you can use default Accelerators in Internet Explorer 8 to get driving directions on a map, translate and define words, e-mail information to others, and search for content. You can also add more Accelerators, such as Bing, eBay, Yahoo!, Wikipedia, Amazon, and Facebook, using the Internet Explorer Gallery. To use an Accelerator, you need to install its add-on. Microsoft provides a Web site gallery where you can quickly install Accelerator add-ons for a variety of different uses, such as map an address using Bing or Yahoo!, find information on eBay, or share information on Facebook. All you need to do is highlight text from any Web page and then click the blue Accelerator icon that appears near your selection to obtain a window with the information you need. If you no longer want to use an Accelerator, you can use the Manage Add-ons dialog box to delete or disable it, or change defaults. ░░░░░ After installing a mapping Accelerator, you decide to use it to get a map of the Quest Specialty Travel corporate offices.

STEPS

1. **Click the Page button** Page▼ **on the Command bar, point to** All Accelerators, **then click Manage Accelerators**

   The Manage Add-ons dialog box opens, displaying a list of the currently installed Accelerators for Internet Explorer. You can also view other installed add-ons.

   QUICK TIP
   To remove or disable an Accelerator, click Accelerators under Add-on Types in the Manage Add-ons dialog box, select the Accelerator you want, click Remove, then click Yes.

2. **Scroll the Accelerator list, if necessary, for** Map with Bing **under the Map category to see if it's installed, then click** Close

3. **If Bing Maps is installed, skip to Step 4. If Bing Maps is not installed, click** Page▼, **point to** All Accelerators, **click** Find More Accelerators, **locate Bing Maps on the Web page, click** Add to Internet Explorer, **click** Add, **then click the** Back button ◉

   The Bing Maps Accelerator is installed and the Quest Specialty Travel Web site reappears.

4. **Click the** About Us **link**

   The About Us Web page opens, which includes the address of Quest Specialty Travel.

5. **Select the address text for Quest Specialty Travel, then click the** blue Accelerator button

   A menu opens, displaying the available Accelerators.

6. **Point to** Map with Bing Accelerator **on the menu**

   A map with Bing appears from the Accelerator, as shown in Figure G-14.

7. **Click the address in the Accelerator window to open it**

   A new tabbed window opens, displaying the larger view of the corporate offices of Quest Specialty Travel in San Diego, California.

8. **Click the** Close button ⊠ **on the Bing Maps tab, then click the** Back button ◉ **next to the Address bar**

   The Bing Maps tab closes and the Quest Specialty Travel home page reopens.

FIGURE G-14: Using a Map with Bing Accelerator

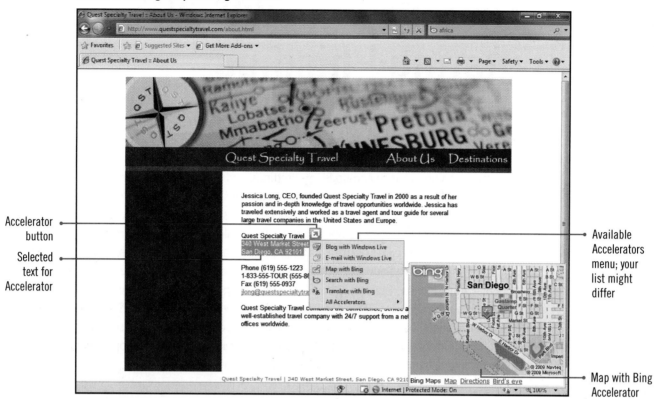

Accelerator button

Selected text for Accelerator

Available Accelerators menu; your list might differ

Map with Bing Accelerator

Managing add-ons and using InPrivate Filtering

Add-ons are programs that extend the functionality of Internet Explorer. An Accelerator is one of many types of add-ons you can use in Internet Explorer 8. There are add-on types for toolbars and extensions, search providers, Accelerators, and InPrivate Filtering, to name a few. To manage add-ons, click the Tools button on the Command bar, then click Manage Add-ons. In the Manage Add-ons dialog box, click the add-on type you want to view or work with, then select an add-on. You can disable/enable or remove an add-on. For InPrivate Filtering, you can import and export filters. **InPrivate Filtering** blocks third-party Web sites, such as maps and advertisements, from gathering and tracking information about you and your browsing habits without your knowledge. InPrivate Filtering is turned off by default and needs to be turned on each time you start Internet Explorer. To turn it on, click the Safety button on the Command bar, then click InPrivate Filtering. To set InPrivate Filtering settings, click the Safety button on the Command bar, then click InPrivate Filtering Settings. You can automatically block content, choose the content to block or allow, or turn it off.

Zooming in and out

Working with Zoom commands gives you another way to control exactly what you see in a Web page. Internet Explorer uses Adaptive Page Zoom tools that allow you to enlarge or reduce everything on the page, including text and images, by relaying out the page. You can adjust the zoom from 10% to 1000%. Zoom commands are located in the lower-right corner of the window or on the Zoom submenu of the Page button on the Command bar. If you have a mouse with a wheel, you can also press and hold down [Ctrl], then scroll the wheel to zoom in or out.

Blocking Pop-ups and Filtering Phishing

The **Pop-up Blocker** in Internet Explorer prevents most unwanted pop-up windows from appearing. A **pop-up window** is a window, typically with an advertisement, that displays in your Web browser without your permission. When Internet Explorer blocks an ad, the Information Bar appears at the top of the current tab telling you that something was blocked. You can click the Information Bar to temporarily or permanently allow pop-ups, change Pop-up Blocker settings, and get Information Bar help. With the Pop-up Blocker Settings dialog box, you can allow or disallow pop-ups from specific sites, choose to play a sound and show the Information Bar when a pop-up is blocked, and set a filter level to block pop-ups. **Phishing** is a technique criminals use to trick computer users into revealing personal or financial information. Typically, a phishing scam starts with an e-mail message that appears to come from a trusted source, such as a bank or credit card company, but actually directs recipients to provide information to a fraudulent Web site. Windows 7 and Internet Explorer 8 provide **SmartScreen filtering** to increase security to help protect you from phishing schemes. You can set SmartScreen filtering options on the Safety menu in Internet Explorer. You can check Web sites to see if they have been reported as a phishing site and report them to Microsoft if you think they are fraudulent.  After receiving an unwanted pop-up window, you decide to enable Internet Options to block pop-ups and check a Web site for phishing scams.

STEPS

1. **Click the Tools button** `Tools ▾` **on the Command bar, then point to Pop-up Blocker**
   If the Pop-up Blocker is turned on, you'll see the command Turn Off Pop-up Blocker; if the Pop-up Blocker is turned off, you'll see the command Turn On Pop-up Blocker.

2. **If the Pop-up Blocker is turned off, click Turn On Pop-up Blocker to enable it; otherwise, click a blank area of the browser window to close the menu**

3. **Click** `Tools ▾` **on the Command bar, point to Pop-up Blocker, then click Pop-up Blocker Settings**
   The Pop-up Blocker Settings dialog box opens, as shown in Figure G-15. You can add specific Web sites for which you will allow pop-ups, select notification options, and specify the filter level you want.

4. **Click Close**
   The Pop-up Blocker Settings dialog box closes with the current pop-up settings intact. If the SmartScreen Filter is turned on, the command on the submenu will allow you to turn it off; if the SmartScreen Filter is turned off, the command on the submenu will allow you to turn it on.

QUICK TIP
If available, you can also click the Smart-Screen Filter icon in the status bar, then click Check This Website.

5. **Click the Safety button** `Safety ▾` **on the Command bar, point to SmartScreen Filter, then click Turn On SmartScreen Filter or Turn Off SmartScreen Filter**
   The Microsoft SmartScreen Filter dialog box opens with the option button corresponding to the command you selected.

6. **Click OK, click** `Safety ▾` **, point to SmartScreen Filter, then click Check This Website**
   The SmartScreen Filter dialog box opens, asking if you want to check this site for phishing.

7. **Click OK**
   The SmartScreen Filter dialog box opens, telling you that no threats have been reported for this website.

TROUBLE
If you need to disconnect from the Internet, click the Network icon in the notification area, click the connection name, then click Disconnect.

8. **Click OK, click** `Safety ▾` **, point to SmartScreen Filter, then click Report Unsafe Website**
   The Microsoft SmartScreen Filter Web page opens in a new browser window, as shown in Figure G-16, asking you to specify information related to the trustworthiness of the Web site you are reporting.

9. **Click the Close button** `✕` **in the browser window, click** `✕` **in the Quest Specialty Travel window, then, if necessary, click Close all Tabs in the dialog box that opens**

FIGURE G-15: Pop-up Blocker Settings dialog box

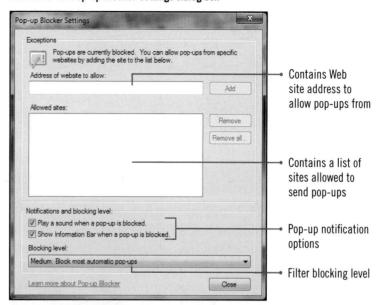

Contains Web site address to allow pop-ups from

Contains a list of sites allowed to send pop-ups

Pop-up notification options

Filter blocking level

FIGURE G-16: Microsoft SmartScreen Filter Web site

Displaying security information in the Security Status bar

While you browse the Web, Internet Explorer 8 automatically checks for valid Web site certificates and any irregularities that might indicate a possible phishing site and for any unwanted or malicious programs that can be installed on your computer from a Web site. If Internet Explorer detects a potential problem, it displays a warning in the Address bar with text in the Security Status bar on the right indicating the problem type, as shown in Figure G-17. The Address bar displays red for certificate errors and known phishing sites, green for sites with high security (connected to the certificate), and yellow for suspected phishing sites. Malicious programs are blocked with the Information bar/Pop-up

Blocker settings that prevent them from working. You can click the security icon in the Security Status bar to find out more information.

FIGURE G-17: Security Status bar

Exploring the Internet with Microsoft Internet Explorer

Practice

Concepts Review

For current SAM information including versions and content details, visit SAM Central. (http://samcentral.course.com). If you have a SAM user profile, you may have access to hands-on instruction, practice, and assessment of the skills covered in this unit. Since we support various versions of SAM throughout the life of this text, you will want to check with your instructor for instructions and the correct URL/Web site to access those assignments.

Match the statements below with the elements labeled in the screen shown in Figure G-18.

FIGURE G-18

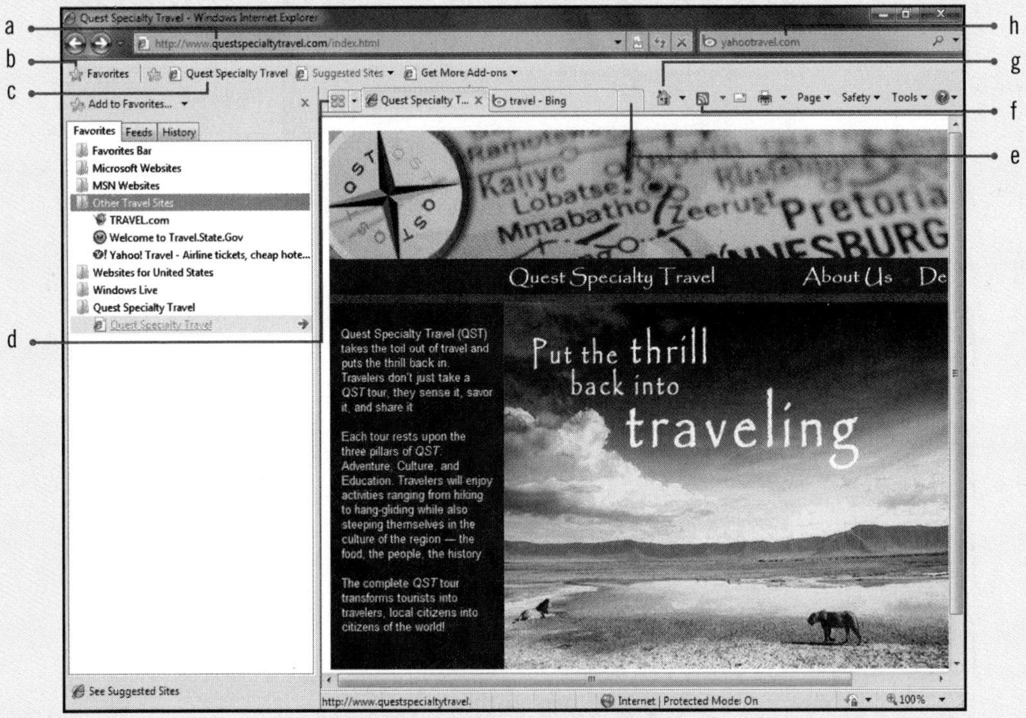

1. Which element opens Quick Tabs?
2. Which element opens a new tabbed window?
3. Which element displays the home page?
4. Which element displays a Web page with a feed?
5. Which element opens the Favorites Center?
6. Which element adds a Favorite to the Favorites bar?
7. Which element displays the address of the current Web page?
8. Which element displays search keywords?

Match each term with the statement that best describes it.

9. hyperlink
10. URL
11. Web
12. Internet
13. ISP

a. Global collection of linked Web pages
b. Web address
c. Global collection of linked computers
d. Provides a connection to the Internet
e. Provides a connection between Web pages

Concepts Review (Continued)

Select the best answer from the list of choices.

14. **Software programs used to access and display Web pages are called:**
    a. Web sites.
    b. Search engines.
    c. Web utilities.
    d. Web browsers.

15. **If you want to save the name and URL of a Web page in Internet Explorer and return to it later, you can add it to a list called:**
    a. Favorites.
    b. Feeds.
    c. Home pages.
    d. Preferences.

16. **Which of the following is a valid URL?**
    a. http:/www.usf.edu/
    b. http://www.usf.edu/
    c. htp:/ww.usf.edu/
    d. http//www.usf.edu/

17. **Text or graphics that you click to jump to another Web page are called:**
    a. Explorers.
    b. Favorites.
    c. Web browsers.
    d. Hyperlinks.

18. **The URL of the current Web page appears in the:**
    a. Title bar.
    b. Document window.
    c. Address bar.
    d. Status bar.

19. **What do you call the words or phrases you submit to find information on the Web?**
    a. Hits
    b. Search engine
    c. Keywords
    d. Menu bar

20. **Which of the following is *not* another name for a feed?**
    a. RSS feed
    b. XML feed
    c. Syndicated content
    d. Blog

Skills Review

1. **Connect to the Internet.**
   a. Use the Connect to the Internet Wizard to create a dial-up connection.
   b. Connect to the Internet.

2. **Open a Web page and follow links.**
   a. Start Internet Explorer.
   b. Click in the Address bar, type **www.cengage.com**, then press [Enter].
   c. Explore the Web site by using the scroll bars, toolbar, and hyperlinks.
   d. Click in the Address bar, type **www.sportsline.com**, then press [Enter].
   e. Follow the links to investigate the content.
   f. Click the Back button to return to any page on Cengage.com.
   g. Click the forward button to return to the Sportsline.com home page.

3. **Use tabs to browse Web pages.**
   a. Open a new tab.
   b. Type **www.loc.gov** in the Address bar, then press [Alt][Enter] to open the page in a new tabbed window.
   c. Press and hold [Ctrl][Shift], then click a link on the page to open the page in a new grouped tabbed window.
   d. Click the Quick Tabs button.
   e. Click any thumbnail to make that tab active.
   f. Click the tab you opened in Step c, and then close it.

4. **Change your home page.**
   a. Click in the Address bar, type **www.perspection.com**, then press [Enter].
   b. Set this Web page as your only home page.

Skills Review (Continued)

   c. Click a link on the page.

   d. Click the Home button.

   e. Type **www.course.com**, then press [Alt][Enter].

   f. Set the current tab as your home page.

   g. Click the Close button for the Course Technology tab, then click the Home button.

   h. Click the Tools button, click Internet Options, click Use default on the General tab to use MSN as your home page or type the URL of your original home page, then click OK.

5. Search the Web.

   a. Select Bing as your search engine.

   b. Click in the Search box next to the Address bar.

   c. Type **job computer training**.

   d. Press [Alt][Enter].

   e. Use the Find on this Page command to highlight the search text.

   f. Click a link to a Web site from the list of search results.

   g. Close the Find toolbar, then click the Back button.

6. Add a Web page and Slices to Favorites.

   a. Display the tab containing the Perspection Web page.

   b. Add this page as a Favorite to the Favorites bar.

   c. Click in the Address bar, type **www.msn.com**, then press [Enter].

   d. Add a Web Slice to the Favorites bar, then preview it.

   e. Open the Favorites list in the Favorites Center.

   f. Pin the Favorites Center in place.

   g. Use the Perspection Home Page Favorite in the Favorites list to jump to that page in the current tab.

   h. Delete the Perspection Favorite and the Web Slice in the Favorites Center.

   i. Close the Favorites Center.

7. View and subscribe to a feed.

   a. With the Bing results tab displayed, click the Feeds button on the Command bar.

   b. Add the feed to the Favorites bar, subscribe to the feed, then preview a feed from the Favorites bar.

   c. Close the tab containing the feed subscription information.

   d. Display the Feeds list in the Favorites Center.

   e. Refresh the feed you saved.

   f. Display the Bing results feed, then click a feed link in the list.

   g. Display the Feeds list in the Favorites Center, then delete the Bing results feed.

8. Get and use Accelerators.

   a. Display the About Us Web page from the Quest Specialty Travel Web site.

   b. Select the top paragraph, then click the blue Accelerator button.

   c. Use the Translate with Bing Accelerator to display the text in Spanish.

9. Block pop-ups and filter phishing.

   a. Open the Pop-up Blocker Settings dialog box.

   b. View the current Pop-up options, then click Close.

   c. Type **www.cengage.com**, then press [Alt][Enter].

   d. Click the Safety button, point to SmartScreen Filter, then click Check This Website.

   e. Click OK.

   f. Click the Safety button, point to SmartScreen Filter, then click Report Unsafe Website.

   g. If the Pop-up Blocker was originally turned off, return it to this setting.

   h. Close all open Internet Explorer windows, close tabs if necessary, then Disconnect if necessary.

Exploring the Internet with Microsoft Internet Explorer

Independent Challenge 1

You will soon graduate from college with a degree in business management. Before entering the workforce, you want to make sure that you are up to date on all advances in the field. You decide that checking the Web would provide the most current information. In addition, you can search for companies with employment opportunities.

a. Use Internet Explorer to investigate the business-related sites listed in Table G-2, or search for other business sites if these are not available. Open three sites in separate tabs as a group.

TABLE G-2: Business-related sites

Career Builder	www.careerbuilder.com
Monster	www.monster.com
Jobs	www.jobs.com

b. Click the appropriate links on the page to locate information about employment opportunities that sound interesting to you.

c. Add each of the sites to your home page.

Advanced Challenge Exercise

- Use the Print button arrow on the toolbar to preview the page.
- Use a button on the toolbar to display the page with and without headers and footers.
- Use a list arrow on the toolbar to display the page as two pages at a time.

d. When you find a relevant page, use the Print button on the Command bar to print the page.

e. Restore the home page to its original Web page.

Independent Challenge 2

You leave tomorrow for a business trip to France. You want to make sure that you take the right clothes for the weather and decide to check the Web for the information. You also want to protect yourself from pop-up windows and check the Web sites you visit for phishing scams.

a. Open Internet Explorer, then turn on the Pop-up Blocker and Automatic Website Checking with the SmartScreen Filter.

TABLE G-3: Weather sites

The Weather Channel	www.weather.com
National Weather Service	www.nws.noaa.gov
CNN Weather	www.cnn.com/WEATHER

b. Use Internet Explorer to access two of the weather sites listed in Table G-3, or search for other weather sites if these are not available. Open the two sites in separate tabs.

c. Check the site you open with the SmartScreen Filter.

d. Click the necessary links on the page to locate information about the weather in Paris.

e. Print at least two reports on current Paris weather.

f. Restore the Pop-up Blocker and SmartScreen Filter back to their original states.

Advanced Challenge Exercise

- Open the Favorites Center, then click the History tab.
- Click Today to list the sites you visited today, then view the list.
- Click the History button list arrow, click View By Order Visited Today, then view the list.
- Click a blank area of the document window to close the Favorites Center.

Independent Challenge 3

Your boss wants to buy a new desktop computer (as opposed to a laptop). He assigns you the task of investigating the options. You decide that looking on the Web would be more expedient than visiting computer stores in the area.

a. Use Internet Explorer to visit at least three of the Web sites listed in Table G-4, or search for other computer company sites if these are not available. Open the three sites in separate tabs.

TABLE G-4: Computer companies' Web sites

Apple	www.apple.com
Dell	www.dell.com
HP	www.hp.com
IBM	www.ibm.com

b. Click the necessary links to find a page from each of the three that you think offers the best deal.

c. Add the pages to your Favorites on the Favorites bar and in a folder called **Computer Deals**.

Independent Challenge 3 (Continued)

d. Use the Print button on the toolbar to print a page from each of the three that you think offers the best deal.

e. Delete the two Favorites and the folder you created. Exit Internet Explorer.

Real Life Independent Challenge

Summer vacations are a great time to visit new places. For example, you might want to visit several National Parks in the United States. You can search the Web for information about places you want to visit.

a. Use the Search box with the Bing engine in Internet Explorer to find Web sites with addresses of the places you'd like to visit.

b. Add the Google Search Suggestions add-on to Internet Explorer, if not already there, then repeat your search in a new tab.

c. Click a link to a Web page with an address, select an address, then use the Map with Bing Accelerator to display a map.

d. Subscribe to the Bing results feed, add it to the Favorites bar, and give it an appropriate name. For example, if you searched for maps of the National Parks, type **National Parks** as the name of the feed.

e. Display the Feeds list, then visit four or five sites listed.

f. Use the Print button on the Command bar to print a page from the site that you think offers the best maps and related information.

g. Delete the feed you saved and close your browser.

Visual Workshop

Start Internet Explorer and re-create the screen shown in Figure G-19, which displays the Internet Explorer window with the Favorites Center pinned and a Web site. Use the Print button on the Command bar to print the Web page.

FIGURE G-19

Exchanging Mail and News

STOP *If you are not connected to the Internet and do not have an e-mail account, you cannot work through the steps in this unit; however, you can read the lessons without completing the steps to learn what you can accomplish using Windows Live Mail.*

Files You Will Need:

No file needed.

Windows Live Essentials is a collection of Microsoft programs, available free for download on the Web, which allows you to interact and communicate on the Web. Windows Live Essentials includes Microsoft Windows Live Mail, a powerful program for managing **electronic mail**, known as e-mail. Windows Live Mail is the successor to Windows Mail and Outlook Express, e-mail programs that accompanied previous versions of Windows. With an Internet connection and Microsoft Windows Live Mail, you can exchange e-mail messages with anyone on the Internet and join any number of newsgroups. **Newsgroups** are collections of e-mail messages on related topics posted by individuals to specified Internet locations. From Windows Live Mail, you can also schedule appointments using the Calendar, an electronic version of the familiar paper daily planner.  Quest Specialty Travel is changing e-mail programs to Windows Live Mail. As the president of Quest Specialty Travel, you need to set up Windows Live Mail to send and receive e-mail messages, join a newsgroup about the travel industry, and set up an appointment.

OBJECTIVES

Start Windows Live Mail

Explore the Windows Live Mail window

Add a contact to the Contacts

Compose and send e-mail

Retrieve, read, and respond to e-mail

Manage e-mail messages

View and subscribe to a newsgroup

Read and post a news message

Schedule an appointment in the Calendar

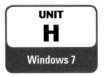
Starting Windows Live Mail

Whether you want to exchange e-mail with colleagues and friends, or join newsgroups to trade ideas and information, Windows Live Mail provides you with the tools you need. To use Windows Live Mail, you need to set up an Internet connection and e-mail account with an ISP. You don't have to use a Windows Live ID e-mail account to use Windows Live Mail. However, if you have or create a free account, you can connect to other online Windows Live services that allow you to access and share information from any computer. Windows Live Mail doesn't come installed with Windows 7; you need to download and install it from Microsoft Windows Live Essentials. When you download and install Windows Live Mail, a menu item for Windows Live appears on the All Programs submenu on the Start menu; from here you can start Windows Live Mail as well as other Windows Live programs, such as Call, Messenger, Photo Gallery, Movie Maker, Toolbar, Writer, Family Safety, and Silverlight. 🔧 Before you can begin using Windows Live Mail to exchange e-mail with your employees, you start Windows Live Mail and create an e-mail account.

STEPS

1. **If the Windows Live Mail program is not installed on your computer, open your browser, type** http://download.live.com **in the Address bar, press [Enter], click** Download, **click** Run, **click** Yes **if necessary, click the** Mail **check box to select it if necessary, deselect any other checkboxes, click** Install, **click** Continue **if necessary, click** Continue, **click** Close **to exit the installer, then click the** Close button ❎ **in your browser window**

   The Windows Essentials Web site opens, where you can download and install Windows Live programs, which include Mail. You can also install Windows Live Messenger, Photo Gallery, Movie Maker, Toolbar, Writer, Family Safety, and Silverlight from this site.

2. **Click the** Start button 🪟 **on the taskbar, point to** All Programs, **click** Windows Live, **then click** Windows Live Mail

   The Windows Live Mail window opens. If you connect to the Internet using a dial-up network connection, you might need to enter your username and password. See your instructor or technical support person for this information.

   QUICK TIP

   If you need help connecting to the Internet or learning how to use Windows Live Mail features, click the Help button 📖 on the toolbar, then click Get help with Mail.

3. **If prompted, click the** Connect to **list arrow, select the** name **of your ISP, type your** username, **press [Tab], type your** password, **then click** Connect

   Your Internet connection is established. When you first start Windows Live Mail, a wizard opens, asking you for e-mail account setup information. See your instructor or technical support person for this information. Refer to the Clues to Use box "Making Windows Live Mail your default email program" for general information about setting up an e-mail account.

4. **If prompted, follow the instructions to set up your e-mail account: for the typical users, type an** e-mail address, password, **and** display name; **click the** Manually configure server settings for e-mail account **check box to select it; click** Next; **select an incoming mail server type; type the** incoming mail server; **type the** outgoing server; **click** Next; **then click** Finish

   A user mail account is set up. If Windows Live Mail is not your default e-mail program, you might be prompted to set it as the default when you start Windows Live Mail.

   QUICK TIP

   To modify or add an account, click Tools on the menu bar, click Accounts, click an account, click Properties, or click Add, click an account type, then follow the wizard instructions.

5. **If prompted, click the** Check this setting when I start Windows Live Mail **check box to deselect it, then click** Yes **or** No **to set Windows Live Mail as the default**

   The Check this setting when I start Windows Live Mail option allows you to disable the check for the default setting when Windows Live Mail starts.

6. **If necessary, click the** Menus button 🔽 **on the toolbar, then click** Show menu bar

   The menu bar appears in the Windows Live Mail window, as shown in Figure H-1.

7. **If necessary, click the** Maximize button ⬜ **on the Windows Live Mail window**

FIGURE H-1: Windows Live Mail window

Menu bar •──

E-mail message; yours will differ

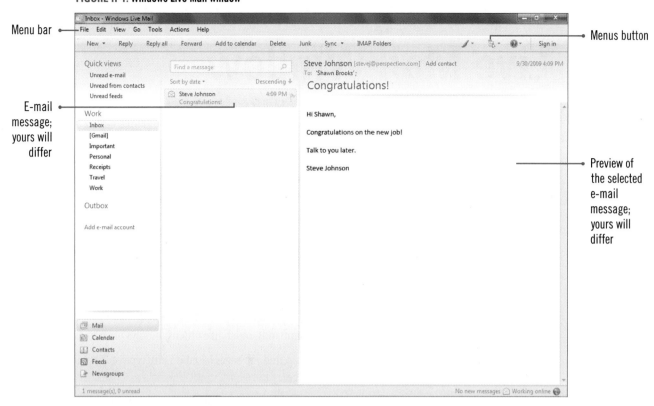

Menus button •──

Preview of the selected e-mail message; yours will differ

Making Windows Live Mail your default e-mail program

You can set Windows Live Mail as your default e-mail program so that Windows Live Mail opens whenever you click an e-mail link on a Web page or choose the mail command in your Web browser. You can also set Windows Live Mail as your default news reader for when you click a newsgroup link on a Web page or choose the news reader command in your Web browser. To set Windows Live Mail as your default e-mail or newsgroup program, click Tools on the menu bar in Windows Live Mail, click Options, then click the General tab. In the Default Messaging Programs section of the Options dialog box, click Make Default next to This application is NOT the default Mail handler and This application is NOT the default News handler. If the buttons are grayed out, then Windows Live Mail is currently selected as the default program.

Understanding e-mail account information

Before you can set up an e-mail account, you need your account name, password, e-mail server type, and the names of your incoming and outgoing e-mail servers from your ISP or network administrator. The Windows Live Mail Internet Connection Wizard helps you connect to, send, and retrieve e-mail messages from different types of e-mail servers. **E-mail servers** are the locations where your e-mail is stored before you access it. Windows Live Mail supports three types of incoming e-mail servers: **POP3** (Post Office Protocol), **IMAP** (Internet Message Access Protocol), and **HTTP** (Hypertext Transfer Protocol). A **protocol** is a set of rules and standards that control the transmission of content, format, sequencing, and error management for information over the Internet or a network. POP3 servers allow you to access e-mail messages from a single Inbox folder, whereas IMAP servers allow you to access multiple folders. HTTP servers are used on Web sites, such as Hotmail, and allow you to send and receive e-mail messages in Windows Live Mail or on a Web site. If you use POP3 or IMAP e-mail servers, you also need to provide an outgoing e-mail server. **SMTP** (Simple Mail Transfer Protocol) is generally used to send messages between e-mail servers.

Exploring the Windows Live Mail Window

After you start Windows Live Mail, the Windows Live Mail window opens, as shown in Figure H-2. The Windows Live Mail window displays tools that you can use to set up and manage multiple e-mail accounts, create and send e-mail messages, use Contacts to store and retrieve e-mail addresses, create stationery or add a personal signature to your e-mail messages, attach a file to an e-mail message, set junk e-mail options and mark e-mail messages as block or safe, join any number of newsgroups, and use the Calendar to make and manage appointments and tasks. The e-mail program you used previously is different from Windows Live Mail, so you decide to familiarize yourself with the components of the Windows Live Mail window.

DETAILS

You note the following features:

- The title bar at the top of the window displays the name of the program.

- The **menu bar** provides access to a variety of commands, much like other Windows programs.

- The **Find a message box** provides an easy way to find messages based on any type of text in the message, including the sender, receiver, subject, and message.

- The **toolbar** provides icons, or buttons, for easy access to the most commonly used commands. Many of these commands are also available on menus; to display menus, click the Menus button on the toolbar, then click the Show menu bar.

- The **Folder pane** displays folders where Windows Live Mail stores e-mail messages. You can also use folders to organize your e-mail messages. The Programs area at the bottom of the Folder pane provides shortcuts to related programs, such as Mail, Calendar, Contacts, Feeds, and Newsgroups.

- The **Message list** displays a list of e-mail messages from the selected folder in the Folder pane.

- The **Reading pane** displays the contents of the current message selected in the Message list.

- The **message header** displays the recipient and sender e-mail address and the subject for the message selected in the Message list.

- The **status bar** displays information about your Internet connection with a mail or newsgroup server.

Changing the Windows Live Mail layout

You can show or hide parts of the Windows Live Mail window to personalize the way you use Windows Live Mail. For example, the Reading pane appears to the right of the Message list by default, but you can have it display elsewhere, such as below the Message list. You can also change the way messages appear in the Message list from the default automatic view to one- or two-line view. Using Folder pane options, you can display the Folder pane in compact view and shortcuts with icons instead of text and show or hide Storage folders and Quick views. The Storage folders provide access to e-mail in the Drafts, Sent Items, and Deleted Items folders, whereas the Quick views provide easy access to unread e-mail and feeds. To change the layout, click the Menus button on the toolbar, click Layout, select a layout option, such as Reading pane (Mail), Message list, Folder pane, or Message header (Mail), select or clear the options you want, then click OK.

FIGURE H-2: Windows Live Mail window

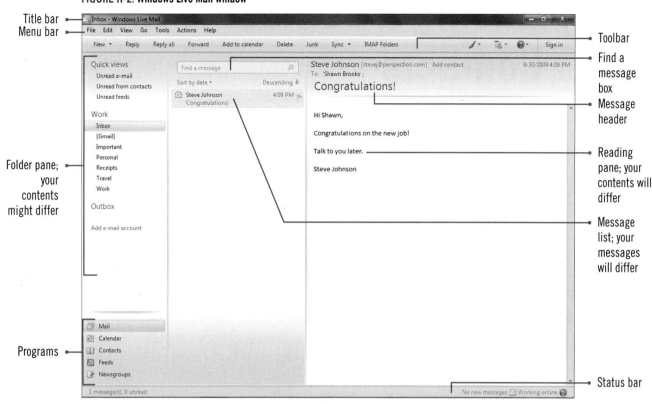

- Title bar
- Menu bar
- Folder pane; your contents might differ
- Programs
- Toolbar
- Find a message box
- Message header
- Reading pane; your contents will differ
- Message list; your messages will differ
- Status bar

Searching for a message

If you can't find a message located in one of your folders in the Folder pane, you can use the Find a message box to help you search for it. You can search the currently selected folder or all the folders in the Folder pane. To search for a message, click in the Find a message box, then type any part of the message. Click the Search in button, click the folder name or All e-mail to narrow or expand the search. If no results are found for a current folder search, you can click the Try searching again in all e-mail link to quickly expand the search. When you're done, click the Close button in the Find a message box to display all the messages in the current folder.

Signing in to Windows Live Mail

You don't have to use a Windows Live ID e-mail account to use Windows Live Mail. You can add and use accounts with another e-mail address without signing in. However, if you have or create a free account, you can connect to other online Windows Live services, such as sending and viewing photo e-mails online, starting instant messaging conversation from Mail, and sharing contacts and calendars. This online service allows you to access and share information from any computer instead of just the one where you set up the account. To sign in, click the Sign in button [Sign in] on the toolbar, type your Windows Live ID, then click Sign in. If you don't have a Windows Live ID, click the Don't have a Windows Live ID? link, then follow the online instructions. To sign in with a different Windows ID, click your display name, click Sign in with a different ID, type a different Windows Live ID, then click Sign in. To sign out, click the Menus button on the toolbar, click Options, click the Connection tab, click Stop signing in, then click Stop signing in.

Adding a Contact to the Contacts

A **contact** is a person or company with whom you communicate. One contact can often have several mailing addresses, phone numbers, e-mail addresses, or Web sites. You can store this information in **Windows Live Contacts** along with other detailed information, such as company name, job title, cell phone number, Windows Live Messenger address for instant messaging (IM), personal information (such as birthday and anniversary dates), or notes. You can also add a **Digital ID** issued by a service to an e-mail address, which helps to validate your identity and sign documents electronically. You can organize your contacts into folders or into **contact categories**, which are groups of related people with whom you communicate regularly. ▰▰▰ You just hired a new employee, Shawn Brooks, so you want to add his contact information to Windows Live Contacts.

STEPS

> **QUICK TIP**
>
> To find a contact, click in the Find a contact box, then type a name. The search results appear in the Contact list. Click the Close button in the Find a contact box.

1. **Click the Contacts button** `📖 Contacts` **at the bottom of the Folder pane in the Programs area**

   The Windows Live Contacts window opens, as shown in Figure H-3, displaying the current contacts. The toolbar for the Windows Live Contacts window appears below the menu bar. Below the toolbar is the Contacts pane along the left side, the Find a contact box, and the Preview pane.

2. **Click the New button on the Contacts toolbar**

   The Add a Contact dialog box opens, displaying the Quick add category. In the Quick add category, you enter the name, e-mail, phone, and company information of the person you want to add. You can use other categories—Contact, Personal, Work, IM (instant messaging), Notes, and IDs (digital)—to enter additional information.

3. **Type Shawn in the First name text box, press [Tab], then type Brooks in the Last name text box**

   The first and last name of the new contact appear in their respective text boxes.

4. **Press [Tab], then type shawnbrooks@cengage.com in the Personal e-mail text box**

   The e-mail address appears in the Personal e-mail text box, as shown in Figure H-4. E-mail addresses are not case sensitive, so capitalization doesn't matter, but they cannot contain spaces.

5. **Click Add contact**

   The Add a Contact dialog box closes and the Windows Live Contacts window reappears with the Shawn Brooks contact in the Contact list.

> **QUICK TIP**
>
> To modify an existing e-mail address, click the Edit button on the toolbar. If an e-mail address is no longer in use, click the Delete button to delete it.

6. **Click Shawn Brooks in the Contact list**

   The contact information for Shawn Brooks appears in the Preview pane.

7. **Double-click Shawn Brooks in the Contact list**

   The Edit Contact: Shawn Brooks dialog box opens, displaying the Summary category, which includes Shawn Brooks' name and personal e-mail information.

> **QUICK TIP**
>
> To create a contact category group, click the New button arrow, click Category, enter a name, select the contacts you want, then click Save.

8. **Click the Work category, type Quest Specialty Travel in the Company text box, press [Tab] to advance to the Work phone text box, type 619-555-1223, then click Save**

   Shawn's work name and work phone number appear in the Preview pane in the Windows Live Contacts window.

9. **Click the Close button** `❌` **in the Windows Live Contacts window**

   The Windows Live Mail window reappears.

FIGURE H-3: Windows Live Contacts window

Find a contact box

Contacts pane; your contacts will differ

Contact list; yours will differ

Toolbar

Preview pane; your contacts will differ

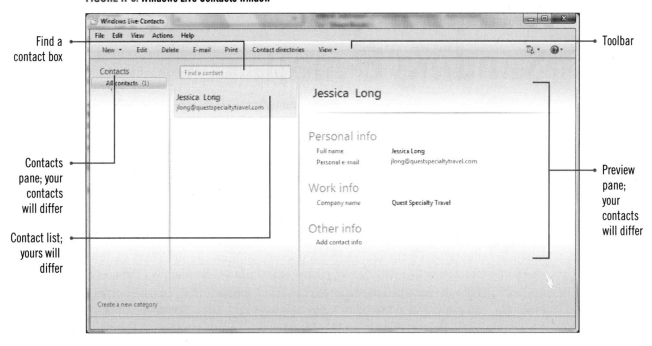

FIGURE H-4: Add a Contact dialog box

Contacts categories

Contact first and last name

Contact e-mail address

Add contact button

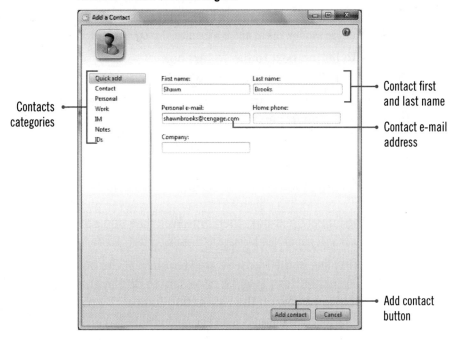

Printing contacts from Windows Live Contacts

You can print your contact information in two formats: Memo and Phone List. The Memo style prints all the information you have for a contact with descriptive titles. The Phone List style prints all the phone numbers for however many contacts you specify. To print contact information, open Windows Live Contacts, select the contacts you want to print, click the File menu; click Print; select a print range, print style, and the number of copies you want to print; then click Print in the Print dialog box.

Composing and Sending E-mail

E-mail is becoming the primary form of written communication for many people. E-mail messages follow a standard memo format, with fields for the sender, recipient, date, and subject of the message. To send an e-mail message, you need to enter the recipient's e-mail address, type a subject, then type the message itself. The subject text is the first information the recipient sees about the e-mail, so it should provide a short, concise summary of the message contents. You can send the same message to more than one individual or to a contact group. You can also use the Cc (carbon copy) button to send a copy of your e-mail message to another person, or use the Bcc (blind carbon copy) button to send a copy of your e-mail message to another person whose name will not appear in the e-mail message. Bcc is useful when sending e-mails to a large group of unrelated people, and allows for privacy for the recipients. You can personalize your e-mail messages with a stationery template, or you can design your own stationery. If you want to send a file along with your e-mail message, you can attach the file to it. If you have not finished composing a message, you can save it in the Drafts folder and work on it later. 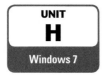 Now that you have Shawn Brooks' contact information in Windows Live Contacts, you want to send him or another specified person an e-mail message.

STEPS

QUICK TIP

To add stationery to an e-mail message, create a new message, click the Stationery button on the Formatting toolbar, click More stationery, select a stationery, then click OK.

1. **Click the** New button arrow **on the Message toolbar, click** E-mail message, **then click the** Maximize button 🔲 **in the New Message window, if necessary**

   The New Message window opens and is maximized, as shown in Figure H-5.

2. **Click the** To button **next to the To text box**

   The Send an E-mail dialog box opens, displaying the contacts from the Windows Live Contacts.

3. **Click the** Shawn Brooks name and e-mail address **or the e-mail address of your instructor, technical support person, or someone else you know, then click** To

   The contact's name appears in the To text box, as shown in Figure H-6.

4. **Click** OK

   The recipient's name appears in the To text box. The recipient's e-mail address is associated with the name selected even though it does not appear.

QUICK TIP

To save an incomplete message, click File on the menu bar, click Save, then click OK if necessary. The message is saved in the Drafts folder.

5. **Click in the** Subject text box, **then type** Welcome aboard!

   The title bar changes from New Message to the subject text "Welcome aboard!"

6. **Click the first line in the** Message area text box **at the bottom of the message window, click the** Format button [Format] **if necessary to display the Formatting toolbar, click the** Font Size button arrow **on the Formatting toolbar, then click** 14 pt Example

   The Formatting toolbar commands allow you to format the text in the Message area.

7. **Type** Dear Shawn:, **press** [Enter] **twice, type** I would like to welcome you to Quest Specialty Travel. We are excited that you have joined our team. Quest Travel is a growing company, and I believe your contributions will make a big difference. Please come to a luncheon for new employees this Thursday at 12:30 in the company cafe., **press** [Enter] **twice, then type** Jessica Long

QUICK TIP

To send a completed message later, click File on the menu bar, click Send later, then click OK if necessary. To send, click the Outbox in the Folder pane, then click the Sync button.

8. **Click the** Send button **on the Message toolbar**

   The New Message window closes and the Windows Live Mail window reappears. The e-mail message is placed temporarily in the **Outbox**, a folder for storing outgoing messages, before it is sent automatically to the recipient. A copy of the outgoing message remains in the Sent Items folder reference later.

FIGURE H-5: New Message window

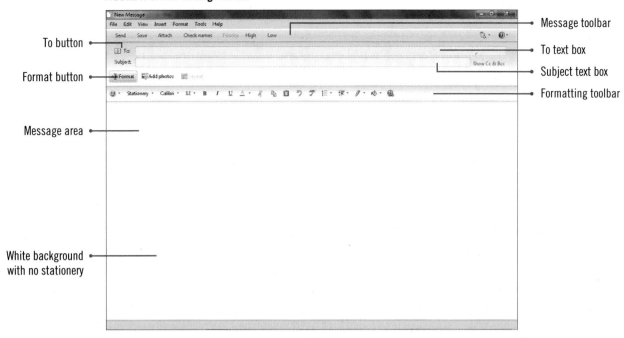

To button

Format button

Message area

White background with no stationery

Message toolbar

To text box

Subject text box

Formatting toolbar

FIGURE H-6: Selecting recipients for an e-mail message

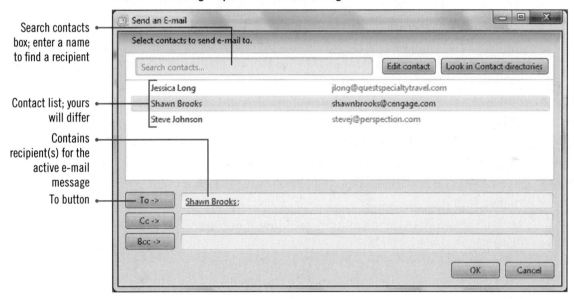

Search contacts box; enter a name to find a recipient

Contact list; yours will differ

Contains recipient(s) for the active e-mail message

To button

Attaching a file to an e-mail message

You can easily share a file, such as a picture or a document, using e-mail by attaching it to an e-mail message. Upon receiving the e-mail, the recipient can open the file in the program that created it or save it. For example, suppose that you are working on a report that you created using WordPad and that a colleague working in another part of the country needs to present the report today.

After you finish the report, you can attach the report file to an e-mail message and send the message to your colleague, who can then open, edit, and print the report. To attach a file to an e-mail message, create the message, click the Attach button on the Message toolbar, navigate to the drive and folder location of the file you want to attach, select the file, then click Open.

Retrieving, Reading, and Responding to E-mail

You can receive e-mail anytime—even when your computer is turned off. When you start Windows Live Mail, the program automatically checks for new e-mail messages and continues to check periodically while the program is open. You can retrieve your e-mail manually with the Sync button or set options in Windows Live Mail to do so automatically. New messages appear in boldface in the Inbox along with any messages you haven't stored elsewhere or deleted. You can also view new messages under Quick views; after you read the e-mail, it's only available in the Inbox. **Message flags** are icon symbols that may appear next to a message. You can respond to a message in two ways: You can reply to it, which creates a new message addressed to the sender(s) and other recipients, or you can forward it, which creates a new message you can send to someone else. In either case, the original message appears in the message response. When you reply to a message that has an attachment, the attachment isn't returned to the original sender. However, when you forward an attachment, it is included along with the message. You can verify that your e-mail message was actually sent by viewing the Sent Items folder. ▓▓▓▓ To prepare for the new employee luncheon, you forward an e-mail message you received to your assistant at Quest Specialty Travel.

STEPS

1. **Have the e-mail recipient to whom you sent the e-mail message send a reply back to you**

2. **In the Folder pane, click Inbox**

   The Inbox folder opens with the messages in your Inbox displayed in the Message list. The Reading pane displays the content of the specific e-mail message selected in the Message list. E-mail messages that appear with boldfaced subject or heading text indicate unopened messages.

3. **Click the Sync button arrow on the toolbar, then click All e-mail accounts**

   An information box displays as Windows Live Mail sends and receives your e-mail messages. When you receive new e-mail, the e-mails are placed in the Inbox and Quick views folders in the Folder pane.

   > **TROUBLE**
   > If you didn't receive a message from Shawn Brooks or another person, click the Sync button on the toolbar again. It might take a few minutes for the message to arrive.

4. **Click the e-mail message you received from Step 1**

   See Figure H-7. The Reading pane displays the e-mail message selected in the Message list.

5. **Double-click the e-mail message you received in the Preview pane, then click the Maximize button 🔲 in the message window, if necessary**

   When you receive a short message, you can quickly read it by clicking the message and then reading the text in the Reading pane. Longer messages are easier to read in a full window. You can reply to the author, reply to all recipients, forward the message, or simply close or delete the message.

   > **QUICK TIP**
   > To print an e-mail message, select the message in the Message list or open the message, click File on the menu bar, click Print, then click Print again.

6. **Click the Forward button on the Message toolbar, then click the Maximize button 🔲 in the message window, if necessary**

   The Forward Message window opens, as shown in Figure H-8, displaying the original e-mail subject title in the Subject text box with the prefix "Fw:" (short for Forward) and the original message in the message box.

7. **Click in the upper-left corner of the message box, then type Please add Shawn Brooks to Thursday's luncheon guest list.**

8. **Click in the To text box, type the e-mail address of your instructor, technical support person, or someone else you know, then click the Send button on the toolbar**

   The e-mail message is sent to the recipient. As you type a recipient name or e-mail address, **AutoComplete** suggests possible matches from the Contact list.

   > **TROUBLE**
   > For some account types, such as IMAP, the Sent items folder is called Sent Mail.

9. **Point to the Folder pane, click the Expand button ▷ next to the e-mail account if necessary, then click Sent items**

   The Sent items folder opens, displaying all the messages sent from the e-mail account.

FIGURE H-7: Windows Live Mail window with Inbox

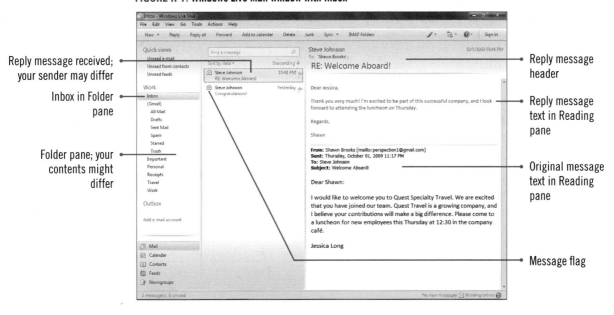

Reply message received; your sender may differ

Inbox in Folder pane

Folder pane; your contents might differ

Reply message header

Reply message text in Reading pane

Original message text in Reading pane

Message flag

FIGURE H-8: Forward message window

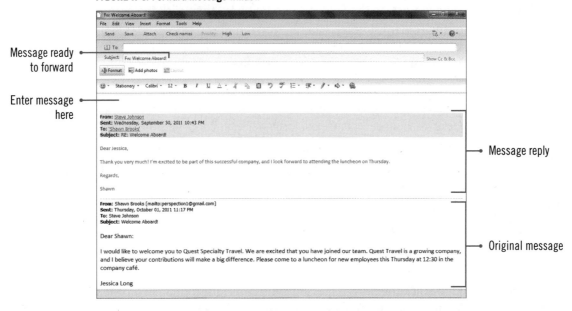

Message ready to forward

Enter message here

Message reply

Original message

Sending a photo file

In Windows Live Mail, you can add photos to an e-mail message as an inline image in the message area or as an attachment. With an inline photo, you can add formatting options to the image, such as frames, color borders, and captions. You can also correct exposure and color, change to black and white, rotate, and change image quality to reduce the size and increase the upload speed. To send a photo file in a message, click the Add photos button, select the photo file you want, click Add, click Done, then use toolbar buttons (Framing, Autocorrect, Black & White, Rotate, or Quality) as desired to modify the selected photo. To change the size and layout, click the Layout button, then click an arrangement/size button on the toolbar. When you're done, click the Send button.

Checking the spelling and content in e-mail messages

Before you send an e-mail message, you should check the spelling of the text and read through the content to make sure your spelling is accurate and your content conveys the desired message to the recipient(s). To start the spelling checker, type your e-mail message, click Tools on the menu bar, then click Spelling or press F7. To have Windows Live Mail automatically check the spelling of all of your e-mail messages before sending them, click Tools on the menu bar, click Options, click the Spelling tab in the Options dialog box, click the Always check spelling before sending check box to select it, then click OK.

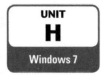

Managing E-mail Messages

A common challenge with using e-mail is managing an overcrowded Inbox. To keep your Inbox organized, you should create new folders and subfolders as you need them. A **subfolder** is a folder within a folder. You should also move messages you want to save to other folders and subfolders and delete messages you no longer want. These tasks make it easier to see new messages in your Inbox and to keep track of messages to which you have already responded. The Folder pane in Windows Live Mail works like the Navigation pane in Windows Explorer. When you create a subfolder, the Expand Indicator ▷ appears next to the name of the folder that contains the subfolder when you point to the Folder pane. If you can't find a message, you can use the Find a message box to quickly locate it. ▓▓▓▓ To help keep your e-mail organized, you want to create a new folder for project-related e-mail messages, move relevant e-mails into this new folder, and delete any messages you no longer need.

STEPS

1. **Click File on the menu bar, point to New, then click Folder**

    The Create Folder dialog box opens, as shown in Figure H-9, displaying the list of folders contained in the Windows Live Mail folder.

2. **Type Projects in the Folder name text box, then click the account name folder at the top of the Folder list**

    The new folder name appears in the Folder name text box and the folder you selected (in this case, the account folder name "Work") specifies the folder location of the new folder.

3. **Click OK**

    The Create Folder dialog box closes and the Sent items – Windows Live Mail window opens. The new folder, Projects, appears under the account name folder (in this case, "Work" in Figure H-9) in the Folder pane.

4. **Click Inbox in the Folder pane, then drag the message you received from Shawn Brooks or someone else you know in the Message list of the Inbox to the Projects folder in the Folder pane**

    The message from Shawn Brooks or someone else you know is now located in the Projects folder.

5. **In the Folder pane, click the Projects folder, then click the message you received from Shawn Brooks or someone else you know in the Message list, if necessary**

    The e-mail message appears in the Message list and its text in the Reading pane, as shown in Figure H-10.

6. **Right-click the moved message you received from Shawn Brooks or someone else you know in the Message list of the Projects folder**

    A shortcut menu appears with options for managing e-mail messages, such as Move to folder, Copy to folder, Delete, Print, and Add sender to contacts.

7. **Click Delete**

    The message is deleted from the Projects folder in the Message list and no longer displays in the Reading pane.

8. **In the Folder pane, right-click the Projects folder, click Delete, then click Yes to confirm the deletion**

    The deleted Projects folder is relocated to the Deleted items folder. The Deleted items folder works just like the Recycle Bin. The folder temporarily stores deleted messages until you automatically or manually delete them.

9. **In the Folder pane, right-click the Deleted items folder if available, click Empty 'Deleted items' folder, then click Yes to confirm the deletion**

    The Projects folder and all of its contents are permanently deleted.

FIGURE H-9: Create Folder dialog box

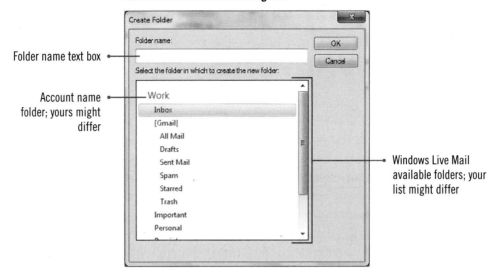

Folder name text box →

Account name folder; yours might differ →

→ Windows Live Mail available folders; your list might differ

FIGURE H-10: New folder in the Folder pane

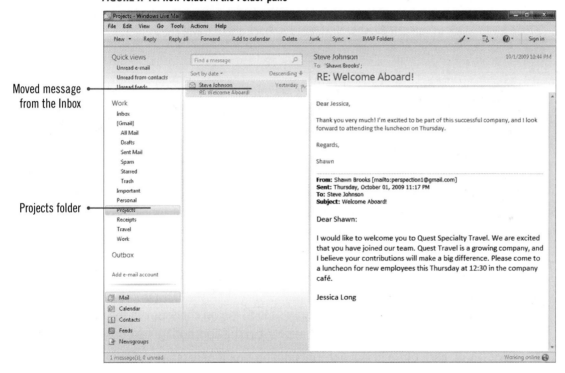

Moved message from the Inbox →

Projects folder →

Diverting incoming e-mail to folders

Windows Live Mail can direct incoming messages that meet criteria to other folders in the Folder pane rather than to your Inbox. For example, your friend loves sending you funny e-mail, but you often don't have time to read it right away. You can set message rules to store any messages you receive from your friend in a different folder so they won't clutter your Inbox. When you are ready to read the messages, you simply open the folder and access the messages just as you would messages in the Inbox. To set criteria for incoming messages, click Tools on the menu bar, point to Message rules, then click Mail. If the Message Rules dialog box opens, click New to create a new message rule. If the

New Mail Rule dialog box opens, no previous message rules exist. In the New Mail Rule dialog box, select the conditions for your rule, select the actions for your rule, click any undefined value (such as the e-mail address you want to divert and the folder where you want to store the diverted messages) and provide information. Type a name to identify the rule, click Save rule, then click OK. If you receive unwanted e-mail from a specific address, you can block all messages from that sender. Simply click the message from the sender, click Actions on the menu bar, point to Junk e-mail, then click Add sender to block senders list or Add sender's domain to blocked senders list.

Viewing and Subscribing to a Newsgroup

A newsgroup is an electronic forum where people from around the world with a common interest can share ideas, ask and answer questions, and comment on and discuss any subject. Before you can participate in a newsgroup, you must select a news server. A **news server** is a computer located on the Internet, which stores newsgroup messages, also called **articles**, on different topics. Microsoft provides its own newsgroups called Microsoft Communities. To select a news server and complete the wizard process, you need to obtain the name of the news server you want to use from your instructor, technical support person, or ISP, and possibly an account name and password. When you add a news server account to Windows Live Mail, it retrieves a list of newsgroups available on that server. Often this list is quite lengthy. Rather than scroll through the entire list looking for a particular topic, you can have Windows Live Mail search the list for that topic. Once you select a newsgroup, you can merely view its contents, or, if you expect to return to the newsgroup often, you can subscribe to it. Subscribing to a newsgroup places a link to the group for easy access in the news server folder in the Folder pane of Newsgroups. Because you need to update the quarterly goals for Quest Specialty Travel, you want to find and subscribe to a newsgroup for travelers so you can monitor the latest feedback about travel companies.

STEPS

1. **Click Tools on the menu bar, then click Accounts**
   The Accounts dialog box opens, displaying a list of available mail and news servers. The Accounts dialog box enables you to add, remove, and view properties for news servers, mail servers, and directory services.

2. **Click Add, click Newsgroup Account, then click Next**
   The Add a Newsgroup Account dialog box opens.

3. **Type your name, click Next, type your e-mail address if necessary, then click Next**
   Individuals participating in a newsgroup need to know your e-mail address so they can reply to your news messages, either by posting another news message or by sending you an e-mail message.

4. **Type the name of the news server provided by your instructor, technical support person, or ISP, click the My news server requires me to log on check box to select it if required by your ISP, then click Next**

QUICK TIP
To remove a news server account, right-click the news server in the Folder pane, click Remove account, then click Yes.

5. **If you selected the My news server requires me to log on check box in the previous step, type your E-mail username and your password in the appropriate text boxes, then click Next**

6. **Click Finish, click Close in the Accounts dialog box if necessary, click the Show available newsgroups, but don't turn on Communities option, then click OK or click Yes when prompted to download a list of available newsgroups**
   The Newsgroup Subscriptions dialog box opens, displaying news servers on the left (if more than one exist) and related newsgroups on the right.

7. **Type travel in the Display newsgroups that contain text box**
   Newsgroups related to travel appear in the Newsgroup list box, as shown in Figure H-11.

QUICK TIP
To download new newsgroup messages, right-click the newsgroup in the Folder pane, point to Synchronization settings, then click New messages only.

8. **Click the newsgroup name from the newsgroup list that interests you, then click Go to**
   The newsgroup name – Windows Live Mail opens, as shown in Figure H-12. The newsgroup name you chose appears selected in the Folder pane, while the newsgroup messages appear in the Message list.

9. **Right-click the newsgroup name in the Folder pane, then click Subscribe**
   The newsgroup is changed from viewing to subscribing. Subscribing to a newsgroup makes it available along with updates the next time you open Newsgroups, whereas viewing a newsgroup does not.

FIGURE H-11: Newsgroup Subscriptions dialog box

Newsgroup topic

Available news
servers; your list
might differ

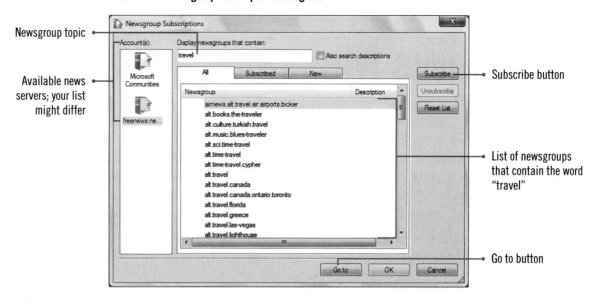

Subscribe button

List of newsgroups
that contain the word
"travel"

Go to button

FIGURE H-12: List of newsgroups relating to travel

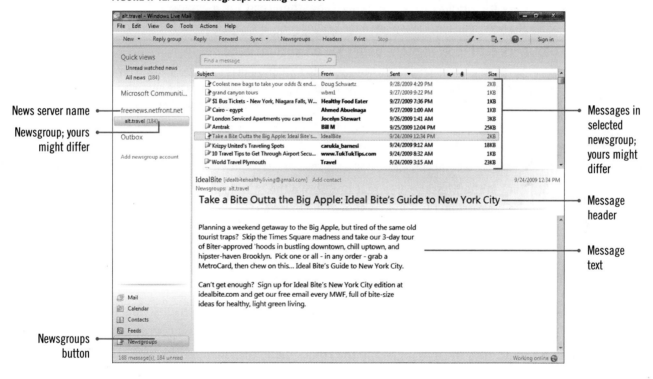

News server name

Newsgroup; yours
might differ

Messages in
selected
newsgroup;
yours might
differ

Message
header

Message
text

Newsgroups
button

Filtering unwanted newsgroup messages

After you become familiar with a newsgroup, you might decide that you don't want to retrieve messages from a particular person, about a specific subject, of a certain length, or older than a certain number of days. This is called **filtering** newsgroup messages. To filter unwanted messages, click Tools on the menu bar, point to Message rules, then click News. If the New News Rule dialog box opens, no previous message rules exist. Otherwise, the Rules dialog box opens, and you click Save rule to create a new message rule. In the New News Rule dialog box, select the conditions for your rule, select the actions for your rule, click any undefined value (such as the newsgroup e-mail address you want to divert and the folder where you want to store the unwanted messages) and provide information, type a name to identify the rule, click Save rule, then click OK.

Reading and Posting a News Message

You can read new newsgroup messages after you retrieve them. Newsgroup messages appear in the Message list, just as e-mail messages do. To view a newsgroup message in the Message list, click the title of the message in the Reading pane. If the Expand Indicator ▷ appears to the left of a newsgroup message, the message contains a conversation thread. A **conversation thread** consists of the original message on a particular topic along with any responses that include the original message. Icons appear next to the news messages to indicate whether a conversation thread is expanded or collapsed, and whether or not it has been read. After selecting a travel newsgroup, you want to read some of the messages in the newsgroup to find out what people want from a travel company, and post newsgroup messages to obtain feedback.

STEPS

QUICK TIP
To view or subscribe to a newsgroup, click the News-groups button on the toolbar, select a news server, select a newsgroup, then click Go to or Subscribe.

1. **Click ▷ to the left of a newsgroup message in the Message list**
   The titles of the responses to the original message appear under the original newsgroup message.

2. **Click the original newsgroup message, then read the message**
   The newsgroup message appears in the Reading pane, as shown in Figure H-13.

3. **Click each reply message under the original message**
   As you read each message, you can choose to compose a new message, send a reply message to everyone viewing the newsgroup (known as **posting**), send a reply message to the author's private e-mail address (rather than posting it on the newsgroup), or forward the message to another person.

QUICK TIP
To view only unread messages, click View on the menu bar, point to Show or hide, then click Hide read messages.

4. **Click the Reply group button on the toolbar, enter user information and click OK if prompted, then click the Maximize button ▣ if necessary**
   A reply message window opens, displaying the news server, newsgroup, subject, and original message.

5. **Click in the Message area text box above the original message, then type a response to the newsgroup message, as shown in Figure H-14**
   Your reply to the newsgroup message is complete.

6. **Click the Send button on the toolbar, then click Yes**
   Your reply message appears in the Message list along with the other replies to the original message. Everyone viewing the newsgroup can download and read your response.

TROUBLE
If another warning message appears, click No to subscribe to the Newsgroup, then click No to view a list of newsgroups.

7. **Right-click the newsgroup name in the Folder pane, click Unsubscribe, then click OK**
   The newsgroup is removed; however, the news server is still available as a news account.

8. **Right-click the news server in the Folder pane, click Remove account, then click Yes**
   The news server is removed.

FIGURE H-13: Reading a newsgroup message

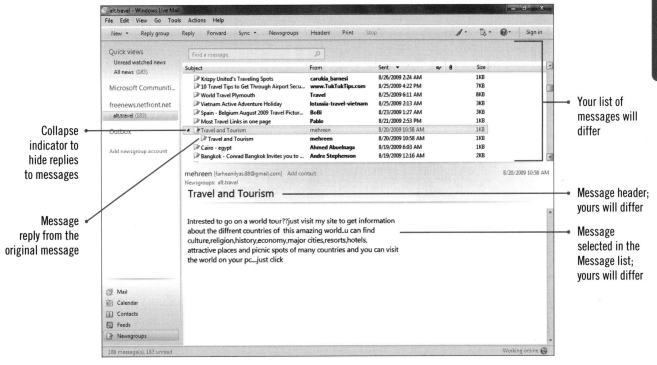

Collapse indicator to hide replies to messages

Message reply from the original message

Your list of messages will differ

Message header; yours will differ

Message selected in the Message list; yours will differ

FIGURE H-14: Posting a newsgroup message

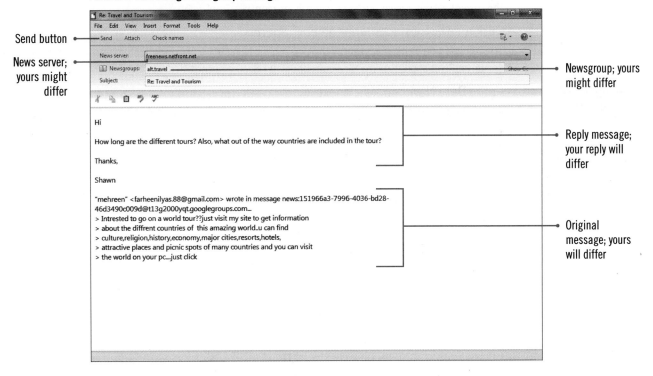

Send button

News server; yours might differ

Newsgroup; yours might differ

Reply message; your reply will differ

Original message; yours will differ

Deleting old newsgroup messages

Newsgroup messages are stored on your hard drive, so you should delete unneeded messages to free disk space. Windows Live Mail provides several cleanup options to help you optimize your hard drive space. You can delete entire messages (titles and bodies), compress messages, remove just the message bodies (leaving the title headers), or reset the information stored for selected messages, which allows you to refresh messages (download again). To clean up files on your local hard drive, select a news server in the Folder pane, click Tools on the menu bar, click Options, click the Advanced tab, then click Maintenance. You can select any of the cleanup options to delete or compress news messages at a specified time, or click Clean Up Now, then click the button for the cleanup option you want to perform.

Scheduling an Appointment in the Calendar

The **Calendar** in Windows Live Mail is an electronic version of the familiar paper daily planner. You can use the Calendar to schedule time for completing specific tasks, meetings, vacations, holidays, or for any other activity. You can adjust the Calendar to show activities using the Day, Week, or Month format. **Appointments** are scheduled activities such as a doctor's visit that don't include other people or resources, and occupy a block of time in the Appointment area. The Appointment area serves as a daily planner where you can schedule activities by the day, week, or month. **Events** are activities that last 24 hours or longer, such as a seminar, and do not occupy blocks of time in your calendar. Instead, they appear in a banner at the beginning of a day. If an appointment or event recurs on a regular basis, such as a Monday morning meeting, you can set the Recurrence option. If you need a meeting reminder, you can specify how long before the appointment you want to receive a reminder alert. To set a reminder, you need to sign in to Windows Live Mail with your Windows Live ID. ⬛⬛⬛ To make sure you don't forget about the new employee luncheon each month, you want to add the activity appointment to your Calendar.

STEPS

1. **Click the Calendar button [🗓 Calendar] at the bottom of the Folder pane**
   The Calendar – Windows Live Mail window opens, displaying the current date in the Date Navigator and, in the current calendar view, either Day, Week, or Month.

2. **Click the Day button on the toolbar, if necessary**
   The calendar view changes to show the currently selected day by hourly increments, where you can view, create, and edit appointments. The current day is selected in the calendar.

> **QUICK TIP**
> To quickly add an appointment, select a time, then type the appointment text you want. To edit the appointment in one of the views, click the appointment, click in the text, then edit the text.

3. **In the Date Navigator, click next Thursday, then select 12:30 to 1:30 p.m. in Day view**
   The Calendar window opens, displaying the selected date and time for the appointment, as shown in Figure H-15.

4. **Click the New button on the toolbar**
   The New Event dialog box opens. The new appointment appears with selected text at the scheduled time in Day view. The start and end times appear along with other information and options you can select. When you enter appointment information in the New Event dialog box, the All day check box remains empty.

5. **Type New employee luncheon in the Subject text box, press [Tab], then type Company cafe in the Location text box**

6. **Click the Recurrence button, then click Monthly**
   The appointment is set to occur every month in the calendar.

7. **Click the Save & close button on the toolbar**
   The Calendar window reappears, displaying the new appointment, as shown in Figure H-16.

> **QUICK TIP**
> To delete an appointment, select the appointment, then click the Delete button on the toolbar. If prompted, select a delete occurrence option, then click Delete.

8. **Click File on the menu bar, click Exit, then click Yes, if necessary, to disconnect from the Internet**
   Windows Live Mail closes.

FIGURE H-15: Calendar window with selected date and time

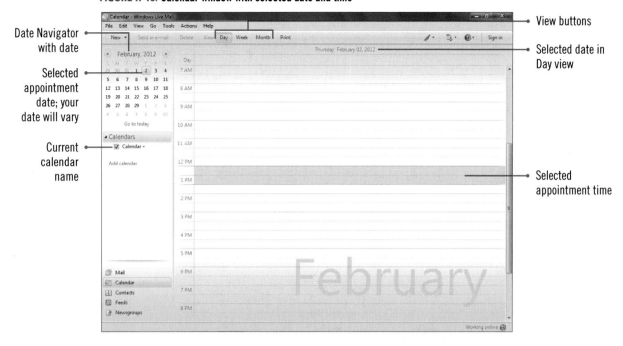

Date Navigator with date

Selected appointment date; your date will vary

Current calendar name

View buttons

Selected date in Day view

Selected appointment time

FIGURE H-16: Calendar window with an appointment

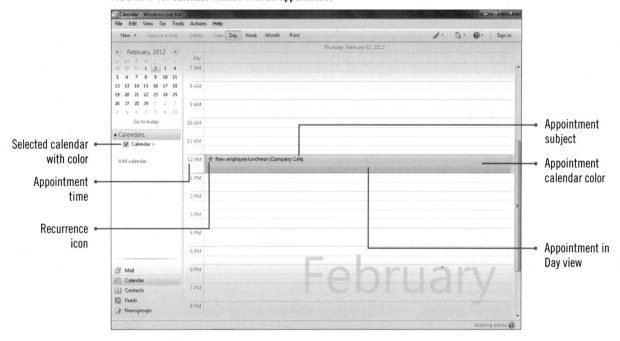

Selected calendar with color

Appointment time

Recurrence icon

Appointment subject

Appointment calendar color

Appointment in Day view

Creating multiple calendars

In the Calendar, you can create individual calendars for multiple people who use Windows Live Mail and share them with each other. When you have multiple calendars, you can view them individually or all at once, side by side, or overlaid to make it easier to compare one calendar with another and check for free time. Appointments for each calendar are displayed in a different color to make them easy to distinguish. If you want to add an appointment from another calendar to yours, you can drag appointments between the two calendars. To create and view a calendar, click the Add calendar link in the Folder pane, type a name in the Calendar name text box, click the calendar color you want, type a description in the Description text box, click the Make this my primary calendar check box to select it if you want to make this your main calendar, then click Save. To view multiple calendars, select the check boxes next to the calendars you want, then clear the check boxes for the ones you want to hide. To create a new event for a calendar, click the calendar name, then click New event. To change the calendar name or other properties, click the calendar name, then click Properties. To delete a calendar, click the calendar name, then click Delete.

Practice

For current SAM information including versions and content details, visit SAM Central (http://samcentral.course.com). If you have a SAM user profile, you may have access to hands-on instruction, practice, and assessment of the skills covered in this unit. Since we support various versions of SAM throughout the life of this text, you will want to check with your instructor for instructions and the correct URL/Web site to access those assignments.

Concepts Review

Match the statements below with the elements labeled in the screen shown in Figure H-17.

FIGURE H-17

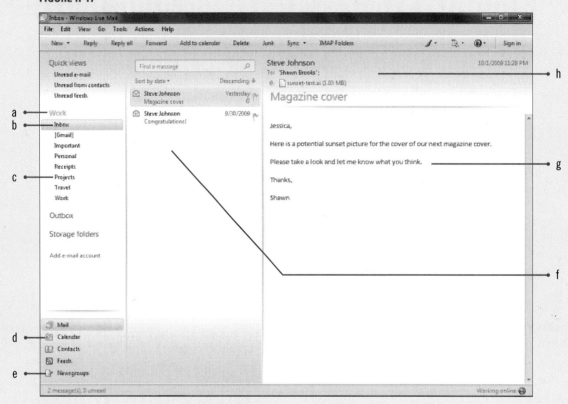

1. Which element displays new e-mail messages?
2. Which element points to the Message list?
3. Which element displays news messages?
4. Which element points to the Message header?
5. Which element points to a new folder?
6. Which element points to the Reading pane?
7. Which element displays appointments?
8. Which element points to the account name?

Match each term with the statement that best describes it.

9. Message flag
10. Newsgroup
11. Windows Live Mail window
12. Windows Live Mail
13. News server
14. Message rules

a. A computer on the Internet that stores articles
b. Displays e-mail, contacts, and newsgroups
c. An icon that indicates e-mail priority
d. Diverts selected incoming e-mail folders
e. A program that exchanges e-mail on the Internet
f. A collection of articles on related topics

Concepts Review (Continued)

Select the best answer from the list of choices.

15. **Which of the following is an outgoing e-mail server?**
    a. POP3
    b. IMAP
    c. SMTP
    d. HTTP

16. **Which of the following is a set of rules and standards that control the transmission of content over the Internet?**
    a. Transfer
    b. Protocol
    c. Hypertext
    d. Flags

17. **A contact is a:**
    a. Person with whom you communicate.
    b. Mailing address.
    c. Newsgroup.
    d. Program.

18. **When you click the Send button on the toolbar in the New Message window, you first send an e-mail message to the:**
    a. E-mail address.
    b. Outbox.
    c. Internet.
    d. Cc and Bcc addresses.

19. **Which of the following means private carbon copy?**
    a. Cc.
    b. Bcc.
    c. To.
    d. None of the above

20. **A newsgroup message is also called a(n):**
    a. E-mail.
    b. Article.
    c. Conversation.
    d. Thread.

21. **A thread consists of a:**
    a. Message only.
    b. Message and any responses.
    c. Responses only.
    d. All of the above

22. **Which of the following is an electronic version of the familiar paper daily planner?**
    a. Windows Live Contacts
    b. Calendar
    c. Windows Live Mail
    d. All of the above

Skills Review

1. **Start Windows Live Mail and explore the Windows Live Mail window.**
   a. Start Windows Live Mail, then connect to the Internet, if necessary.
   b. If prompted, enter your username and password, then click Connect.
   c. Identify the title bar, menu bar, Find a message box, toolbar, Folder pane, Message list, Reading pane, and status bar.
   d. On the toolbar, identify icons or elements for opening Windows Live Contacts, sending and receiving e-mail messages, composing a message, and finding a message.

2. **Add a contact to the Windows Live Contacts.**
   a. Click the Contacts button.
   b. Click the New button on the Contacts toolbar.
   c. Type **Grace** in the First name text box, press [Tab], then type **Wong**.
   d. Click in the Personal e-mail text box, then type **gwong@questspecialtytravel.com**.
   e. Click Add contact.
   f. Double-click the contact, add Quest Specialty Travel to the Work category, then click Save.
   g. Click the Windows Live Contacts Close button.

3. **Compose and send e-mail.**
   a. Click the New button, then click the Maximize button, if necessary.
   b. Click the To button.

   c. Click the Grace Wong name and e-mail address or the e-mail address of your instructor, technical support person, or someone else you know.

   d. Click To, then click OK.

   e. Type **Financial Update Request** in the Subject text box.

   f. Click in the message window, then type **Grace: Please send year-end financial report ASAP. Thanks.**

   g. Click the Send button.

4. Retrieve, read, and respond to e-mail.

   a. Have the e-mail recipient to whom you sent the e-mail message send a reply back to you.

   b. Click the Sync button.

   c. In the Folder pane, click Inbox, then click the message you just received.

   d. Click the Forward button, then click the Maximize button if necessary.

   e. Click the To text box, type your e-mail address, then compose a response in the message window.

   f. Click the Send button.

5. Manage e-mail messages.

   a. Click File on the menu bar, point to New, then click Folder.

   b. Type **Archive**, click the account name folder, then click OK.

   c. Drag the message received from Grace Wong or someone else you know from the Inbox folder to the Archive folder.

   d. In the Folder pane, click the Archive folder.

   e. Right-click the message received from Grace Wong or someone else you know, then click Delete.

   f. Right-click the Archive folder, click Delete, then click Yes.

   g. Click the Contacts button.

   h. Click Grace Wong, click the Delete button, click OK, then click the Close button.

6. View and subscribe to a newsgroup.

   a. Click Tools on the menu bar, then click Accounts.

   b. Click Add, click Newsgroup Account, then click Next.

   c. Type your name, click Next, type your e-mail address, then click Next.

   d. Type the name of a news server (see your instructor, technical support person, or ISP for a name), then click Next.

   e. Click Finish, click Close if necessary, then click Yes.

   f. In the News server list, click the news server you just added (if available).

   g. Type **finance** in the Display newsgroups that contain text box. (*Hint*: If no items appear, type **budget**.)

   h. Click a newsgroup, then click Go to to open the newsgroup.

   i. Right-click the newsgroup in the Folder pane, then click Subscribe.

7. Read and post a news message.

   a. Click a newsgroup message with a ▷.

   b. Click ▷ next to the newsgroup message.

   c. Click and read each reply.

   d. Click the Reply group button, then type a response.

   e. Click the Send button, then click OK.

   f. Right-click the newsgroup in the Folder pane, click Unsubscribe, then click OK.

   g. Right-click the news server in the Folder pane, click Remove account, then click Yes.

8. Schedule an appointment in the Calendar.

   a. Click the Calendar button.

   b. Click the Day button on the toolbar, if necessary.

   c. Select a day and time to schedule an appointment.

   d. Click the New button.

   e. Type a title for the appointment, press [Tab], then type a location.

   f. Set the recurrence to Weekly, then click the Save & close button.

   g. Click File on the menu bar, then click Exit to exit Windows Live Mail.

Independent Challenge 1

You are a new lawyer at Kenny & Associates. You have a home computer with Windows 7 and Windows Live Mail that you often use to do work on while you are at home. Because e-mail is an important method of communication at the law firm, you want to use Windows Live Mail and Windows Live Contacts to enter e-mail addresses of colleagues with whom you need to communicate while working away from the office.

a. Start Windows Live Mail, then open the Windows Live Contacts.

b. Enter the following names and e-mail addresses:

Kristen Kenny, kkenny@kenny_law.com

Jennifer Kenny, jkenny@kenny_law.com

Karen Quan, kquan@kenny_law.com

c. Print the Windows Live Contacts in both the Phone List and Memo styles.

d. Delete the names and e-mail addresses you just entered in the Windows Live Contacts.

Independent Challenge 2

As president of Auto Metals, you just negotiated a deal to export metal auto parts to an assembly plant in China. Your lawyer, Jack Blea, drew up a preliminary contract. You want to send Jack an e-mail indicating the terms of the deal so he can finish the contract. When Jack responds, move the e-mail into the Legal folder. If you do not have a connection to the Internet, ask your instructor or technical support person for help completing this challenge.

a. Open a New Message window using the stationery called Money, or another option.

b. Type **jblea@blealaw.com** in the To text box in the message window, then type **China Deal Contract** in the Subject text box.

c. Enter the following message:

Dear Jack,

I have completed the negotiations with the assembly plant. Please modify the following terms in the contract:

1. All parts shall be inspected before shipping.

2. Ship 100,000 units a month for 4 years with an option for 2 more years.

Sincerely yours,

[your name]

Advanced Challenge Exercise

- Set Windows Live Mail as your default e-mail program.
- Set spelling options to always check spelling before sending a message.
- Check the spelling in your e-mail message.
- Attach a file to an e-mail message.
- Set and run a rule to divert mail messages from a specific sender to a folder.
- Delete the message rule.

d. Send the e-mail, then print the e-mail you sent to Jack Blea.

e. Create a new folder called **Legal**, then move the e-mail message you received from Jack Blea to the new folder.

f. Delete the Legal folder.

Independent Challenge 3

You are a legal assistant at a law firm specializing in international law. Your manager asks you to research international contracts with China. You decide to start your research with newsgroups on the Internet.

a. Select a news server. (See your instructor, technical support person, or ISP to obtain a news server.)

b. Subscribe to a newsgroup about China, then read several newsgroup messages and replies.

c. Reply to a message, then post a new message.

d. Print the newsgroup messages, including the original message and replies.

Independent Challenge 2 (Continued)

Advanced Challenge Exercise

- Set Windows Live Mail as your default news client.
- Set and run a rule to divert news messages on a specific topic to a folder.
- Set options to delete old news messages on your computer.
- Delete the message rule.

e. Unsubscribe to the newsgroup, then remove the newsgroup server.

Real Life Independent Challenge

You have a very busy schedule this week, so you want to schedule all your appointments and set reminders so you don't forget anything.

a. Open the Calendar.

b. Specify all the appointments you have for the week. Include at least four appointment and one all-day event.

c. Specify recurrences for at least two appointments.

d. Change the view to Week and Month to see your appointments.

Advanced Challenge Exercise

- Create a new calendar, then add some appointments to it.
- Sign in to Windows Live Mail with your Windows Live ID.
- Specify reminders for at least two appointments.
- View the appointments on both calendars, then delete the new calendar.

Visual Workshop

Re-create the screen shown in Figure H-18, which displays the Calendar in Windows Live Mail with appointments on a specific day using multiple calendars.

FIGURE H-18

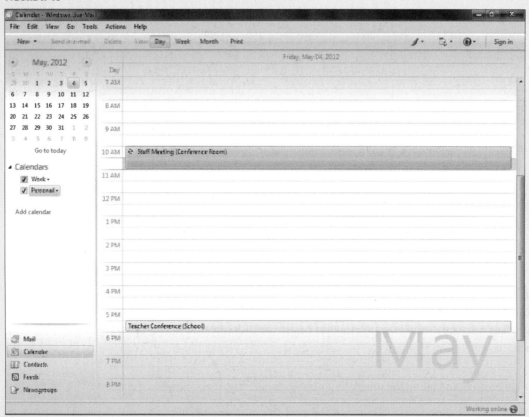

Glossary

Accelerator An add-on program that extends the functionality of Internet Explorer.

Accessories Built-in programs that come with Windows.

Action Center A place in Windows that makes it easy to find information about the latest virus or security threat, check the status of essential security settings, quickly get support from Microsoft for a security-related issue, and access Control Panel utilities that allow you to set additional security and privacy settings.

Active Refers to the window you are currently using.

Active window The window that is open. The title bar changes from light blue to a darker blue when active.

Address bar Displays the address of the current Web page or the contents of a folder or local or network computer drive.

Administrator A computer account for the person who needs to make changes to anything on the computer as well as manage user accounts.

Antivirus software A program that examines the files stored on a disk to determine whether they are infected with a virus, then destroys or disinfects them.

Applications *See* programs.

Appointments Scheduled activities that don't include other people or resources, and occupy a block of time in the Appointment area of Calendar in Windows Live Mail.

Articles Another name for newsgroup messages.

AutoComplete A feature that suggests possible matches with previous filename entries or Web addresses.

Auto-hide A feature that helps you automatically hide the taskbar.

Automatic Updating A feature that provides protection when you update your Windows software to make sure it's safe.

Background The primary surface on which icons and windows appear; you can customize its appearance using the Display Properties dialog box.

Bitmap A file that is a map of a picture created from small dots, or pixels.

Bitmapped characters Fonts that are created with small dots organized to form a letter.

Blind carbon copy (Bcc) An e-mail option to send a copy of your e-mail message to another person whose name will not appear in the e-mail message.

Broadband High speed connections to the Internet that are continually turned on and connected.

Buffer A temporary memory storage area that transmits streaming media to play continuously.

Burn The process of copying files and folders to a compact disc. Also known as burning.

Burn in When the same display remains on the screen for extended periods of time and becomes part of the screen; this can be avoided by enabling a screen saver.

Byte A unit of storage capable of holding a single character or pixel.

Cable modems Cable television lines that provide a completely digital path from one computer to another.

Calendar A program in Windows Live Mail that allows you to schedule time for completing specific tasks, meetings, vacations, holidays, or for any other activity with the Calendar.

Canvas area The white drawing area within the Paint window that doesn't include the gray area.

Carbon copy (Cc) An e-mail option to send a copy of your e-mail message.

Cascading menu A list of commands from a menu item with an arrow next to it. Pointing to the arrow displays a submenu from which you can choose additional commands.

Case sensitive When a program makes a distinction between uppercase and lowercase letters.

CD or CD-ROM *See* Compact Disc-Read-Only Memory.

CD-R *See* Compact Disc-Recordable.

CD-RW *See* Compact Disc-Rewritable.

Certificate A statement verifying the identity of a person or the security of a Web site.

Classic style Refers to the Windows user interface setting where you double-click icons to open them.

ClearType A feature that smoothes out the edges of fonts on portable computers or flat screen monitors to look the same as fonts on the printed page.

Clicking The act of pressing a mouse button once and releasing it.

Clip A video or audio segment.

Clipboard A temporary storage space on a hard drive that contains information that has been cut or copied.

Cluster A group of sectors on a disk. Also known as an Allocation unit.

Command A directive that provides access to a program's features.

Compact Disc (CD) *See* Compact Disc-Read-Only Memory.

Compact Disc-Read-Only Memory (CD-ROM) An optical disk on which you can stamp, or burn, up to 1 GB (typical size is 650 MB) of data in only one session. The read-only disc cannot be erased or burned again with additional new data.

Compact Disc-Recordable (CD-R) A type of read-only CD on which you can burn up to 1 GB of data in multiple sessions. The disc can be burned again with additional new data, but cannot be erased.

Compact Disc-Rewritable (CD-RW) A type of CD on which you can read, write, and erase data, just like a removable or hard disk.

Compress Storing data in a format that requires less space than usual.

Computer virus A program that attaches itself to a file, reproduces itself, and spreads to other files, usually meant to cause harm to the infected computer.

Contact A person or company with whom you communicate.

Contact categories A group of contacts that you can organize together.

Content Advisor A security feature that allows you to prevent access to Web sites that contain material you deem inappropriate, such as language or violence.

Control Panel A central location for changing Windows settings. A window containing various programs that allow you to specify how your computer looks and performs.

Conversation thread The original message on a particular topic along with any responses that include the original message.

Cookie A file created by a Web site that stores information on your computer, such as your preferences and history when visiting that site. Also known as a first-party cookie.

Default The standard way of displaying information or performing a task in Windows.

Definition Instructions that determine how to defend against malicious software.

Delete To remove a file or folder from a disk.

Desktop A graphical background on screen that represents a desk. The screen that appears when you first start Windows, providing access to your computer's programs and files and to the Internet.

Destination file The file where you store a representation of a linked object.

Destination program The program where you store an embedded object.

Dialog box A window that opens when you choose a menu command that is followed by an ellipsis (. . .); many dialog boxes have options you must choose before Windows or a program can carry out a command.

Digital ID Another name for a certificate in some programs, such as Microsoft Outlook; *see* Certificate.

Digital Subscriber Lines (DSL) Wires that provide a completely digital path from one computer to another.

Digital Video Disc (DVD) A type of read-only optical disc that holds a minimum of 4.7 GB (gigabytes), enough for a full-length movie.

Digital Video Recordable (DVD-R) A type of read-only DVD on which you can burn up to 4.7 GB of data in multiple sessions. The disc can be burned again with additional new data, but cannot be erased.

Digital Video Rewritable (DVD-RW) A type of DVD on which you can read, write, and erase data, just like a removable or hard disk.

Disable To turn off a feature.

Disk label A name you assign to a hard or floppy disk using the Properties dialog box.

Display adapter A hardware device that allows a computer to communicate with its monitor.

Document A file created using a word processing program such as WordPad.

Document window The work area of the WordPad window.

Dots Per Inch (DPI) The number of dots that a device can display or print per linear inch. The greater number of dots per inch, the better the resolution.

Double-clicking Clicking the left mouse button twice.

Drag and drop A method that allows you to move text from one location to another using the mouse and without placing the information on the Clipboard.

Dragging Moving items or text to a new location using the mouse.

DVD *See* Digital Video Disc.

DVD-R *See* Digital Video Disc-Recordable.

DVD-RW *See* Digital Video Disc-Rewritable.

Edit The process of changing the contents of a file.

Electronic mail A system used to send and receive messages electronically. Also known as e-mail.

Ellipses In a dialog box or on a menu, indicates that you must supply more information before the program can carry out the command you selected. *See also* Dialog box.

E-mail *See* Electronic mail.

E-mail servers An Internet location where your e-mail is stored before you access it.

Embedding Inserting an object created in one program into a document created in another program.

Enable To turn a feature on.

Events Activities that last 24 hours or longer and do not occupy blocks of time in the Calendar area of Windows Live Mail.

Extract To uncompress a file or folder.

Favorites Center A feature in Internet Explorer that stores and organize Web addresses.

Feed A way to deliver text content in the form of news headlines or blogs, or digital content in the form of pictures, audio, and video; *see* RSS (Really Simple Syndication) feed.

File An electronic collection of information that has a unique name, distinguishing it from other files.

File extension A three letter extension at the end of a filename that refers to the program Windows uses to distinguish, create, and open files of that type.

File hierarchy A logical structure for files and folders that mimics how you would organize files and folders in a filing cabinet.

File management The process of organizing and keeping track of files and folders.

Filter A management feature that allows you to view only events matching specified criteria, such as all events associated with a certain user.

Filtering A way to display only files with the properties you select by heading type.

Firewall A security system that creates a protective barrier between a computer or network and others on the Internet.

First-line indent marker The top triangle on the ruler in WordPad that controls where the first line of the paragraph begins.

First-party cookie *See* Cookie.

Folder list A file hierarchy in the Navigation pane of a file management window that displays all drives and folders on the computer and connected networks.

Folder pane A feature in Windows Live Mail that displays folders where e-mail messages are stored, and shortcuts to related programs, including, Mail, Calendar, Contacts, Feeds, and Newsgroups.

Folder template A collection of toolbar options for working with specialized content. Windows 7 comes with five folder templates: General Items, Documents, Music, Pictures, and Videos.

Font The design of letters, numbers, and other characters. For example, Times New Roman.

Format To change the appearance of information but not the actual content.

Frame A separate window within a Web page.

Gigabyte A file size measurement equal to 1,024 megabytes.

Graphical user interface (GUI) Pronounced "gooey." An environment made up of meaningful symbols, words, and windows in which you can control the basic operation of a computer and the programs that run on it.

Gadget A mini-program that resides on the desktop.

Grouping A way to display a sequential list of files by heading type.

Hanging indent marker The bottom triangle on the ruler in WordPad that controls where second and subsequent lines of the paragraph begin.

Hard copy *See* Printout.

Help and Support A book stored on your computer with additional links to the Internet, complete with a search feature, an index, and a table of contents to make finding Windows-related information easier.

Hertz A unit of frequency to measure a monitor display.

Hibernation A state in which your computer first saves everything in memory on your hard disk and then shuts down.

Hits The results of an Internet search that, when clicked, open a Web page or category.

Home page The page that opens every time you start Internet Explorer.

Hyperlinks (links) Highlighted text or graphics in a Web page that open other Web pages when you click them.

Hypertext Transfer Protocol (HTTP) A type of incoming e-mail server that is used for Web sites, such as Hotmail, and allows you to send and receive e-mail messages in Outlook Express or on a Web site; *see* Protocol.

Icons Graphical representations of computer elements, such as files and programs.

Indexed location A file that Windows has kept track of in the background and stored information about using an index to make locating files faster and easier.

InPrivate browsing A way browse the Web without of keeping track of browsing history, searches, temporary Internet files, form data, cookies, and user names and passwords.

InPrivate filtering A filter that blocks third party Web sites, such as maps and advertisements, from gathering and tracking information about you and your browsing habits without your knowledge.

IMAP (Internet Message Access Protocol) A type of incoming e-mail server that allows you to access multiple folders.

Insertion point A blinking vertical line that appears in the work area of the WordPad window, indicating where the next text will appear when you type.

Internet A communications system that connects computers and computer networks located around the world using telephone lines, cables, satellites and other telecommunications media.

Internet account A set of connection information provided by an Internet Service Provider (ISP) or Local Area Network (LAN) administrator that allows you to access the Internet, and send and receive e-mail.

Internet Service Provider (ISP) A company that provides Internet access.

Jump list A submenu on the Start menu or shortcut menu on the taskbar that displays a list of recently opened files for the program or Windows item for easy access.

Keyword A word or phrase you submit to a search engine to find various Web sites on the Internet. *See also* Search engine.

Kilobyte A file size measurement equal to 1,024 bytes.

Landscape The page orientation when a page is wider than it is tall.

Left indent marker The small square under the bottom triangle on the ruler in WordPad that allows you to move the first-line indent marker and the left indent marker simultaneously, which indents the entire paragraph at once.

Library A special folder that catalogs files and folders in a central location, regardless of where the items are actually stored on your hard drive.

Linking Connecting an object created in one program to a document created in another program so that any changes will be reflected in both places.

Links *See* Hyperlinks.

Live File System A disc burning format that allows you to copy files to a disc at any time, like a USB drive, even if you are using a CD-R or DVD-R instead of a rewriteable disc.

Live icons Thumbnails that display the first page of documents making it easier to find exactly what you are looking for.

Load The process of displaying a Web page in a browser from a server.

Loop An option that repeatedly plays a media clip until you stop it.

Malware Malicious software, such as viruses and spyware, that can delete or corrupt files and gather personal information

Margin The space between the text and the edge of the document.

Mastered A disc-burning format that copies files all at one time.

Maximize A button located in the upper-right corner of the window that enlarges a window so it fills the entire screen.

Megabyte A file size measurement equal to 1,048,576 bytes, which is equal to 1,024 kilobytes.

Menu A list of available commands in a program. *See also* Menu bar.

Menu bar A list of menu names in a program that display a menu. *See also* Menu.

Message flags An icon associated with an e-mail message that helps you determine the status or priority of the message.

Message header A feature in Windows Live Mail that displays the recipient and sender e-mail addresses for the message selected in the Message list.

Message list A feature in Windows Live Mail that displays the e-mail message selected in the Reading pane.

Microsoft Internet Explorer A program that helps you access the World Wide Web.

Minimize A button located in the upper-right corner of the window that reduces the size of a window.

Mouse A hand-held input device that you roll across a flat surface (such as a desk or a mouse pad).

Multitasking Working with more than one Windows program at the same time.

Narrator A text-to-speech Windows program that gives users who are blind or have impaired vision access to the computer; an Ease of Access Center program.

Navigation pane The left side of a dialog box or window used to open or save files that contain common locations or recently used files and folders.

News server A computer located on the Internet that stores newsgroup messages.

Newsgroups Online discussion groups about a particular topic, usually in an e-mail format.

Notepad A Windows text editing program that comes as a built-in accessory.

Notification area Located on the right side of the taskbar and used to display the time, system icons, and icons for currently running programs and related processes.

Object A picture, chart, video clip, text, or almost anything you can create on a computer.

Object Linking and Embedding (OLE) The process of placing and working with common objects in different programs.

Office Open XML Document (DOCX) A file format available in WordPad that saves documents for use in Microsoft Word 2007.

OpenDocument Text (ODT) A standard office file format available in WordPad that saves documents for use in Office programs, such as OpenOffice.

OpenType font A font type based on a mathematical equation that creates letters with smooth curves and sharp corners.

Operating system A computer program that controls the basic operation of your computer and the programs you run on it. Windows 7 is an example of an operating system.

Orientation The direction text is printed on the page.

Outbox A storage folder in Windows Live Mail where an outgoing e-mail message is placed temporarily before it is sent automatically to the recipient.

Outline fonts A font type (TrueType and OpenType) based on a mathematical equation that creates letters with smooth curves and sharp corners.

Paint A Windows accessory you can use to create and work with graphics or pictures.

Pane Refers to a part of a window that is divided into two or more sections.

Partition A section of a disk drive that operates like a separate drive.

Path A location to a file from the drive to the folder.

Personal folders A storage area designed for managing business and personal files and folders; for example, Documents.

Personal certificate A type of certificate that verifies your identity to a secure Web site; *see* Certificate.

Phishing A technique criminals use to trick computer users into revealing personal or financial information.

Pinned Item Refers to putting items on the Start menu, where they will be easily accessed. Pinned items remain on the Start menu until they are unpinned, or removed.

Pixel A single point on your monitor's screen. *See also* Screen resolution.

Podcast A feed that can deliver audio content usually in the MP3 format.

Point A unit of measurement (1/72nd inch) used to specify the size of text.

Pointer A small symbol on the screen that indicates the pointer's position.

Pointing Positioning the mouse pointer over an icon or over any specific item on the screen.

Pointing device Hardware connected to or built into the computer you use to position the pointer on the screen that indicates the pointer's position.

Pop-up notification An informational message in the notification area of the taskbar that appears when you need it.

Pop-up Blocker A feature in Internet Explorer that prevents most unwanted pop-up windows from appearing.

Pop-up window A window that gets displayed in your Web browser without your permission.

POP3 (Post Office Protocol) A type of incoming e-mail server that allows you to access e-mail messages from a single Inbox folder.

Portrait The page orientation when a page is taller than it is wide.

Posting The process of composing a new message or sending a reply message to everyone viewing the newsgroup.

Power plan A predefined collection of power usage settings.

Print Preview A feature that shows the layout and formatting of a document as it would appear when printed.

Printing A process to create a printout. *See also* Printout.

Printout A paper document that you can share with others or review as a work in progress.

Program Task-oriented software you use to accomplish specific tasks, such as word processing, managing files on your computer, and performing calculations. Also known as applications.

Properties The characteristics of a specific element (such as the mouse, keyboard, or desktop) that you can customize.

Protocol (component) The language that the computer uses to communicate with other computers on the network.

Quick **Access Toolbar** A customizable toolbar at the top of the WordPad and Paint programs.

Quick Tabs A user interface that displays thumbnails of each page currently open in a tab in order to open and close Web pages.

Random **Access Memory (RAM)** A temporary storage space whose contents are erased when you turn off the computer.

Raster *See* Screen font.

Reading pane A feature in Windows Live Mail that displays the selected message in the Message list.

Recycle Bin A temporary storage area for deleted files that is located on your desktop.

Restore Down A button located in the upper-right corner of the window that returns a window to its previous size.

Ribbon A tab-based toolbar used in WordPad and Paint to display buttons for easy access to commands.

Rich Text Format (RTF) A standard text format that includes formatting information and provides flexibility when working with other programs.

Right-clicking Clicking the right mouse button to open a shortcut menu that lists task-specific commands.

Right indent marker A triangle on the right side of the ruler that controls where the right edge of the paragraph ends.

Rip Copying individual music tracks or entire CDs to your computer and creating your own jukebox or playlist of media.

RSS (Really Simple Syndication) feed A way to automatically deliver Web content, such as headline news, to your desktop, browser, or e-mail; *see* Feed.

Scalable *See* Outline fonts.

Scheme A predefined combination of settings that assures visual coordination of all items.

Screen font A font that consists of bitmapped characters. *See also* Bitmapped characters.

Screen resolution The number of pixels on the entire screen, which determines the amount of information your monitor displays.

Screen saver A moving pattern that fills your screen after your computer has not been used for a specified amount of time. *See also* Burn in.

ScreenTip A description of a toolbar button that appears on your screen when you position the mouse pointer over the button.

Scroll bar A bar that appears at the bottom and/or right edge of a window whose contents are not entirely visible. Each scroll bar contains a scroll box and two scroll arrows. You click the arrows or drag the box in the scroll bar in the direction you want the window display to move.

Scroll box A box located in the vertical and horizontal scroll bars that indicates your relative position in a window. *See also* Scroll bar.

Search box A text box that searches to find installed programs and other Windows items.

Search engine A program you access through a Web site and use to search through a collection of information found on the Internet.

Search provider A company that provides a search engine directly from Internet Explorer to look for information about any topic throughout the world.

Sector The smallest unit that can be accessed on a disk.

Select To click an item, such as an icon, indicating that you want to perform some future operation on it.

SmartScreen Filtering A filter that provides increased security to help protect you from phishing schemes; *see* Phishing.

Shortcut A link that you can place in any location that gives you instant access to a particular file, folder, or program on your hard disk or on a network.

Show the desktop button The blank button next to the time and date on the taskbar that minimizes all the windows on the desktop.

Shut down The action you perform when you are finished working with Windows to make it safe to turn off your computer.

Skin The Windows Media Player's appearance.

Sleep A state in which your monitor and hard disks turn off after being idle for a set time.

SMTP (Simple Mail Transfer Protocol) An outgoing e-mail server that is generally used to send messages between e-mail servers.

Sorting A way to display files and folders in alphabetical order, either A to Z or Z to A.

Source file The file where a linked object is stored.

Source program The program where you create or insert an object.

Spyware Software that tries to collect information about you or change computer settings without your consent.

Standard A computer account for people who need to manage personal files and run programs.

Standby *See* Sleep.

Start button Located on the taskbar and used to start programs, find and open files, access the Windows Help and Support Center and more.

Start menu A list of commands that allows you to start a program, open a document, change a Windows setting, find a file, or display Help and support information.

Status bar Used in a program to display information about the program or a currently selected item.

Streaming media A technique for transferring media so that it can be processed as a steady and continuous stream. The Windows Media Player delivers streaming video, live broadcasts, sound, and music playback over the Internet.

Subfolder A folder within a folder.

Submenu A menu that opens when you select an item with an arrow next to it from another menu. *See also* Menu.

System tray *See* Notification area.

Tab stop A predefined stopping point along the document's typing line.

Tabs A user interface at the top of dialog boxes that organizes options into related categories. *See also* Dialog box.

Tags User-defined file properties.

Taskbar Located at the bottom of the screen, and may contain the Start button, program buttons, and the notification area.

Taskbar button A button on the taskbar that represents open windows on the desktop.

Terabyte A file size measurement equal to 1,024 gigabytes.

Text Document (TXT) A file format available in WordPad that saves documents in plain text.

Text Editor A program that you can enter and edit text only with basic document formatting.

Theme A set of visual elements, such as desktop background, screen saver, mouse pointers, sounds, icons, and fonts that provide a consistent look for Windows.

Third-party cookie A file created by a Web site you are not currently viewing, such as a banner ad on the current Web site you are viewing, that stores information on your computer, such as your preferences and history while visiting the current site.

Thumbnails *See* Icons.

Title bar The name of the document and program at the top of a window.

Toggle A button or option that acts as an on/off switch.

Toolbar Used in a program to display buttons for easy access to the most commonly used commands.

Touch Pad A point device for laptop or notebook computers.

Trojan Horse A program that appears to be useful and comes from a legitimate source, but actually causes problems.

TrueType font A font type based on a mathematical equation that creates letters with smooth curves and sharp corners.

Undo A command that reverses the last change made.

Uniform Resource Locator (URL) A Web page's address.

Vector *See* Outline fonts.

Visualization A visual effect that displays color and shapes that change with the beat of the sound in Windows Media Player.

Wallpaper *See* Background.

Web Part of the Internet that consists of Web sites located on computers around the world connected through the Internet.

Web address A unique address on the Internet where you can locate a Web page. *See also* URL.

Web browser A software program that you use to "browse the Web," or access and display Web pages.

Web pages Documents that contain highlighted words, phrases, and graphics that open other Web pages when you click them.

Web site A location on the World Wide Web that contains Web pages linked together.

Web site certificate A type of certificate that verifies its security with a Web site before you send it information; *see* Certificate.

Web Slice A portion of a Web page that lets you know when an update is available.

Web style Refers to the Windows user interface setting where you single-click icons to open them.

Window Rectangular frame on your screen that can contain several icons, the contents of a file, or other usable data.

Windows Aero The advanced Windows 7 user experience that expands visual effects, such as glass-like interface elements, see through, subtle window animations, window colors, and live thumbnails on the taskbar.

Windows Live Contacts A program in Windows Live Mail that allows you to enter, store, and organize detailed information, such as job title, cell phone number, and Web page address, about a person.

Windows Explorer A Windows file management feature that uses two panes to help you organize your files and folders on your local, Homegroup (a shared home network), and network computers.

Windows Firewall A Windows feature that monitors all communication between your computer and the Internet and prevents unsolicited inbound traffic from the Internet from entering your computer.

Windows Media Player A Windows program that allows you to play video, sound, and mixed-media files.

Windows program Software designed to run on computers using the Windows operating system.

Word wrap A feature that automatically places text that won't fit on one line onto the next line.

WordPad A Windows word-processing program that comes as a built-in accessory.

WordPad button A Wordpad button that provides file-related commands.

Word Processor A program that you use to enter, edit, and format text and graphics.

Work area *See* Canvas area.

World Wide Web (WWW) *See* Web.

Worm A virus that can spread without human action across networks.

XML Paper Specification (XPS) A secure fixed-layout format—similar to an Adobe PDF file—developed by Microsoft that retains the format you intended on a monitor or printer.

Zone Internet security areas (Internet, Local intranet, Trusted sites, and Restricted sites) where you can assign different levels of security.

Index